Morning

Dan Batson

Morning

ISBN: Softcover 978-1-951472-63-4

Copyright © 2020 by Dan Batson

All rights reserved. No part of this book may be reproduced or transmitted in any form or by any means, electronic or mechanical, including photocopying, recording, or by any information storage and retrieval system, without permission in writing from the publisher.

www.parsonsporch.com

Parson's Porch Books is an imprint of Parson's Porch & Company (PP&C) in Cleveland, Tennessee. PP&C is an innovative organization which raises money by publishing books of noted authors, representing all genres. Its face and voice is David Russell Tullock (dtullock@parsonsporch.com).

Parson's Porch *turns books into bread* by sharing its profits with the poor.

For Donna Lynn

"Weeping may linger for the night, but joy comes with the morning."

~Psalm 30:5

Acknowledgements

University professor of English and artist, Betty Hodges, painted a picture for my wife, Donna, capturing a sunrise, Donna's favorite part of the day. Betty's gift to Donna is the cover art for this book. I will always be grateful for this gift. I am also grateful for Betty's inspiring words given to me about a year later. She simply and confidently told me: "You have your story. Now you just need to write it."

Many thanks to my faithful and unfaltering beta readers, Bill and Margaret Baker, Penny Wesley, and Jayne Ferrer who not only offered many improvements but also great advice.

My appreciation to my editor, Andrea Hitefield, who I met on a sidewalk at a writer's conference, and who helped polish this work while also believing in the importance of the message. I also appreciate David Tullock of Parson's Porch Books for reaching out to me about publishing a collection of my sermons. Thank you, David, for being willing to take this book instead.

My devotion to Donna's mother, Thelma Smith, who deserves much credit for her loving care of the entire family and her unfaltering strength and faith.

My indebtedness to all of my church members over the years who have patiently taught me what it means to be a servant of God, of God's church, and the people of God.

My deep gratitude and love to Rene', my wife, editor, critic, and greatest fan. She found my true voice and gave it to me.

Chapter 1
Underwater

WE OFTEN SWAM IN THE COLD MOUNTAIN waters of Table Rock Lake to escape the summer heat. After an afternoon of splashing and swimming, we would begin to play more risky games.

One of our favorites involved seeing how long we could stay on the bottom of the lake in the deeper waters. I quickly learned from the mutual experiences of my brothers and cousins that the best way to sink to the bottom included not only diving and swimming to the lake bed but also to expel all the air from our lungs.

Even though we thought of this game as harmless fun, a big part of the attraction involved the thrilling difficulty in getting back to the surface.

Sometimes I would do practice runs while the others were playing.

I would start by getting as much air in my lungs as possible and then jumping from the platform feet first. Once the initial decent took place, I would try to make my body as sleek as possible with legs tight together and arms held close at my sides. Just when my descent seemed to be slowing to nothing, the exhaling would begin.

With every muscle in my chest, I would force the breath out of my lungs. The air would make wonderful bursts of bubbles which frantically rushed to the surface as if in a great hurry to join the air of the skies above.

With the release of the life-giving air from my lungs, I would again be descending. Eventually, I would push my palms in upward motions to complete the final few feet until my feet hit the bottom.

There, in the cold murky darkness, I would realize no one actually knew where I was. As my feet slowly sank into the soft brown mud, I would wonder if they might become so mired in the lake bottom as to be trapped. I would open my eyes trying to see through the dark waters only to find very little visibility. Looking up to the surface, I could see some shimmering light and hear distorted sounds resembling voices.

The object of the game was to simply stay down there with my feet in the mud in the darkness until I felt I could not hold my breath any longer. The great risk involved the fact that I never knew exactly how long to stay down there. I also did not know how long it would take me to swim to the surface.

We were never scientific in playing the game. We would jump from any side of the platform without considering that the depths of the lake changed every few feet. We also never thought of counting off the seconds so as to have any indication of the time passing.

Instead of taking any safeguards, we would foolishly play the game thinking we could always make it to the surface before it was too late.

When my lungs were screaming for air and my heart began to race, I would kick off the muddy bottom and start my frantic race to the surface.

Just then, a quiet panic would begin. My chest would burn, and my head would grow dizzy.

As I struggled to swim through the dark waters, I would lose all of hope of ever seeing the light of another morning.

Chapter 2
Clemson 1978

SHE SIPPED HOT CHINESE TEA FROM A CUP with no handles, and I knew I would love her forever. Donna wore a high collar, cream blouse. Small ruffles gently caressed her neck and matched the rows of soft pleats covering the front of her blouse. A camel colored wool skirt held her elegantly tight and then flowed full below her knees. The cuffs of the blouse peeked out from the sleeves of her brown velvet jacket.

Her open-toed, high heels made from exotic woods and bamboo echoed the tones of brown and cream in her outfit. Using her thumb as a ruler, she had measured the heels carefully before purchasing. She laughed and told me about the shoe store clerk stating that care had to be taken to make sure one did not end up being taller than one's date.

A dark red garnet in her ring glowed gently in the light of the candle on our table in the restaurant. The color of the stone brought out the rich hues of her hair. Waves of mahogany brown framed her face as she energetically spoke about her day.

Life made sense. I knew beyond any doubt or question, I loved her. Even though I had not started dating her thinking that it would lead to something so serious, I knew this love changed everything. Instead of dating, instead of just spending time together, instead of just exploring who we were as we transitioned into the realities of adulthood, I knew this love would continue.

Just a few months before, she laughed and smiled as she held out her hand to me in greeting. After we shook hands, she gave a quick amused look at her suitemate and then back at me. I confusedly smiled back at her.

I found out months later that I had been the object of an ongoing joke between them. Much to her suitemate's consternation, I never seemed to remember Donna even though she walked with us every Sunday morning to church. Each time I saw her, I would hold out my hand and say, "Nice to meet you."

Since I used the same greeting week after week, my ignorance of Donna became absurdly obvious.

Determined to keep me from saying the same inappropriate greeting to her again, Donna quickly held out her hand and said, "Nice to meet you."

During the morning worship service, the pastor asked us to stand and greet those who sat near us. Instead of shaking Donna's hand again, I asked her about her major.

"I'm going to be an elementary school teacher," she said with a smile. "After graduation, I'm going to live with my grandmother in Kansas."

With a twinkle in her eye, her smile widened and then took on firm determination.

"I'm never going to get married," she stated as though I had asked the question, "and I never plan on having any children."

I'm sure I can change your mind, I thought in a rare moment of bravado.

Our first date almost didn't happen since I had difficulty getting her to answer the phone in her dorm room. As it turned out, she had become convinced another young man from one of her classes was calling her. Since she did not want to date him, she had decided not to answer the phone. Finally, my brother's girlfriend, Diane, heard her tell someone she wished he would stop calling. Pulling her gently aside, Diane told her who was really calling.

Donna and I had gone to Greenville to eat at a Mexican restaurant and then watch a movie. The salsa at the restaurant made me cough almost uncontrollably, and then we arrived late to the theater. On our drive there and back, she had spoken at length about anything and everything, and I had remained quiet.

As we each spoke privately to our friends about our first date, we expressed concern.

"She never stopped talking."

"He hardly said a word."

Those words summarized the experience. I complained to my twin brother, Don, about my date as we sat in our high-rise dormitory, and Donna complained to Diane in the identically built dormitory standing next door on campus.

With the insistence of Don and Diane, we decided we would give a second date a try.

After several dates, Donna playfully pulled me to her and smiled. I felt the soft pressure of her warm chest next to mine through the thin white sweater I had worn on that autumn evening.

It had become obvious to her that if she wanted our first kiss to happen, she would have to take it from me. With a smile and a laugh, she did.

Morning

    Realizing permission had been given and the invitation still stood, we lingered over our next kiss. We embraced in the night on the dormitory porch next to giant dark windows.

    She continued to sip her hot tea from the cup with no handles and looked at me questioningly as I sat in silence. Appreciating who was before me, I returned her look with a smile.

Chapter 3
Marietta

ON HER FIRST VISIT TO MY SOUTH CAROLINA HOME in the small rural community of Marietta, I welcomed Donna to my world.

In the fields, pastures, and woods, Dad taught us what it meant to be one who grew things. Our home kept us safe and warm, but the growing took place outside. The farm became not just the source of food but the identity of purpose and being. There we played, toiled, cried, and laughed. There we learned what it meant to love family as we found meaning and faith. Even though Dad continued to work Aunt Helen's farm in the country, our home in town also included a large garden. In these gardens, we put down our own roots and grew.

When Donna and I arrived at my home, Dad took us down to a small stand of pine trees. He continued to talk as he lifted one of his hands above his head. Two unshelled peanuts he had grown and harvested, rested in his palm as though being offered to the lesser gods of the pines. He stood on the edge of the woods near the fenced area where at different times either ducks, chickens, turkeys, calves, or dogs lived and thrived. As he stood there with his peanut offering, we heard a scraping sound of fast claws digging their way quickly across the dry pine bark. Before Donna or I could look up, two squirrels jumped onto Dad's strong outstretched hand. The squirrels began to eat their peanut treats while ignoring us as we stood there with our mouths open in astonishment.

This amusement of feeding the squirrels was just a passing moment to Dad. He smiled at our bewilderment. To him, it was just that the squirrels knew him and wanted peanuts. To us, it demonstrated his mystifying connection to nature.

We walked past the iris bed, situated perfectly on the small rise where the driveway curved around the house and separated the woods and the garden from the backyard. At the back of the irises stood an old row of mountain laurel bushes still in the place they had naturally grown with their twisted branches and dark green pointed leaves. Those old mountain bushes faithfully offered their small pale pink blossoms strangely marked with burgundy accents as they had since before our little town existed.

Pointing out the border of large smooth white river rocks taken from the creek, I asked Donna if her mother ever used eggshells to fertilize her irises.

Morning

Donna looked at me as though she had not heard my question correctly and then quietly said her mother did not grow irises in large beds.

I explained how our relatives and friends had provided all the bulbs.

"Mom would always try to find new colors for her iris bed. But, sadly enough, every time she would receive some plants, they always produced beige blossoms. Pretty soon, her whole bed was mainly dull tan."

"An old farmer once told Mom to use eggshells as fertilizer for her iris bed. So we washed and crushed our eggshells and spread them over the bed. One day, Dad thought the beige irises with beige eggshells would look better with some nice green grass to give the bed some needed color. Without checking with Mom, he spread his best fescue seeds over the entire bed. My brothers and I spent many long summer afternoons weeding out very healthy grass that thrived on the eggshells better than the irises."

While we walked near the woods behind the house, I told her about Aunt Helen's old farm in the country. I described how the forest wrapped around the whole area protecting and preserving it from the changing world. At the farm, little had changed for at least three generations, and modern agriculture meant you did what had always worked.

I described the corn crib where the wooden barrels filled with sweet feed were stored and how we enjoyed opening those barrels and smelling the variety of grains mixed with molasses. I shared with her stories about the strong, yet aged, log barn. I helped her imagine its large loft and the bales of hay stored there for the winter where we would play for hours as young children had done in the past.

"I can't wait to walk with you down the trail running beside the back pasture and past the old pig pen," I told her hoping she would be as interested in the place as I had always been. "Once you get past the pasture, the forest deepens. You can stand on a wide area covered in club moss on the edge of the ravine and see the river."

I tried to help her fully understand the wonder of an almost sacred place in the forest. On the side of a hill surrounded by tall oaks and poplars, a hemlock grove grew. "One massive hemlock stands in the center circled by many of its offspring," I told her. "We always loved walking through the smaller trees until we finally stood at the base of the mother hemlock. It looks like it's been there forever."

"It all sounds amazing," Donna responded. "I can't wait to see it."

Dad walked proudly through the neat rows of many varieties of vegetables which grew in abundance on every available inch of well-tilled soil. As Donna quickly surveyed the lush plants, I realized how many other things I wanted to tell her. She had no background of tending a garden. She couldn't begin to understand what it meant to work the corn fields at Aunt Helen's. With crook neck hoe in hand, we would strain to see the end of the row knowing every inch of weed-laden soil between the corn plants had to be cleared.

She would never experience the tiredness that came from knowing when you finished one section countless rows awaited. She would never truly know the joy and the frustration with the old ways of country life and farming.

I could only tell her how it felt when, as a young boy, I struggled with my hoe trying my best to avoid damaging the beautiful young stalks of corn sprouting from where my brothers and I had planted the seeds. Aunt Helen stopped her hoeing on the next row and came to instruct me to hoe with rhythm. With a gentle circular movement, she demonstrated how the hoe could quickly and almost effortlessly cut through the soil moving from one plant to the other. Feeling the rhythm of the hoe in my sweaty hands, I understood the connection with all those who had used this same practice so long ago.

I could never express to Donna the amazement of the first time I realized the joy of planting one kernel of corn and saw a whole plant emerge. She would never completely appreciate the wondrous economy of our farm in the old ways of using every stalk and piece of growth as fodder for the cows. Nor could she appreciate the ways in which even the forest surrounding the pastures provided blackberries, wild blueberries, locusts pods, hickory nuts, black walnuts, squirrels, rabbits, and fish to supply our needs and desires.

She would never remember the small red clay yard my Aunt Helen swept clean with her homemade thin, tree branch broom. Donna never heard my aunt mimic the birds of the field as we sat on the front porch of the old farmhouse in the country on a summer evening.

"Bob White, Bob White," Aunt Helen would say in answer to a bird's call from the fields. Donna could never fully realize how we knew it was our aunt's way of answering the Bob White's call and letting the little bird know it was not alone as the sun began to set.

In the quick journey through our house garden, I knew I could never adequately convey to her how all the aspects of farm life influenced my whole way of facing every challenge.

Everything contained a story; memories surrounded every leaf. As we walked past the rose trellis beside our house in town, I told her how Dad had decided to purchase three rose bushes for Mom and plant them for Mother's Day. He had purchased the very best red velvet rose bushes he could find and installed three trellises.

Morning

Despite his amazing ability to grow all things, two of the bushes quickly died leaving only the middle one. As though knowing it needed to fill all three trellises, the sole surviving rose bush exceeded all expectations. With branches growing in perfect symmetry, the rose bush reached out to both sides and filled the end of the house with some of the best blossoms in town.

As Donna and I walked past the trellises filled with large red velvet roses, she commented on the beauty of the large blossoms which begged to be touched and cradled in both hands. She also asked about the white powder covering the bush and most of the blossoms. Chuckling, I told her Dad's cure for any kind of insect or infestation was simply bean dust.

Donna smiled and nodded as Dad took her past the rows of cucumbers growing on a fence running the length of the garden. The dark green cucumber vines with their contrasting and simple little yellow flowers obediently grew on the fence as though they understood by doing so their fruit would be given a better chance to grow larger. Little did she know Dad's quiet invention of this cucumber fence had yielded amazing results. Little could she appreciate the fact these cucumbers were the awe of all the local farmers and resulted with a picture of him and some of his prized cucumbers in the local newspaper.

We walked past the tall rows of okra as she commented on how much she enjoyed fried okra and okra in soup. I made a mental note to tell her later about the summer mornings spent harvesting the rows of okra almost daily so no pod became too large and therefore too tough to be used. I wanted to share with her the amazement of seeing the small perfectly round gun-metal gray okra seeds. I felt compelled to share with her Dad's practice of soaking the little seeds in a large bowl of water overnight on the kitchen counter before planting. I wanted her to feel the prickliness of the tiny spines covering the okra plants, to know the sensation of the okra itch and the great relief of washing bare arms with the garden hose once the harvest for the day was complete.

In those very few minutes of a casual walk upon soil that looked to be too red to grow anything, I knew words would not convey life. My young experiences seemed to already contain too many expressions of sweat, joy, and unsatisfied longings to ever be expressed to someone else completely. All I could really do was walk through the garden and comment on how well the bell peppers were growing this year.

I stood in the garden, my feet firmly planted upon the soil he had cleared from the forest by his efforts. His will formed my brothers and me from the bareness of the soil, also. His plants always grew and thrived due to his relentless attention to every detail of their needs. I had witnessed the care he demonstrated for every plant as he took an old bucket and a small cup and poured water at the base of a struggling young plant in the heat of late spring. Envy almost overtook me as I realized his garden claimed and received the attention of the farmer who by birth and practice knew how to make things grow.

Here we stood in his garden as its imperceptible movements of the complicated processes of life took place right before us and witnessed the completed proof of what one man could create. A good creation, even though not without its flaws, but a creation slowly yielding a harvest. A creation of plenty in the midst of a world of scarcity.

By this time, Dad and Donna had already moved from the impressive rows of peppers to the small apple orchard on the upper corner of the garden next to the workshop. This corner also contained a pear tree taken as a sapling from Aunt Helen's.

Old tin buckets of pears were always on the back porch of Aunt Helen's house. The porch was on the high end of the house facing one of the side pastures. Underneath the porch, a cellar had been dug. Protected by a small door covered with chicken wire to keep the animals out, many colorfully filled Mason jars sat on the shelves dug into the cellar's red clay walls. Proudly displaying the preserved harvest of the season, the jars contained tomatoes, green beans, corn, okra, and whole pickled peaches. Beyond the cellar, the small pillars of field rocks collected long ago and stacked without mortar acted as the foundation of the little farmhouse.

The plump little green pears never remained in the tin buckets for very long. My aunt would take them to the kitchen to be cooked. As though by magic, the green speckled pears would be converted to sweet golden preserves filled with the flavor of the old farm.

Next to Aunt Helen's flower garden filled with varying colors of gladioluses, stood the only apple tree on the farm. We never knew exactly what variety of apple it produced, but the small green apples always tasted as though the old tree had forgotten how to make fruit that would ripen.

From its wide and wrinkled trunk, the branches of the tree produced many of the strange little apples. Since the tree grew next to the side pasture fence, the cows claimed all the produce of any branch they could reach. If we sat on the fence, the cows would come from the pastures and the woods as though a silent signal had been given.

Without making a sound, they would line up in cow custom and get as close to us as possible without knocking us off our perches. We, in turn, would begin to feed them one little green apple after another. Their eyes would show a strange appreciation for this midafternoon snack as their long tongues took the apples offered in our hands and with a single loud crush turn the offering into apple sauce and apple juice all at once.

Dad took Donna to the upper edge of the garden to show her his trailing vines of muscadines and scuppernongs. Dad's vines grew on an old fence even though most of our relatives grew muscadines and scuppernongs on arbors where the large grapes could be easily harvested and turned into jams and jellies. I watched as Donna walked with Dad from those vines past the row of fig bushes to the carefully staked Concord grape vines where perfectly shaped clusters of deep purple grapes would soon ripen.

As I stood in the small orchard of my Dad's garden watching him talk with Donna, I remembered the winter mornings when we would be getting ready to go to school. Mother always served a hot breakfast before dawn. The small radio cheerfully gave the morning news while fresh eggs were scrambled, sausage fried, grits boiled, and biscuits baked. Many times our grits would be cold firm paddies on our plates by the time we made it down to the table. Dad would be reading the morning newspaper while sipping hot coffee. We knew he had already been out to check on his prized chickens. He kept them well-sheltered in pens he fashioned himself and hung from the rafters of the car shed next to the garden. Polish Top Notch, Blue Silver Wing, Rhode Island Red, White Feather-legged, their names sounded as different as the chickens looked. They seemed to enjoy their special little pens Dad had built. He always kept the numbered pens supplied with clean hay as though the specialty chickens deserved only the very best.

Dad would finish eating and then make the long slow journey to feed the cows at Aunt Helen's before coming back to town to open the gas station for the early morning customers taking their children to school or going to work in the mill in the nearby village of Slater. It was a long and slow journey to the farm, not because of distance or poor roads, but because Dad drove an old 1958 Chevy truck that never seemed to move more than twenty miles per hour to any destination.

After we finished our sturdy breakfast, we would go upstairs to get dressed. The ritual consisted of going up the stairs and sitting with our backs to the heat vent of the old oil furnace which, on cold winter mornings, spewed forth great quantities of slightly petroleum scented heat into the house.

Much to our mothers' dismay, we would sit on the floor at the top of the stairs with our backs to the vent and sleep until we heard her coming up the steps. Sleep quickly turned into a frenzy of getting bathed and dressed so no one would be late to school. Mom taught at the high school which served as one of the main centers of activity in the town.

On those sleepy winter mornings when all the world seemed as frozen as the mountain gorges surrounding us, one great surprise would come each year. The solitary plum tree would have blossomed overnight.

Standing at the bathroom window and looking through the bare branches of the trees in our backyard into Dad's small orchard, we could see the plum tree. Defying the bitterness of the frost, the small white blossoms clustered themselves together and covered the branches. Nothing spoke a louder voice of the grandeur of ancient cycles of nature like that little plum tree covered in blooms.

By this time, Dad and Donna had moved past the fig trees. Now they were standing next to the rhubarb bed, and I listened as Dad spoke of the apple-rhubarb and strawberry-rhubarb pies Mom baked using the dark red stalks of those plants. As I started to make my way to where they stood, I passed a large, strange looking plant I could not identify. At the back of the orchard near the fence separating the woods from the garden, stood this very healthy bush. It was beautiful, not so much because of its great health, since all of Dad's gardens grew with great enthusiasm, but because of the unusually deep green color. This bush seemed so out of place at the edge of the garden, at first I thought it must have been a weed Dad had purposely left to grow.

But something about it looked familiar.

I touched one of the leaves and felt the ridged edges of the palm shaped formation of finger length leaflets as a realization crept over me.

"Dad, what is this bush?" I called out over the garden as foreboding over a new discovery and fear of knowing the truth swept over me. I wanted to know if my suspicions were correct, but I also knew that if correct, I might have to find another girlfriend.

Morning

"Oh, that's my pot plant," Dad said with a smile as he started to walk toward me. "It's done really well there."

I heard my sweet Donna utter a word of polite surprise as she followed Dad to the corner of the orchard where I stood. Now embarrassed, I thought for a moment about trying to pull the bush quickly out of the garden by its roots and tossing it over the fence into the woods before she walked the short distance to where I stood with the marijuana bush. My efforts would be in vain partly because the bush was as big as a barrel and partly because I didn't want my girlfriend last's memory of our relationship being of me struggling to pull this bush out by its roots as she walked to the car in disgust.

"Why are you growing marijuana next to the cucumbers?" I asked in utter astonishment.

Completely unbothered by my discovery, Dad brought Donna over to his very healthy and very illegal plant.

"A. C. gave all of the local famers some pot seeds they got from an arrest and told us to grow a plant so we would know what it looked like," Dad said referring to the local constable in town.

A. C. Simmons worked during the day at our local hardware store and at night sat on watch in his ancient patrol car making our little hamlet safe from all who would dare disturb our haven of slumber.

"A. C. is the local constable," I quickly explained to Donna, hoping she would not be quite so quick to call the DEA.

"A. C. said people were growing pot on any field or pasture where they think the farmer won't notice, and he wanted us to be able to identify it. I think mine looks really healthy," he added while gently caressing one of the marijuana leaves in his hand as though carefully assessing the health of a prized sweet potato plant.

"It's looking unbelievably healthy," I added in disbelief, "but you could always grow anything."

Sheepishly I looked at Donna and tried to gauge her reaction.

"Dad doesn't have a green thumb," my voice began to betray my concern, "he has green fingers."

"One time the log posts he used to make a shed on the side of the barn sprouted leaves the next spring…" my voice trailed off as a realized I was rambling.

My fears of myself, of who I was and ever would be, surfaced as I quickly searched her beautiful green eyes for either acceptance or rejection. In spite of everything I might try to accomplish in this life, the best person I gave to her as the first fruits of myself would be forever inadequate to all she deserved. Now I understood the limitations of who I was in this life. Even though I might strive to change and to improve, the person of my birth and time and place remained to forever haunt me. All I could hope to offer her as we stood together in the garden was simply red velvet roses covered in bean dust.

Returning my searching and yearning gaze with a look of complete acceptance and the sure and unmistakable look of love, she laughed and smiled.

Chapter 4
Jekyll Island

SHE SAT IN THE COOL SHADE OF A SMALL, Jekyll Island pier off the Georgia coast near Brunswick. The sea breeze captured her laughter and made it forever a part of that place.

Just the day before in the midst of everything—in the midst of family and friends gathering—in the midst of the start of the wedding music – in the midst of the voices of those around me, a clear sound had broken through and given clarity. Beyond the sweetest note of music, beyond the tolling of the distant bell, beyond the greeting call of wind gently whistling through the pines, and beyond the songs of the birds celebrating forest life around us, the sound of laughter joyfully seared itself into me. It forced me to grow beyond myself. The sound of her laughter gave me air and told me to breathe.

Laughter. Her laughter. Donna's laughter as she prepared with her bridesmaids in the gray stone room of the open air chapel next to the courtyard where I sat with my brother. Her laughter made all other sounds simply cease. Her laughter filled the mountaintop with unmistakable joy.

From strength of ancient cliffs possessed with all the wisdom of lives lived and ages of creation unfolding, her laughter became immortal. This mountain had seen the dawning of the first light of the first day, and now gave witness and companionship to the uniting. Donna's voice on the mountain, her heart, her spirit could be heard in her laughter.

For a precious moment, I could hear nothing else but the sound of her joy. A few minutes later, she walked down the long row of center aisle steps in the chapel and joined me at the altar on the very precipice of the blue mountain and united her precious laughter with mine.

Late the next morning, we drove through the old terra cotta roofed entrance gates of Jekyll Island and began the journey down the long causeway across the beautiful marshes to our destination.

In Jekyll Island fashion, our hotel consisted of small single-story buildings in the midst of a grassy field surrounded by wind twisted oak trees. The trees covered most of the island near the northern end next to the nature preserve where the island ceased. At the rounded point of the island, the white skeletons of old oak trees were scattered across the sands as though waiting for the tides to take them to other shores. These massive displays of driftwood invited us to endless exploration of this nautical wonderland. As if the beach, framed by the undisturbed landscape and the point surrounded by the inlet, were not enough, across the channel the quiet beauty of another island in the land of the Golden Isles beckoned.

Black and white stripes climbed in spiral fashion up the ever narrowing dimensions of the lighthouse on St. Simon's Island. This amazing structure could be seen across the channel and completed the seascape. Standing on the point of Jekyll Island while holding each other tightly in the gentle breeze, I felt lovingly contained in a carefully constructed landscape someone had built in a bottle to preserve forever.

Jekyll wrapped its island splendors around us and welcomed us as though we had always belonged there. The natural beauty and quietness of the island intensified our intimacy to build a solid foundation for continued discovery of each other as man and wife.

After several days, Donna mentioned she wanted to create a souvenir of our island honeymoon paradise. She thought the perfect remembrance would be a shell lamp we made ourselves using shells we found on the beach. Since this was before the clear glass shell lamp kits could be easily found, we spent the better part of one morning going from store to store in and around the island looking for the necessary components to fashion our lamp. The most helpful place ended up being an old antique store where the owner also repaired lamps. When we told him what we were trying to accomplish, he gladly helped us design one using an intricately carved wooded base from an old broken lamp and the glass chimney from a kerosene lamp. Complete with electrical parts and a small pleated shade, we knew we could now carefully select the perfect shells to complete our treasure. Sealed in the glass of the lamp, those shells would forever remind us of this place and time.

Exploration of the island included not just walks on the beach but also long bicycle rides. In my youthful enthusiasm, the first bicycle trip became a marathon of sorts as I became determined to travel the circumference of the island. After spending most of the afternoon on our bicycles, we finally finished our exhausting trek almost too tired to have appreciated the beauty of everything we saw. On the next afternoon, we decided the best way to enjoy the island involved a much slower appreciation of inner trails winding through the undisturbed marshes.

These trails became our favorite. On the edge of the marshes where the oak trees had been sculptured by the salt filled winds, the trails invited us to ride for hours. As though we were the only ones on a deserted island, our marshes and forests beckoned us to stay and enjoy what we had discovered. Without the unnecessary complication of trying to accomplish a goal, we both relaxed and enjoyed each moment of beauty.

Morning

Our times varied in exploring the marsh trails. Some days the water from the sea would greet us with a reminder that it still claimed this part of the island as its own. On other days the dark brown shiny mud of the marsh bottom could be clearly seen through the waist high grass. This marsh grass thrived there as though salt water and the endlessly brutal sun only made it love life all the more.

During low tide when the sea receded from the marsh, we could see small crabs running between the tall blades of grass hurriedly trying to accomplish their natural marketing before the water returned. At places near the trail, intimate refuges of white sandy soil invited us to step away from our bicycles and venture out on the dry baked trails and walk in the marshland as far as we dared.

Our journeys over the trails would eventually and reluctantly end on the small wooden bridge connecting the marsh to the shore near the fishing pier. Continuing from the pier to the campground and past the small marina, the story of the island's past met us as we entered into a small village of large unoccupied homes from the early 1900's. We had heard this "Millionaire's Village" with its large Victorian white frame hotel in the center had been the winter playground for some of the wealthiest families in the country. The hotel, known as the Jekyll Island Club, showed signs of not being occupied for many decades. The homes, now empty, invited visitors to browse through their inner halls and imagine the privileged life on the island so very long ago.

One guide told us Jekyll Island's future had been determined by warfare. During the time of World War II, the federal government recommended the wealthy residents no long gather on their beloved island. Since a German U-Boat had already sunk a freight ship off the coast of the Golden Isles, the threat existed that one U-Boat could surreptitiously capture the island along with its inhabitants which would have represented a very large percentage of the wealth of the world.

Under this threat, the families sold the island to the state of Georgia. As we rode our bicycles through the deserted village, the abandoned homes amazed us. Their emptiness spoke of the glamor and beauty of the past.

At the marina on the edge of the village, we parked our bicycles and walked out to the piers. The fishing boats had been coming and going as we approached, and we saw several larger tourist boats as well. On one of these boats we noticed a sign about a moonlight dinner cruise around the island.

Most of our evenings, Donna and I would attend a show at the amphitheater on the island near the historic village. A summer troupe of university students performed famous Broadway musical hits. The same cast outdid themselves in presenting a different show each evening as the audience relished the music and laughter under the island's beautiful trees. Donna and I decided this evening we would forgo the pleasure of the show and take the moonlight dinner cruise.

Our journey began as the boat pulled away from the pier and slowly ventured around the island under the opulence of the clear golden light of the setting sun. After a delicious meal of fresh fish complete with coffee and dessert served in the galley, we made our way to the top deck to witness the full moon as it shimmered across the waters.

As we turned from the broad water into a channel between these Golden Isles, a gentle stream of light reached out from the old lighthouse on St. Simon's Island and pointed to the vastness of the Atlantic as though giving guidance for an unknown destination.

Gracious words greeted us on the top deck from a kind and charming lady well dressed in casually elegant evening attire. In true southern charm this fellow passenger calmly invited us into her world.

As we shared with her the reason for our stay, fascination with our new beginning became evident in her quiet and polite tones. Within a few moments of sharing, we knew quite a lot about her. As the boat completed rounding the island and the quaint marina once again could be clearly seen, she added some parting thoughts.

"I have spent the last several years in treatment for cancer," she said with soft words. In the subtle glow of the full moon across the waters, I could see a resolve in her eyes running through her core to a faith being tested with fire.

"I thought everything was going very well, but at my last check, the cancer has returned."

In silence, Donna and I looked at our fellow traveler. We simply did not have words to adequately convey our thoughts.

"I'm going to my doctor tomorrow to hear what lies ahead."

After the moonlight cruise on the still, dark waters surrounding the island, Donna and I disembarked into the quietness of the empty village. Holding hands, I knew she continued to worry for the elegant lady of the boat and what awaited her.

"That didn't sound very good," she said softly. "I'm going to remember her in my prayers."

We both knew we would never hear any news of this lady who had impressed us with her graciousness. As we stepped out into an island's rich history, our thoughts ran not in the direction of the past, but into all the future held. Existing now at its beginning, our story briefly intersected with

Morning

another story. We knew our journeys briefly ran together as though guided by currents beyond our ability to direct.

The next morning our quest to find the perfect shells for the lamp continued. Undaunted by the lack of large shells on the stretch of beach bordering our resort, we decided to sift the sands to collect some tiny lavender bivalve shells. Working at a shaded spot beside an unused pier, we laughed in discovering many small shells hidden just beneath the surface of the sand.

A rude awakening came when we returned to our room and discovered our afternoon's carefully selected miniature shells amounted to barely an inch of space in our treasure lamp. We realized it would take us a month of sifting the sands on Jekyll to finish the job.

Thinking the shell-less-ness was just a peculiarity of our honeymoon destination, we decided to collect what we could on this trip and then add to our collection on each trip back to our island.

The next morning, we rented bicycles and rode the beloved paths through the marshes. This time we made a new detour and went in another direction not caring if we were lost in the marshes since we would contently stay there forever. Much too soon the trail ended on the shore of another side of the island we had seen as we passed by on our moonlight cruise. As we ventured out to this new shore, we made an amazing discovery.

On this side of the island, like pearls gleaming in the sands, beautiful shells abounded. We laughed at ourselves for spending an entire afternoon sifting for the small shells when this great bounty existed. Hand in hand, we walked across the moist sands and gathered what the ocean tides had provided as together we created our everlasting treasure.

Chapter 5
Pendleton

BUILT FOR THE RETURNING COLLEGE-BOUND War World II veterans and their families, prefabricated houses originally dominated a section of campus at Clemson University near the athletic fields. The small structures, designed as much as possible to resemble a regular house, seemed to contain more metal than wood. As undergraduates, we found amusement in the silver-sided flat roofed relics from the past now used as housing for married students. During the hot days of spring semester's end and the first months of the fall semester, garden sprinklers could be seen on the roofs of these tiny houses. We always laughed while watching steam rising off the tops of these residences baking in the fields.

When Clemson decided the prefabs no longer served a useful purpose they were either sold or destroyed.

A dairy farmer in nearby Pendleton decided to transform one of his pastures into a little village of prefabs. This country gentleman and his wife, along with their three Scottish Terriers, lived in a nearby large farmhouse they named "The Retreat". Our village of reworked, rewired, and air-conditioned prefabs bore the name of "Retreat Homes".

The units sat in a perpetually green pasture next to a small creek beside a quiet country road. Covered in new white siding, the homes resembled giant pastry boxes waiting to be opened on Easter.

Selecting just the right upholstery fabric to cover an old couch from her parent's home became one of Donna's first thrills in setting up our house. Great expectation surrounded the arrival of the beautiful couch followed too soon by disappointment. The couch would not fit through the small prefab entrance. Since all of the windows were narrow and the back entrance was built like the front, the couch made the trip back with Donna's parents.

Another smaller couch from my Aunt Wilma and Uncle Buck's basement soon replaced our newly covered couch. Not letting this setback deter her, Donna threw herself into decorating our first little home. Nothing would stop her from making it beautiful.

I came to appreciate the fact that either because of her father's early death, or her own battles with health problems, Donna knew life could be bitterly disappointing. Her green eyes perceived the world as one in which strength and faith provided the needed balance. Always the teacher, she modeled for me that desires, wishes, and dreams are wonderful, but the utter failure of those things to become reality did not mean we would stop moving forward.

Every time I sat on our used brown couch covered in Naugahyde, I felt stronger.

Donna relished the opportunity to take on the challenge of her first job. Teaching one of the two fifth grade classes in a school where only one elementary teacher per grade was normally needed, she made the trip from our prefab to her mountain village school each day.

Each weekday morning after Donna left to go to work, I cleaned the entire house before leaving to go to my job at the university. Up to this point in my life, work meant chores. Starting early in life, working around the house became the normal expectation of each day. Skills had been gained by endless chores at home and on the farm. Skills had been sharpened through the interaction with customers while working in my father's business and helping out with customers in my aunt and uncle's drugstore. Even with those preparations, nothing compared to going into the workforce for the first time. Excited and frightened, Donna and I stood at the deep end of the pool, and even though we weren't sure if we could really swim, we jumped in together.

We ventured forth into each sunrise to do the thing life expected—whether we felt ready or not. We had longed to be allowed into the depths of the water, and now we had to prove we could swim.

My job at Clemson University came with an impressive title and a tiny paycheck. Graduate Counselor of Career Services. I worked for four hours each weekday afternoon and then attended three hours of graduate level classes in the evenings. In over my head, I relished the opportunity of providing some guidance to students as they prepared for their interviews. Recruiters from large corporations came each semester to pick the best of the eager harvest.

"I know in the first three minutes of an interview whether or not I am going to make a job offer to any particular student," a recruiter once reported.

I knew he did not mean the statement in a harsh or judgmental way. He simply stated the facts. With all things being equal—decent grades, a desirable degree—it all boiled down to whether or not this person would fit into their corporate work team.

We did not tell the students they only had three minutes to succeed. It didn't seem fair. I did, however, stress to them the great importance of first impressions.

Diving into my work meant trying to figure out what to do when no teacher, no role model, no mentor, no facilitator was present to say, "Pick up your pencil. Open the test booklet. Begin."

It meant the test was upon you in an instant with no chance of preparation, no careful time to refine the choices, and no experience to guide. It meant every breath and every word, every action and every thought existed in the new, the unexplored.

These moments of struggling and finding the best way to maneuver one's self in the water, even though unnerving, were also exhilarating.

In our evening discussions, we spoke of how experience taught and guided but also began the process of making things routine.

"I know these days are exciting," Donna said one evening as we sat on our small couch, "it's sort of sad because this time can never be repeated."

Diving into the deep end of the pool also meant I became the one to guide and answer questions for all of the summer internships available for our students. Sitting at a round table in the room I had carefully prepared to showcase the internship opportunities, I found myself one afternoon speaking with an eager student about different possibilities for summer work.

She showed great interest in an internship and demonstrated characteristics for such a position. I became excited about her efforts to dive into the deep water.

From cheery pleasantness appearing to come from seeing a world filled with endless possibilities, I watched her begin to falter in her speech and manner. She turned to me with distressing sadness.

"All of my life," she said as sorrow began streaming down her perfect face, "I have wanted to be a teacher. It's the only thing I have prepared for— the only thing I know I can do."

Her words flowed through quiet sobs as, in spite of her best efforts, she realized all pretense had vanished and her world of disappointment had opened itself up to me.

"But I just found out I failed the National Teacher's Exam. I will not be certified. I cannot teach. I'm graduating, but I have to find something else to do. I don't know what to do."

As she sat at my round table in her fury of disappointment, the excitement of the new collided with a roadblock of reality. Life saying, "Not so fast." The deep waters turning treacherous.

I wrenched in pain as I experienced her worst fears becoming real. Instead of finding a counselor's words and guiding the process of self-awareness to the point of self-discovery, I simply said nothing. We became fellow strugglers not yet equipped with sufficient skills in keeping afloat, and in the midst of her pain, I simply began to sink with her.

I remembered on a beautiful spring morning before our wedding in August, Donna arrived at the front door of my apartment. I swung the door open delighted to see her. Before I could speak, I noticed the white fear and anguished astonishment beading out from the cold sweat of her forehead as she stood clutching a piece of paper.

"I failed the NTE," she said as she rushed into my arms and began to cry. "I don't know what to do."

Her world wrapped itself so completely into my world I knew she was referring to the National Teacher's Exam. I also knew that passing or failing this exam meant continuing to work at the bank where she had worked since her junior high school days or beginning her much desired career in teaching.

She fell into my arms still holding the small piece of paper stating her apparent failure. In the midst of sobs, I heard her state her disbelief but also her confusion.

"There are two scores," she cried. "I don't know why there are two scores. But neither one is high enough to qualify me."

I knew the magic number existed. Someone or some committee or perhaps some machine calculated the score every person wishing to enter the teaching profession in the United States of America had to obtain to be a certified teacher. This score simply and coldly stated in mathematical logic whether or not one's education had been sufficient. No point of grace extended. No forgiveness offered. Welcome to the deep end of the pool.

In an effort to be more than just understanding and sympathetic, I gently took the crumbled piece of paper from her hand and looked at the two scores.

"Maybe you add them together," I said quietly.

In her frustration and disbelief, she stated she had never heard of adding the scores together to get a total. Looking at my watch I realized with relief the College of Education office would still be open for another fifteen minutes.

"I'll call the office," I said reassuringly.

Too shaken to stand with me as I called, she went into the other room sobbing. The kind lady who answered the phone gave me a quick and greatly relieving answer.

I found Donna in the bathroom holding onto the sink and hardly able to stand. For a fraction of a second, the deep waters closed in around her. I reached out with hardly a moment to spare.

"You add the scores together," I said quickly knowing the pain would stop and knowing she would immediately begin to swim again with eagerness. "You easily passed."

From one moment of complete despair to the new moment of relief, she traveled through the darkest of the waters to the security of accomplishment. Now, her life and her efforts over the last four years made complete sense, and her new teaching position at Holly Springs Elementary School would actually begin. As her tears stopped, she hugged me and laughed.

I had helped her conquer the deep water at just the right moment. Exhilaration filled me as I realized with blinding certainty how I had completely changed her world. I had taken the facts of her situation and examined them and then rearranged them so they made sense and worked for her. She needed me. I needed her. My deep emptiness began to recede as I realized for the first time how I had become a vital part of her life. Without fully comprehending it, the resolution established itself with me that I would always make her world right, no matter what.

I had helped someone to see they were already swimming in the deep end of the pool even though they thought they were drowning. Looking at Donna, I knew she would always be there to do the same for me.

Weak hope swelled up within me as I looked across the small table at the student in the Career Services office. Knowing my words could possibly offend her, I threw her a lifeline that had worked once before.

"You did add the two scores together to get your total score?" I said with as gentle a voice as I could muster.

The student nodded yes through her tears. I realized her work in our office could not be completed at the moment, and the young student stood and quietly left the room. I would never see her again.

I had not counseled, I had not helped, I had not even been able to console. Her world had broken into pieces. She showed me the pieces, and I had simply become a witness to her drowning.

Morning

Newness in all things. Frustration at the lack of ability to handle all things. Excitement over where life would take us. Every meal prepared in newness. Every evening, a new experience of being together. Each picture placed, each curtain hung, each chair positioned, created a new way to live together as husband and wife. Each pot of beans, each biscuit or cake or cookie baked became our first together. Each sunrise and each sunset, a new experience of days running into years.

We sat at our kitchen table as Christmas approached. We knew our small collection of ornaments for our tree would hardly cover one branch. Since we wanted our first tree to have some sort of enduring remembrance, we decided we would make our own ornaments. In our tiny oven of our tiny kitchen, carefully shaped and colored dough slowly dried. The cheerful Santas, wreaths, stars, and reindeers would soon be cooled and then painted with cute details and finished with a clear coat of lacquer.

I remembered watching my parents when I was very young as they sat at our kitchen table and carefully blew eggs to make Christmas decorations. Dad used his extremely sharp pocketknife to make small holes on both ends of a fresh egg. Placing one of the holes to his lips, he blew with just the right amount of strength to force the contents of the egg out of the small hole on the other end. Somehow, both holes remained small. Mother carefully rinsed and dried the empty whole eggshell.

Following what I observed as a child, I had great success in creating whole egg shells ready to be decorated. Covering the eggs with glitter and tinsel or cutting a small window into the side of the eggs and placing a tiny scene of Christmas joy inside became a challenging adventure in dexterity.

Finally, our decorations for our first Christmas tree were complete. We stood and held each other while feeling pride in our accomplishment. I knew we still didn't have enough ornaments to cover an entire tree, but it really didn't matter. Being together and experiencing this season of joy and hope for the first time as husband and wife meant everything. Each tomorrow eased the fear of the newness. Each sunrise gave a new trust in our abilities, and even though the newness would never be felt again, the gathering of velvet memories made each treasured sunset more golden. The waters of the deep end of the pool did not seem so threatening anymore.

Chapter 6

Azure Moon

ON ONE OF OUR FIRST VACATIONS SINCE THE honeymoon, Donna and I traveled up north to visit my twin brother, Don, and his wife, Diane. For the trip back home, we decided to leave a day early so we could stop and see interesting sites without feeling rushed.

At an old gas station near the interstate, Donna found a brochure about a hotel built on top of a cavern. While we waited for the attendant to ring up our purchases, we asked him about the place.

"Oh," he said in a friendly tone, "I didn't know I still had a brochure for that place. I think they might have closed a long time ago."

He took off his cap and scratched his head while examining the brochure.

"I haven't seen one of these in forever," he said with a confused grin. "It must have been misplaced or else I would have thrown it out."

He handed the brochure back to Donna.

"Where is it from here?" she asked. Even though we were still newlyweds, I knew from her tone of voice she would not be stopped from finding the old hotel and cavern.

The man gave us directions and told us it would not take long to travel to it.

"But I really think it has been closed for a long time," he added while shaking his head.

Donna thanked him and then handed me the brochure as we walked to the car. I had paid very close attention to the directions the attendant had given us even though I knew Donna had them memorized as well.

The old brochure showed its age not just by the yellowness of the paper and the torn and dirty condition but also from the fact it was done without color, just a few words and even fewer old pictures.

The front of the brochure pictured an interesting and somewhat stately hotel. A few faded pictures of a cavern adorned the inside along with a description that included something about a river.

"It's not far out of our way, and it sounds interesting," Donna said as I pulled away from the gas station in the opposite direction of the interstate. "I'm sure the station owner can't believe we are going to drive out there, but I want to see it."

Morning

As we pulled out onto the street, I noticed in the rearview mirror the station attendant standing near the door with his hands on his hips watching us.

The drive took us deeper into the country than we had expected, but we laughed about our new adventure to a destination that would probably not be worth the effort. I had the very firm impression Donna had decided to satisfy my desire to see different things.

On each of our evening walks down the quiet country road near our house, I would say, "Every time I see high tension power lines running over hills and down through valleys, I want to start following them to wherever they might lead me" as we passed the giant power lines. We would talk and laugh and share our ideas about everything. We would also share our dreams and plans.

"I want to go on a trip one day and take photos of all the different types of power lines," I would say with enthusiasm. "Just think of all the great places we would see! We could go to places no one would ever want to visit and find every imaginable type of power poles and lines and transformers. People drive past those all the time and never take any time to really see them. Each place has their own type and in some weird sort of technical way, they are really amazingly beautiful."

Donna would laugh at my desire to travel and explore different places. I knew she understood my desire to escape all the demands and worries of life. She laughed as I would plan out my career of photographing telephone poles.

We saw the old hotel from a distance. The photograph on the worn brochure captured it very well. As we got closer we realized the structure possessed a great amount of stateliness as though at one time it might have been a small palace for a long forgotten princedom.

Turning from the road onto the well-worn gravel driveway, we saw no other cars.

"I believe the man at the gas station was right," Donna said while bending forward to see further. "I don't see any cars, and the hotel does not look open for business."

Glancing up from the driveway while still driving, I noticed the building, though impressive, looked completely empty. No signs of curtains or blinds as though the entire façade stared out with an empty gaze upon a deserted lawn and road.

Just as we pulled up to the front steps, we noticed a woman on the porch. She turned toward us, smiled, and then started to walk away as though she had nothing to say to us.

We quickly got out of the car and started walking toward her to ask about the place.

"If you want to go to the cavern," the lady said as she continued to walk away, "you'll have to follow the little path right here."

In walking away from us, she had led us to the path that ran from the side of the old hotel to a riverbank.

"I think Helen is down there," the lady continued. "She will help you. Just follow the path."

The woman disappeared around the corner of the hotel as though she had never existed. She left us standing beside the empty old hotel in a treeless yard with instructions to walk down a deserted path. Looking down the trail, we could see it led to a river that seemed to slowly cut through the old estate and then simply vanish.

Just when I was getting ready to say we should leave, Donna smiled and took my hand.

"We've come this far," she said with a smile. "Let's go on down and see what we find!"

The winding path led us to the riverbank. From this point, we could see why the river appeared to vanish because here we could see the rather massive opening of the cavern. The river ran extremely slowly and calmly past us and then glided quietly into the wide dark abyss. As though standing guard over the entrance, the old hotel stood on top of the cavern.

Donna giggled as she walked down the well-worn gravel path. We outpaced the flowing water as though we were much more eager to reach our destination than it was. With no fear of what awaited us in the cavern, we ventured forth holding hands.

Immediately inside the opening, the path transformed into a pier beside the water. With each step, we descended to the level of the water. The pier barely protected us from getting wet. Old bare lightbulbs dangled on an electrical line fastened to the rock walls of the cavern. Other lights could be seen across the river which at this point seemed to spill out from the confinement of the riverbank and become a large pool, almost a lake in the midst of the cavern.

As we stepped upon the pier, we immediately realized we were not alone. Up ahead at the end of the pier stood a lady.

"You must be Helen," Donna said loudly so the lady could hear. I wondered if Donna had asked so as to make sure we shouldn't make a hasty retreat if the lady wasn't who she was supposed to be.

Morning

"Yes," the lady called back with a surprisingly calm voice that echoed across the still waters. "I was expecting you. Welcome to the cavern. I'm so glad you came."

Long grey hair flowed to her shoulders. Her black dress with accents of white came down to the ground and puddled slightly at her feet. She wore a short jacket that almost looked like a shawl. As we approached her, she smiled gently and held out her hand to point us to our destination. At the end of the pier, a small boat awaited.

The gondola sat still in the waters unaffected by the very slight current of the river. Donna looked at me and smiled. I knew it pleased her greatly that our little side trip was turning into an occasion we would always remember.

"Please take a seat," the lady said while pointing to the boat. "I've made sure everything was ready for you."

I wondered how long it took us to walk down the path from the hotel to the riverbank and then into the cavern. Looking at the rock wall next to the pier, I did not see a phone.

"You must have seen us coming," I said in a friendly tone as Donna and I took our seats. "I guess you normally have a lot of people coming to see this amazing sight."

The lady smiled at me but did not answer. She stepped gently from the pier to the front of the boat. A small platform on the gondola stood slightly higher than our seats. The lady stood on an old black velvet cushion on the deck and then reached down with great agility and untied the boat from its mooring and took a long pole from the side of the pier.

Her motions demonstrated many years, perhaps decades, of practice. With a slight motion of the pole in the water, she pushed us away from the pier as we began our journey deeper into the cavern. I wanted to look at the cavern walls but the boat itself drew my attention. Built like a Venetian gondola, the ends of the boat curved upward and toward us as though ready to embrace. The black paint with gold trim glistened in its glossiness as though freshly prepared just for this adventure. A curious old lantern hung from the gondola on a rod over the water.

The lantern's frosted blue glass allowed the flame to shine with amazing clarity without being too bright to obscure the view of the cavern. The flickering lamp seemed to be the only thing that moved as we found ourselves captured in the eternal stillness of this breathtakingly beautiful underworld.

I found out years later that normally the tourists would explore the cavern in rather long narrow red boats with small outboard engines. I guess since we were the only visitors that day or even for many days, Helen must have decided to use one of the old gondolas for our excursion.

A short distance from the pier we rounded a slight bend in the river pool and a side cavern opened for us to see. Hidden lights made the walls of this new cave visible. Beautifully delicate stalagmites and stalactites futilely reached for each other as they had for centuries before.

"The view is overwhelming," I said quietly. "I could stay here forever." Our gondolier stopped poling and looked across to the side cave.

"My great-grandfather found this cavern in the river," she said quietly. "We used to have many visitors here. People loved to stay in the hotel he built. He spared no expense. It was said he spent all of his fortune on this place because he wanted it to be a destination like no other."

She turned and looked at us with sadness and with a look that let us know we were indeed privileged to have her speak to us at all.

"Many people used to come here to see the beauty and go away refreshed. They were beautiful people, young people. Everyone was young then, it seemed. They danced and laughed and glowed in the grandeur of each evening. It's all so still now. It seems like that never happened."

"You are the first people to come here in a very, very long time," she said with unmistakable gratitude. "I'm so glad you find it...wondrous."

She returned to her poling. Donna looked at the lady and then turned and looked at me.

"She seems so sad," she whispered. "It's almost as though she feels there is no future."

I nodded and found myself feeling her bitterness over a past that would probably never be repeated. I wondered at the sights she must have seen and experienced. I imagined the gondolas full of laughing people celebrating the sights.

Donna leaned over the side of the boat and looked into the water.

"That's so strange," she said pointing at the reflection of the lamp on the dark waters. "It looks just like a moon. It looks like an azure moon."

Our gondolier ceased to pole and stood above us. Looking at the reflection of the lamp in the water, she began to speak once again.

"The lamp was made to give the reflection of the full moon in the water," she said mysteriously. "The story used to be that people would come to the cavern not just for the ride in the gondola but also to see their future in the azure moon. Great care was taken with the shaping of the glass so the reflection mimics even the craters of the moon's surface."

I looked down to the reflection and understood. Floating on the surface of the still water, the azure moon shone back at me. It looked almost as though it had come and rested just below the surface of the water.

Morning

"The legend used to be widely shared that if you looked into the azure moon, you would see your future unfold."

I marveled again at how she kept everything in the past and wondered if she had gazed into the azure moon and seen that the cavern and the hotel had no future.

Donna leaned over once more and drew her face closer to the reflection of the azure moon. Smiling and serene, she held out her hand to see if the reflection could be seen there. Her hand and her face captured and reflected the light as her eyes examined what tomorrow would be.

As I watched, her face began to capture the rich luster of the lamp's reflection upon the calm water. She looked at me and smiled once more almost as if she knew the light enhanced her beauty. Her face absorbed the blue of the waters. More than simple beauty, the azure moon created its own impression upon her. In awe, I accepted what I saw as an almost magical moment of grace.

"The azure moon has filled your face with wonder," I said to her as I joined her in gazing into the waters.

"What does it mean?" she whispered softly.

Chapter 7
Seneca

SUNRISE, SUNSET. EACH DAY STARTS LIKE ANY OTHER. Finding a rhythm in our lives, contentment became our established way in the world. Instead of unexpected wonder, we discovered the joy of living out each sunrise and sunset together.

Just as the first light of dawn approached, our days began with a hasty breakfast and a quick kiss goodbye. Our little townhouse with two bedrooms and two bathrooms, felt like a mansion after our prefab. Built on the road connecting two of the three towns in this rural county, our second home possessed a beautifully efficient stylishness. To Donna's delight, the couch fit through the door. With curtains hung and newly acquired artwork mounted, the warmth of our new home and the continuing journey of our lives blended with the eternal rhythms of the sun.

Donna's trek to the nearby county where she taught fifth grade took her on a twenty-mile journey early each morning. We had moved from Pendleton to Seneca because I had taken a job in the area of our state called the Golden Corner. My second job presented itself to me in much the same manner as the first. Each had come while I had been pursuing other things.

My job with the career center at Clemson had been the result of a fellow graduate student telling me to apply for an open position at the office where she worked. My second job came one evening as I sat in class with another graduate student. She introduced herself to me as the agent-in-charge of the Oconee County office of Probation and Parole which at present had an opening for an agent. She asked me if, like my older brother, Jim, I had ever considered a job in the field of criminal justice. She explained that she knew my brother and the fine work he was accomplishing in the Greenville County office of Probation and Parole.

My first reaction was to tell her I was going to continue my studies and hopefully obtain an advanced degree in clinical psychology. Before I could speak those words, I hesitated. Instead of telling her I had already chosen my path, I asked her about the application process.

After several interviews to make sure I was cut from the same cloth as Jim, I found myself completing six weeks of training at the South Carolina Criminal Justice Academy. Surprisingly, I discovered great satisfaction in doing something completely new and different. The shift from my preconceived notions excited me as I began to live out the seemingly inexhaustible possibilities of each day.

Each morning Donna left for work, and I would leave soon afterward. On many bright and clear winter mornings, the mountains would greet me with a faint whiteness indicating a snow flurry had passed through their heights during the night.

One morning, not long after Donna left, I was getting ready to walk out the door when the phone rang. I wondered who would be calling at this time of the day.

"Does your wife drive a blue car?" a female voice questioned.

I stopped myself from saying our new car looked dark blue but was actually dark green. All of a sudden, the color of the car did not seem to be the important part of the conversation.

"Yes," I said without asking why she was inquiring or who she was.

"Well, she has been in a wreck right out of Seneca," the lady stated. "It's a pretty bad wreck."

"Is she alright?"

"The car is very badly damaged, but I really can't tell how much," the lady replied.

"Is my wife alright?"

"The ambulance is here and the Highway Patrol and the police, I think a wrecker is driving up now. Lots of people have gathered."

I repeated my only concern.

"Is my wife OK?"

"The wreck is on the Clemson highway not far out of town. She must have been going to work. I think another car is involved."

I stood to my feet wanting to go to the scene as quickly as possible, but I had to have the answer to my question first. In spite of myself, I screamed into the phone as my hands began to tremble.

"IS SHE OK? IS MY WIFE ALRIGHT?"

"Oh, yes, I think she's fine," the lady said with a startled voice. "She gave me your phone number and asked me to call you. She's sitting on the ground near the wreck. She appears to be unharmed."

Apologizing for shouting and feeling more relief than I had ever experienced in my life, I thanked her for calling and then ran out the door.

As I raced up the highway, I remembered a similar time of panic just a few months ago. While far from home, my fears had taken me on a search for assurance.

During our one summer of living in the prefab, we flew to the Mayo Clinic in Rochester, Minnesota, for Donna to have surgery.

Born with a defect in her kidneys discovered when she was six years old, Donna had undergone extensive corrective surgeries at the Egleston Children's Hospital at Emory University in Atlanta. These surgeries continued, throughout her childhood and ended with what was hoped to be the last one when she was in the sixth grade.

When she spoke of those days, her strength and calm assurance could be felt as well as her relief in her present good health. Her mother, Thelma, told many stories of the trips to Atlanta to see one specialist after another.

Donna's kidney troubles had not been discovered until she was in the first grade. After a routine trip to the doctor's office to handle what they thought was just another childhood illness, the long succession of hospital visits began. Thelma laughed as she retold how six-year-old Donna grew increasingly impatient with the doctors and the long stays in the hospital. On one occasion, a young doctor walked into the room and started his friendly examination. Jumping from the bed, Donna bolted for the door before anyone could stop her. Thelma said by the time she and the doctor got to the door, all they could see was her mahogany brown ponytail waving at them as she ran down the corridor. The doctor took off after her and a little while later returned with Donna in his arms. As he put her back on the bed, Donna triumphantly grinned at the doctor.

"There can't be too much wrong with you," the doctor said while trying to catch his breath. "Anyone who can run that fast must be in pretty good shape."

My job at the Mayo Clinic consisted of sitting in extremely comfortable chairs in the pleasant waiting rooms as Donna saw one doctor after another. Everything had been prepared and coordinated with her doctors in South Carolina. Assurances were given this would be the last surgery she would face to correct her condition.

The whole trip lasted longer than we had anticipated but turned out to be a final chapter in this part of her life. Since Donna's childhood days, many things had improved with this type of surgery including the recuperation time. When she had undergone procedures like this in the past, they had confined her to bed and tied her legs together so no movement could undo the reconstructive work of the surgery. After the confinement finished, she received therapy to help her relearn how to walk.

Morning

We took the trip to the Mayo Clinic expecting this restrictive recuperative procedure would have to be followed. I even asked one of the flight attendants on the plane how they would transport someone who was still confined to bed. She assured me they had handled this situation before, especially coming and going from the Mayo Clinic, and it would be no problem at all.

Much to our delight, one of the first doctors who saw her said they would be using a new procedure he had developed and she would be up and walking the day after surgery. In excitement over this good news, we spent the rest of the day finding a small apartment in Rochester within walking distance to the clinic and the hospitals. The apartment building was older but very well preserved and clean. The small suites had been designed especially for people who had come to stay for a few weeks. The lady who managed the building welcomed us as though we were long lost relatives.

All of these memories surfaced as I raced up the highway in search of Donna. In near panic and desperation, I tried to calm myself with the words of the lady on the phone saying Donna appeared to be uninjured. Even as I worked my way through the morning traffic and started down the long stretch of highway toward Clemson, my mind went back to that time in Rochester.

I remembered a small sanctuary glowing in the early morning light as the colors of the old stained-glass windows began coming to life. The dark wooden pew felt amazingly comfortable somehow forming itself to me as I sat in solitude seeking relief through prayer. I had stopped on my way to the bright modern hospital across the street from the clinic. The day of Donna's much anticipated surgery had finally arrived. I needed a moment of prayer before seeing my beloved wife who awaited me in her hospital bed in the ward where she had been assigned on the previous afternoon.

After she had been admitted, I had spent an anxious evening in the apartment. My youthful determination and my confidence in this famous place of healing weakened as we approached the hour of surgery. Sitting in the pew, I studied one votive candle burning near the altar. Unlike all of the other candles, this flame remained unmoving.

This candle's flame seemed to represent the faith and prayers of the people of this place. Even though my resolve to make everything right for Donna stretched thin at this moment, I knew many others were praying for her. In this place where she was not known, the faithful brought the attention of the always present God to the plight of travelers who had come on their pilgrimages from distant places seeking healing.

My prayer became one of gratitude. Strengthened not by my weak faith but by the faith of others seen in the light of one small candle, I lit another candle for her in the quiet sanctuary of hope and walked out into the brightness of day bolstered by peace and hope.

The surgery and the trip turned out very well. Even though I knew these events could have taken place without me, I was grateful for being with Donna during this time in her life. My role as her protector continued.

As I raced up the Clemson highway in search of Donna, I realized how her joys, anguish, fears and even her health now completely filled my life. I knew I had to be with her at this moment to hold her and offer what I could of my imperfect strength.

My anxious journey came to an end as soon as I saw cars parked on the roadside, bystanders and flashing lights of emergency vehicles gathered on the highway. I ran to the scene in my frantic search for Donna. Confused by everything, I could not find Donna nor our car. The only car I saw was upside down, and from looking at the bottom of it, I mistakenly thought it was too large to be ours.

Later, Donna told me she had been driving in the left lane of the four-lane highway when the driver in front of her quickly pulled to the right. A car was stopped in the left-hand lane while another car waited in the cross-over lane to make a left turn. Having no time to slow her car, Donna decided to drive into the wide grassy median separating the four lanes. Being her only choice, the median became a point of safety for her and the other drivers except for the deep ditch in the median. When her car hit the ditch, it flipped. The driver waiting in his car in the cross-over lane said he saw dirt landing on his hood. He turned to see where the dirt was coming from and saw Donna hanging upside down by her seatbelt in her car sliding right at him. Without having an opportunity to move his car, he held on for what he thought would be an impact, but Donna's car stopped just in time.

Just as I almost started screaming her name, Donna suddenly appeared. I ran to her and embraced her tightly. My joy in seeing her unharmed renewed my resolve to always be there for her and make all the bad things disappear.

I felt her strength leave her body and knew she had contained her poise during the ordeal for as long as she could. Now in my arms, her true emotions surfaced and she began to cry. She buried her face into my neck and I held her all the more tightly as the crowd became quiet and focused its attention

Morning

on us. For just a moment, the sun stopped rising as the golden strands reached across the heavens and glowed in stillness. Eternity existed in the light of the early morning. I held her with the embrace of lives forever joined.

A loud sigh from the large crowd of bystanders broke the spell of the moment, and the sun continued its dance across the skies.

Chapter 8
Walhalla

"Lord, I believe, help thou my unbelief."

Pastor Ben Locklair preached from the pulpit of St. Luke United Methodist Church in Walhalla. Wearing the brightest white robe and stole I had ever seen, he preached a very effective sermon. His brilliant attire matched the paraments and flowers of the chancel. The brightness also perfectly complemented his impossibly continuous cheerfulness. Donna and I held hands as we sat with our new church family in the beautiful old pews.

From time to time during the sermon, I would look up at the dark wooden beams running across the cathedral ceiling from one side of the small sanctuary to the other. Demonstrating their strength made perfect through the past century, those beams continued supporting the vaulted ceiling in quiet witness of the lives of sitting worshippers. The dark beams, whose existence probably began in the undisturbed mountain forests surrounding our little town, continued to live out their preserved life while symbolizing eternal truths. Silently they assured us the values preached in worship existed all around us. Strength, clarity of purpose, faithful service, selfless giving of life, glorifying the Living Lord all seemed to be stated by these massive structures. While listening to Pastor Ben's words, I wondered how the church sexton kept all of the beautiful dark wood dusted and polished.

As though someone wanted to make sure I was paying attention to the truth of the matter at hand, awareness of the significance of the spoken word took priority over my random thoughts. A different consciousness marked the moment as sacred.

This awareness became evident as Pastor Ben kept repeating piercing words from the Gospel of Mark.

"Lord, I believe, help thou my unbelief."

Memories from my childhood began to crowd into the moment.

"And what do you want to be when you grow up?" a nice older lady asked me one day as I left the worship service with my mother, father, and two brothers from the church of my childhood in Marietta. I knew she was asking in order to hear me say the answer so she could be slightly amused.

"A preacher," I said with a shy smile.

Morning

"Oh, how cute!" she said as she patted me on the head. Perhaps she did not mean to be condescending, but even at that early age, I understood she did not take my calling seriously. My biggest fear seemed to be confirmed with each well-meaning adult patting me on the head while smiling and unknowingly strengthening all of my feelings of inadequacy.

They did not understand I had sinned and my calling was a result of my sin. In tearful confession before God for stealing my older brother's small cloth bag filled with pennies and a few quarters, I pleaded with God to forgive me and not send me directly to hell. In determination to demonstrate to the Almighty, who then seemed to be a God who always punished wrongdoers with instant death and damnation, I blurted out a quick prayer and promise while hiding in my parent's bathroom. I promised to become a preacher if God would forgive me.

Somehow the word soon got out in our little town of my calling to the ministry. In seeing it as a childhood fascination with things I didn't truly understand, the townsfolk slowly and inadvertently confirmed my worst fears: becoming a preacher because of guilt could not be a legitimate call.

In my high school years as others around me began to explore all the possibilities of amazing careers, I put an end to all presumptions of my calling. I then sought forgiveness for calling myself into ministry.

Much to my amazement, I realized no one noticed this change of career choice. I came to the conclusion that other people must have known more about the call than I did. They seemed to be quietly relieved as though wanting me to have a regular life.

Even as I made up my mind to abandon what appeared to be a false call, I still wondered.

"Lord, I believe, help thou my unbelief."

Now, as I sat in the pew of our little church in Walhalla listening to the words of the scriptures being expertly applied to my adult life, I realized the comfortable and satisfying life Donna and I fashioned into existence might have to change.

Just a few weeks before, we walked through the rooms of an almost new house and knew it could be a place where we would happily raise a family and live for many years. In a quiet subdivision just off the Westminster Highway, this split-level half brick home with three bedrooms and two and a half bathrooms sat on a large lot and appeared to have everything we could have ever imagined in a house. I dreamed about living there and how we would make each room the perfect space for ourselves and our future family. The house seemed to be the final brick and mortar evidence and perfect assurance that together our search was finished. A happy future awaited us on Stone Drive where the yearning of our young twenty-something year old lives would finally be satisfied.

Donna needed that assurance much less than I did. Her clear, green eyes saw the passing clouds and the movement of the sun across the sky as the uncomplicated part of the journey we all shared. At the same time she embraced clarity of all things with faith, she also understood my constant search for reassurance.

Down at the river bordering our old family farm, a wide place existed. The old North Saluda River always appeared to be just a pale faded version of a real river. It had been abused in the past, and in our walks down by the small but steep sandy banks, my Aunt Helen would tell me stories of how grand it used to be. She relished in telling me stories of the strong, swift, and clear waters of yesteryear. She pointed to the nearly hidden stone foundations of the spring house that at one time stood in a clearing at the bottom of a steep hill near the river. Aunt Helen would laugh about those olden days of storing fresh milk within the always chilled stone walls of the spring house and the trips into the woods from the farmhouse to gather milk for the day. On several occasions she would take me to the spring itself. We would watch as it quietly bubbled forth the clear and cold waters from the depths and formed a little shallow stream flowing to the river.

With her perpetual laughter, she explained how even though she and her sisters and brothers used to play in the strong currents of the river, she never learned to swim.

"When we came to a deep part," she said while pointing to a dark green area in the water, "Father would simply put me on his back and swim through the water to the other shore."

She smiled at the place in the river as we continued to walk on the shore under the giant poplars. They grew just beyond the hemlock grove on the side of the forested hill.

My grandfather's oldest daughter walked beside me on the riverbank. Somehow her life seemed trapped in the currents of the small river. She never married nor had a home other than the old farmhouse with its tin roof and coal heaters and a straight path back to a past that was quickly vanishing during my childhood.

Even though the old river never seemed particularly impressive, it did possess one area right at the edge of the farm property where everything changed. As the river slowly turned to leave the woodland of the farm, it became wider. Just at this point, the river gained strength reminiscent, I thought, of the glory of its past.

There in the riverbed an island arose. It was much more than just a random sandbank since it had full-grown river birch trees on it. Their white and tan slender trunks sprouted up through the dark soil. The thin bark peeled away from the sides of the trees and seemed to be nature's version of natural paper. The small heavily veined and perfectly tinted green leaves added just the right contrast to the tan paper bark as though an artist had contrived the island as a beautifully perfect Appalachian setting. The dark sandy soil rose above the waters and held them at bay. The little island appeared inviting and yet treacherous since the soil looked as though it might simply give way to the weight of our footsteps. I wondered at times if anyone had ever walked on its shores.

The river begrudgingly divided at the point of the island as the waters flowed with faster pace along the shorelines of this unexplored isle. This place in the river always gave me an unexplainable thrill. The small island and the wideness of the divided river made our little old farm seem to be on the edge of something significant. The river became, in my mind, a real river at this juncture. Here the reality of the natural force of moving water linked it with all significant waterways. It lost its hesitancy and demonstrated the force and purpose of why it existed.

On our side of the island, the water took drastic turns as it cut through the sandy riverbed and exposed many pale white rocks. Smoothed by the relentless flow of the waters, the rocks beckoned for someone to come and examine them to see if their quartz veins held flakes of mountain gold.

The water flowing on the other side of the shoreline must have faced less of a rocky riverbed and succeeded in pushing the river's domain wider. On that side, fallen tree trunks from our neighbor's woodlands formed obstacles in the stream. The water rushed over and around these obstacles to continue the journey. Standing on the tall banks on our side and looking across at what the quiet river had become, I realized by its presence, this waterway created a formidable boundary for the farm.

As the old river approached the island and began the process of dividing, an eddy existed. In a deep green pool possibly hiding many long-forgotten artifacts of ancient people from this forest, the water turned in slow motion counter to the current of the river.

The water reached this point in its relentless flow of hundreds of miles to the ocean's shore and here had to decide which way it would go. One side of the island claimed the run of interesting turns and shallow rocky beds. The other side possessed the wideness and the old blackened tree trunks creating amusing obstacles. The water hesitated in the slow churning of the eddy and seemed to be caught in thought for just a moment as more water cascaded into the pool and forced a decision in the relentless curse of constant motion.

"Have you ever thought you were called to go into the ministry?" I asked Donna one Sunday as we left St. Luke with Pastor Ben's word still quietly echoing in my ears.

"No," she replied without hesitation, "and I've never thought I was called to be a pastor's wife, either."

Her smile spoke words that broke through the present and became a part of the forever in our lives. Her smile moved beyond just mere knowing, as Donna affirmed and accepted my call in simple directness. Without a word of grief over the shattered perception of the future we were planning together, she took my hand.

The river had chosen its course.

Chapter 9

Central

STANDING AT OUR KITCHEN SINK FILLED WITH cold soapy water, I grasped a greasy pan, but my mind could not fully grasp my new reality. I tried to comprehend the fury of events that had changed our lives and brought us here. I looked out the small kitchen window into the backyard which seemed to be a continuation of all the other nondescript backyards.

After all the decisions Donna and I made and the endless activities those choices demanded, our lives were beginning to settle down once more into a routine. Just as things began to appear to be comfortable, the questions started to arrive.

"Let's go on a walk," my mother said as soon as Donna and I had arrived at my parent's home in Marietta. "We need to talk."

I looked at Donna and with a quick nod let her know this was not a walk she needed to complete with me. She went into the house with my Dad and brother as Mom began to walk with a purpose around the circle driveway.

"I'm not sure you have considered the impact this decision will have on Donna," she said with directness. After teaching high school for over three decades, Mom often counseled her students as they began to make major life choices. She had seen her beloved pupils make good and bad decisions.

Mom reared my brothers and me to make our own decisions. She promoted our strength and only offered her advice if she thought our chosen course might lead us to difficult circumstances. At times such as these, she carefully considered her words so they would have maximum impact and deliver her concerns with unmistakable clarity.

"You married her, and she expects you to work with her in providing a home and a future," she said while looking down at the asphalt as the beautiful April day welcomed us with the splendor of spring. Oblivious to the flowers and the bird songs, we continued our intensely focused walk.

"Are you sure she is happy with your decision?" Mom asked. "I'm not sure she will be happy enough to stay with you if you continue with the choice you have made."

I recalled Mom lecturing students to resist the tendency to be "spoon-fed" as she was so fond of saying.

"You have to search for the answers before you can really understand," she would say with teacher sternness.

I had listened to her as she stood before her classes and presented new concepts and ideas. Teaching classes in typing, record keeping, shorthand, business law and math, she unquestionably demonstrated her love of the importance of learning. In her world, the teacher validated the acquisition of knowledge through testing.

Mom would not be at peace with my decision until she tested it to the best of her abilities. Her words hit their intended mark, but instead of producing uncertainty, I found great relief in knowing I would pass this test. I gave her my assurance that Donna's happiness and contentment with this decision mattered more to me than my own.

My agent-in-charge at the Probation and Parole office in Walhalla had given me a sad smile as I placed my badge on her desk. All of the paperwork and reports had been completed to her satisfaction and my case files had been temporarily transferred to her care. My last action before I left the oversized offices consisted of the simple act of relinquishing this final vestige of my position, authority, and duty.

My fingers lingered on the leather case holding my badge. The golden stamp of the state seal had not even had time to wear thin. The thick protective cloth cover inside the leather case still kept the badge shining. I wanted to flip open the case to see the artfully designed brass once more but decided it was time to leave.

My fingers also lingered on the doorknob of our townhouse as I began to shut the door for the last time. I looked over the small living room remarking to myself how much it reminded me of when we had entered for the first time. I tried to glance back into the kitchen but could not see it without entering the townhouse once again. Fighting off my feelings of despair for not being able to remain in such a perfect home, I closed the door and joined Donna in the car.

The evidence of her strength could always be seen in her smile. Without a word, she conveyed to me her understanding of my need of place and things. She also conveyed to me another way of approaching life. As a teacher, still new to the profession but gaining skills every day, she began to help me grow in my understanding and took responsibility for all of my future testing.

Morning

"Things are just things," she said as we drove away from our beloved home. "People matter more than things."

Our new duplex apartment in the little community of Central near Clemson consisted of two bedrooms, one bath, kitchen and a large living room. With well-kept but out-of-date cabinets and an old avocado green refrigerator, which sounded like a locomotive when running, the kitchen completed the slightly run-down appearance of everything.

The old linoleum floor of the kitchen continued down the hallway and into the bathroom. Its pattern matched the paneling of the apartment which, at one time, had been very popular. Donna and I tried everything to remove what appeared to be centuries of floor wax on the linoleum. Finally, remembering a trick my Aunt Pat had described in dealing with a similar situation in her home, we found two old wooden rulers in our still boxed possessions. Using these rulers as scrapers, we forced the soapy ammonia water to remove the wax buildup. Side by side on our knees we attacked the grime with the dull wooden edges of our rulers. "Do unto others as you would have them do unto you" was printed with bold black letters on the rulers and seemed a fitting way to describe the efforts we were making to prepare our new home for ourselves and those who would follow us.

As we made our bed for the first time in our freshly cleaned duplex, Donna went to one side of the bed and gave a shriek. From her reaction, I thought she had found something unimaginably horrible. As I came around the corner of the bed, a tiny field mouse hid in the corner and shivered in fear.

Donna did not find my amusement with her situation appropriate nor did she agree with my decision to scoop up the little helpless animal in a bowl and take it to the field.

"I'm sure he will beat you back in here," she said. "He obviously knows his way around here better than we do."

The old hardwood floors of the living room and bedrooms helped to soften the reality of our downsizing. We both knew this duplex would be less expensive and also more suitably located to both Donna's school and my seminary. A piece of carpeting my brother and I had used in our dorm room completed our interior designing in what Donna deemed as "Early Make Do".

My hands ached while they continued to grasp the pan soaking in the cold water. Stillness overcame my continuous stream of movements which had been taking place in those few months since the decision had been made.

I realized I could not move my hands through the cold water in the sink as a bird landed in the small bare tree outside the kitchen window. The bird seemed not to care about my presence as it intently stared across the field as though contemplating a new journey.

Even though I wanted to finish my task at the sink, the only motion I could muster was a tightening of my fingers on the pan in the dishwater and a tensing of every other muscle in my body as I refused to accept the reality of our present situation.

Donna had helped me decide not to obtain a part-time job as I began seminary. I needed to focus my attention on my studies. Outside of church, I had never taken a class at Clemson or elsewhere in any sort of theology or Biblical studies. I feared I would always be far behind the other seminarians who probably arrived with undergraduate degrees in this field of study.

Even though those fears seemed justified, I remembered a young high school chemistry teacher giving me words of encouragement in a similar situation. She taught interesting and animated classes in which we explored the world of science.

One day after class, I went to her with my anxieties about the students from other schools being better prepared for college since they would have taken advanced classes that our school did not offer.

"The only difference," she said to me, "will be while those other students may be hearing the information for the second time, you will be hearing it for the first time."

Her words gave comfort then and now.

Before the onslaught of other decisions could be made, Donna and I had to choose which seminary I would attend.

Pastor Ben immediately started letting me know of the advantages of the closest United Methodist seminary, Candler School of Theology at Emory University in Atlanta. His cheerful assertiveness pushed itself on me as though to say this was the only logically course of action. He also mentioned the Divinity School at Duke University not knowing I had visited at Duke while at Clemson and had almost transferred there after my freshman year.

Morning

Both choices seemed to have great merit. They also seemed, for some reason, to be completely wrong.

Atlanta had been home to Donna and her family for a few years. Her father, Ken, had been stationed there while in the Navy. Donna's mom, Thelma, had met him on a blind date while Ken was stationed at the Charleston naval shipyard. After marrying, they had lived in Connecticut and then Memphis and finally Atlanta.

The image of a nine-year-old girl standing in the driveway to flag down the ambulance as it made its way to their home became vividly real the very first time Donna shared it with me. Ken, just thirty-nine years old and the father of three young children, had come home early from work and complained of not feeling well. A former basketball player at the University of Nebraska, he had been forced to give up his athletic scholarship when he suffered a heart attack in the middle of a game.

In those days, the doctors dismissed his condition and told him to go and lead a normal life. Donna had been sent out to the driveway when Ken lost consciousness and began to have difficulty breathing while Thelma stood by him watching helplessly.

Reliving the fear and sharing it with me so it became a part of our shared life, Donna told me how she knew the moment her father died. While dutifully waiting in the driveway as instructed by her mother, Donna's world turned dark.

"All of a sudden, I couldn't see anything," she said with a look of blind terror in her eyes. "Somehow I made it back into the house and to the bedroom. I had to be near my Dad."

The ambulance arrived too late, and after everything changed for this young family, Thelma moved from Atlanta to be closer to her parents.

Donna's pain was evident in her experiences there, but her Midwestern roots of being able to face anything with unwavering strength, ran deep. She assured me she would not mind living in Atlanta again as we continued to discern wisdom in the midst of the decisions to be made.

As a logical course of action, we decided I would visit three seminaries. The third choice for us would be Erskine Theological Seminary in Due West.

This Associated Reformed Presbyterian college and seminary along with the Lutheran Seminary at Columbia constituted the entire list of seminaries in South Carolina accepted by the United Methodist Church for its candidates to ordained ministry. We started this process by visiting the closest first.

As I walked from the main entrance to the dean's office, oil portraits from the last century lined the main room and flanked a large and stately fireplace glowing with flames dancing through the logs obviously gathered from the rural area surrounding this small community. The couches, chairs, oriental carpets and even the architecture of the room spoke to a well-preserved elegance.

The dean of the seminary sat behind a large desk in his dignified office at McQuiston Divinity Hall on the campus of Erskine. Donna's brother, Wayne, had played basketball at the college, and his team went all the way to the national championship. He would later be inducted into their athletic hall of fame. Donna had decided to attend Clemson because she feared that at a school as small as Erskine, she would be forever labelled as "Wayne's sister".

Dean Ruble spoke with tones of authority with an undercurrent of great kindness. An immensely talented Princeton and Edinburgh graduate who would later become the president of the college, he radiated a natural ability to lead.

As he told me about the seminary and the courses involved, he demonstrated a devotion to this task even though he had probably accomplished this discussion with many other people, young and not so young, who answered the call. I asked my prepared questions, and realizing I had gained all of the information possible, gave him my thanks for taking the time to see me.

"Before you go," he said in a teacher's tone, "let's pray."

Closing my eyes and bowing my head as I sat in the Chippendale chair in front of the white bookcases stacked neatly with many volumes, I wondered how a seminary dean would pray.

Dean Ruble gave praise to God and then asked for direction and guidance for me and all students.

To my amazement and embarrassment while Dean Ruble prayed, I began to cry. I successfully held back my sobs but the tears ran down my face and splattered on the lapels of my suit. Through the sudden onslaught of emotions, my tears unmistakably assured me I had found my home for the next three years.

Dean Ruble looked surprised and perhaps a little startled when he concluded his prayer and then looked across his desk to me. I tried to be as

Morning

inconspicuous as possible in wiping my face with my handkerchief but failed miserably. He looked at me for a few silent seconds assessing with his discerning eyes if I needed to speak with him about the trauma of my days, and when I nodded and smiled at him, he returned a knowing smile.

Still gripping the old greasy pan in the cold soapy water of our kitchen sink, I wondered why, after all of these assurances, I felt such anxiety. More than regular worries, this new fear ran rampant through my mind and put me into a catatonic state. Frozen, I realized I would never accomplish this task and I could never be the pastor of any church.

"It's OK."

My hands let go of the pan and with dripping, sudsy fingers I turned from the window to see who had spoken the words releasing me from my terror.

No one greeted me. I stood alone in the kitchen of our new home which now seemed to glow with remarkable warmth and peace.

Chapter 10
Homeland Park & John Wesley

"WELL, SHE'S A LIVING DOLL!" EXCLAIMED AN OVERLY exuberant member of the committee when he saw Donna. His words greeted us as we walked through the threshold and into the narthex of the church. I laughed because I knew his exclamation would put Donna at ease. We had spent more than a few hours in several stores looking for just the right outfit for her to wear to this important meeting.

Donna always selected her clothes with great care not only because she hated to spend a lot on herself, but also because she had to make sure the clothes worked on her. Born with uneven hips, she learned to accept the fact that one hip was several inches higher than the other and how certain clothes could help conceal the condition.

Remarkably, she developed a method of making both hips appear even in height. Later in life, one of her doctors studied this almost undetectable procedure. Donna said he wanted to understand the method she used to accomplish the subterfuge.

"He shook his head and laughed as I walked up and down the hallway at his office," she later told me. "He said he had worked with other people with the same birth defect but had never seen anyone develop a way of standing and walking which made it appear to disappear. He also said even though he watched me do it, he didn't understand how I did it."

Outfit purchased and accessorized, the evening arrived when we found ourselves making the quick car ride to the district parsonage where we would meet with the district superintendent and his wife as they took us to this meeting.

"I don't understand why I have to be a part of this," Donna said as we drove to the district parsonage. Her mild apprehension showed while she checked her makeup in her compact mirror one more time. "When I interviewed with the school district for my job, they didn't need to have you present." She gave me a quick smile and a funny look while sticking out her tongue at me.

"Only you could pick a profession where I would be examined to see if I will fit in," she said with a pretend scowl on her face.

I knew this entire process made her nervous and wasn't exactly fair. In many churches the pastor's spouse played a very important part in the work of the ministry. She would indeed be under examination by this committee representing the congregations. I smiled at her nervousness while trying to reassure her.

I knew these churches would fall in love with her. I doubted if they could possibly be excited with a pastor who had only preached one sermon. The one sermon had been in my first preaching class my freshman year of seminary. The sermon and the peer examination went well, but I knew my qualifications to preach and lead two congregations of the faithful remained very slim. I received this committee member's words of greeting as we walked through the threshold as a small token of mysterious grace. I watched as Donna laughed and smiled in her new royal blue suit with shiny black buttons.

Everyone chuckled with the church member who was known for his off-the-wall comments and his unending joy. A year later, Donna and I would sit with him all through the night as he mourned the sudden death of his wife. His tears replaced his normal laughter as together we recounted his wife's life and journey of faith.

The meeting with this committee of nine elected church members would determine if they thought effective ministry could take place with me as the pastor. Our district superintendent, who oversaw the United Methodist churches in this and several other surrounding counties, would preside over the meeting.

Uniquely, my first introductory visit took place in the choir loft of the church. One of the committee members, Marguerite, kept smiling and nodding at us as though we had been longtime friends.

"I knew the second you walked through the doors," she would later tell me, "you were the pastor for us."

Due in part to the extreme friendliness of the group, the meeting went very well. I didn't even have to recite the books of the Bible even though I had prepared for it and any other theological or doctrinal question I thought they might ask me.

Donna had gently laughed at my preparation.

"I think they just want to get to know us a little," she said while standing beside the kitchen table in our duplex in Central. I stood as I began to pack away all my notes on these two churches I had studied the prior evening. I did not know how to prepare for this meeting but I thought some sort of preparation must be necessary.

"They will be much more interested in who we are and what sort of personalities we have and whether or not we will fit in with the congregations than in how much information or how many skills you have," she said with a gentle teacher's voice.

After our meeting, the district superintendent and his wife took us to visit the other church and the parsonage where we would be living.

"You need to remember something while serving here," he said with flat authority once we were back in the privacy of his car. "Seminary must come first. You are here to serve these two churches, but you must not let this work keep you from graduating seminary on time. Seminary is your priority."

I was grateful for this appointment and for the fact these parishioners understood the role of the student pastor. I was also grateful for the salary which made it easier for Donna and me to pay for the next two years of training. The fact that McQuiston Divinity Hall was just eighteen miles from the carport of the parsonage gave me assurance that all was as it should be.

The first Sunday I drove to the John Wesley church my nervousness almost got the best of me. My first sermon as pastor would be preached right after the Sunday School hour. As I turned into the driveway, I suddenly realized I could not preach to this or any other congregation. The mere thought of the intense scrutiny of my words and the delivery of the words to the congregation terrified me. I took my foot off the gas pedal and the car coasted to a stop.

Donna looked at me with raised eyebrows as though waiting for an explanation.

"This is over and done with!" I started to say. "I'm not going through with it. I just realized I can't do it."

"Of course you can!" my mother's voice stated clearly and authoritatively in my mind. "You can do anything you put your mind to doing!"

It was Mother's standard answer when any of us doubted ourselves. With all the force of a seasoned high school teacher and all the confidence and assurance of unfailing love, her words continued to hit their mark.

Just like the athlete who depends on muscle memory to perform complicated maneuvers to perfection, her words now forced my emotions into their proper perspective. I looked at Donna and smiled as I put my foot to the gas pedal once more.

In August, I returned to seminary for my middler year.

"Look at Dan," one of my seminary friends, Karen, said to the administrative assistant in the office at McQuiston as the autumn classes resumed. "He looks different now. Last year you looked so carefree! Now your shoulders are set back as though you can see the weight of responsibility on them."

I knew Karen meant her comments as a joke, but I also knew she stated something she observed. One of our more experienced seminarians, she had

Morning

served many years in the Peace Corps in Africa before deciding to answer the call to ordained ministry. Her quest for knowledge and her desire to make a difference inspired all of us to do the same.

My responsibility took many forms as the church members immediately invited me into their world and expected me to be very comfortable there.

"When you see Bert," an older man said as soon as he introduced himself to me, "When you see Bert," he repeated as he leaned into me and smiled, "say, 'Poor, old Joe!'"

The gleam in the man's eyes and the expression on his face reminded me of a little boy. For a second, I tried to imagine what he must have looked like at age eight or nine when he had decided to pull a prank. I wondered about the love his mother must have felt as she looked down into his eyes realizing he was up to no good, but loving him for being the mischievous rascal she knew he was. He later shared with me his story of being just ten years old when his mother died instantly after being struck by lightning while standing in the threshold of the kitchen door. When he spoke of her sudden death, he voiced a very real and present sadness going back through at least seven decades of his life.

"Even her hair pins melted," he repeated from time to time as though I had never heard him say it before. The heartbroken ten-year-old boy still existed within him.

Now the eighty-something year old man had stood before me pulling a prank on an old friend. The introduction and his instructions about my part in the prank took place as I stood outside the front doors of the Homeland Park church to speak to each of the forty-two members as they departed from my first Sunday morning worship service with them.

I had no idea as to the identities of two men named Joe and Bert, but I laughed with him and nodded. He repeated it for emphasis and then walked down the steps still laughing. I now understood how the pastor becomes privy to even the strangest inside jokes.

A few more friendly and smiling people came through the line and then finally a nice looking older couple stood in front of me.

"Hi, I'm Bert," the lady said with an engaging smile and some of the whitest hair I had ever seen. "And this is my husband, Joe."

I smiled at her and then said, "I've been instructed to say, 'Poor old Joe!' when I met you."

She laughed a laugh I would come to love and respect. Bert and her friend, Sadie, wisely and gently mentored me during those first years of serving a church as a novice pastor. Sadie called me several times each week about different issues but never took more than a few minutes with each call. Bert tended to talk to me in person. Both shared from their great common sense about how to run a church.

"We train 'em up and send 'em out," Bert later told me. "It's our mission and our purpose, and we're good at it!"

Eager for every bit of advice and institutional knowledge I could obtain, I became their very willing student. Their wisdom mirrored the instructions of my very skilled, educated, and experienced seminary professors. Their guidance formed my foundation of how to try to be an effective pastor.

Looking into the faces of my kneeling parishioners as I offered them the bread, the Body of Christ, for the first time, I became aware of how this act of worship brought the participants into a unique experience of the presence of God.

"God with us," took on a new meaning. "The Body broken and given for you," became very real. These people looked to me to perform worship so they might become living participants in the ancient and the new.

Sacrifice and grace, mercy and forgiveness, passion and love, filled me as we shared the sacrament. I tried, as best I could, to express to each person just how much God loved them and how God was counting on them to love and serve others.

Standing before them and offering Christ was a unique blessing for me. I knew the moment would never be repeated. I hesitated before giving the table dismissal. Several of my parishioners looked up at me from their kneeling positions at the altar rail with puzzled expressions.

"Go in peace to serve God and the world in the name of Christ," I said with reluctance since I had to end their confusion and to carry out the rest of the service.

They did not rise. Thinking they had not heard my words of dismissal, I repeated the words.

"Go in peace to serve God and the world in the name of Christ!" I said with a little more volume and authority.

One of the ladies kneeling closest to me looked up into my eyes. I wondered if she also found the moment to be so filled with grace and the presence of the living Savior that she was going to tell me no one wanted to leave.

With a quick motion of her hands, she held an imaginary cup and then pretended to drink from it.

I had given them the bread but not the cup. I tried not to laugh as I heard sacred chuckles completing the precious moment.

Morning

The next week at Sunday School someone asked Donna to pray to begin the class. In the midst of her very thoughtful prayer, she uttered the phrase, "And dear Lord, please help those who are sick to get sicker."

At the close of the prayer, the teacher paused as though too confused to begin the lesson. I thought I must have misheard what Donna had just prayed. Everyone in the class seemed lost in thought and reflection and a few of the members were visibly frowning.

As though on cue, one of the ladies laughed and said, "Remind me never to ask you to pray for me when I'm sick!"

Everyone in the class erupted in laughter, and Donna said she meant to pray for God to heal those who were sick and seemed to be getting sicker. I watched as she laughed at herself and joined in the moment of celebrating new friends who through humor and growing experience gathered trust in her.

We continued into the next week accomplishing as much as we could each day. Late at night when studies were finished, I would tell Donna stories of the latest amazing church member I had met. When the activities of living hushed and the evening became the threshold leading to the dawn of a new morning, we softly spoke about where this journey was taking us.

Donna would talk about her students while sipping a cup of herbal tea. She would then smile at me as I prattled on about everything I had encountered. I would find myself speaking to her in quiet tones as though the information I gave contained the most exciting discoveries of all time. Her green eyes gazing sleepily at me told me she shared my general amusement with life.

My weekly routine involved the amazing task of discovering what the Word called me to preach each Sunday. As part of our training, we received strict and often repeated instructions about how to write a sermon.

"The eleventh hour always approaches," one professor after another would say. "When you are the pastor, you will be called upon to proclaim the Word to people who are anxious and ready to hear a message to sustain them through the week."

"When this happens, no matter who is listening, no matter what sort of accomplished scholar might be present in the congregation, YOU are the only one who can speak what the passage has to say. No one else has the authority. No one else can speak the Word right then. It is a great responsibility."

"Therefore, you must not come to the Word with what you want to say to your congregation. The Word tells you what to preach and how to preach it. It is the power of the Spirit. Never write a sermon and then say, 'I wonder what text will sound right with this sermon?' What you have accomplished is not a sermon. The Word creates the sermon. The Word calls on you to proclaim the sermon."

While feeling entirely inadequate for the task, I also found the wonder of going to a text and seeing, almost immediately how the text called me to preach. Much preparation had to take place once the message was received, but I knew the message came from somewhere other than me. This understanding gave great energy for getting the work done.

On Sunday afternoons, we would prepare for the youth of the churches to come to the parsonage for their weekly fellowship. After the meeting, we rushed over to either the Homeland Park or John Wesley church for evening worship services. Those services were not held at each church every Sunday evening but rotated between the two. One week I was at one church and the next week at the other one.

A fifth Sunday in a month meant no evening activities took place. No youth meeting and no worship service. At first I felt a little embarrassed to stay home on those evenings, but soon came to relish those quiet times when Donna and I could pause from our week of non-stop motion.

On one particular fifth Sunday afternoon, Rev. Goodson stood at the side door of the church and knocked with increasing intensity.

A cousin of a rather well-known retired Bishop who taught at the Candler School of Theology at Emory University, Rev. Goodson had adopted the Homeland Park church as one of his special projects. A thin man with a booming voice, he would appear at random times during the week and do carpentry jobs in our building.

When he realized the bell in our little steeple no longer worked, this retired United Methodist clergyman crawled up into the attic in the middle of July and spent many scorching days reworking the roping mechanism so the bell could once more be heard in our neighborhood. His devotion to every aspect of church life remained steadfast even though he rarely preached.

Now he stood at the church door and knocked. I wondered why he was not at his church across town but then decided, as I headed across our backyard to the church, they must not have evening services on the fifth Sunday either.

"Good afternoon, Rev. Goodson," I said as I walked across the parking area. "I'm sorry no one told you we don't have evening services on the fifth Sunday."

"I'm deeeegusted and reeegusted!"

Morning

Donna said she could hear his response from inside the parsonage. His version of 'disgusted' and his invention of the word 'regusted' amazed me so much I found it impossible to be angered at his outburst of venomous frustration with the state of the world.

He did not stop at just showing his exasperation over the church schedule, but also continued with his frustration at just about everything. I respected him too much to argue any point and simply stood there trying not to look too amused but thinking about the many living room curtains being discreetly drawn back so the neighbors could spy on the odd sight of an old pastor yelling at a new pastor.

"Some of your church members," a seminary professor stated in one of our classes, "will seek you out so they can vent all of their frustrations at you." The professor stopped while we politely chuckled and nodded our heads in agreement as though we had already experienced this phenomenon.

"It will happen," the professor stated with a serious look on his face. "Many times they are not mad or annoyed with you or with your style of ministry. Most of the time they just need someone safe to receive the brunt of their anger."

"You are safe because pastors will generally listen to whatever is being said and not get into an argument. You may be the only person in their life who will listen to their rantings and not retaliate."

I thought about the professor's words and realized my turn had arrived. Rev. Goodson finished his shouting which had finally turned into incoherent muttering. Without waiting on any response from me, he got into his car and drove off. I wondered how many times in his different pastorates he had been on the receiving end of someone shouting at him. I also wondered if he had remained silent.

Since I spent all my available free time studying for seminary classes, Donna decided she might as well be in school herself. She enrolled as a graduate student in education at Clemson while keeping her teaching position.

On a regular weekday, we would eat dinner and hit the books. Donna would spread her materials on the couch while I sat in an overstuffed chair in the corner of the den. It became our ritual of being together while studying.

On Wednesday evenings, Donna and I rehearsed with the John Wesley choir and then drove to the Homeland Park church to attend a Bible study group.

"We don't like to follow any sort of curriculum or book," Ernie White told me on the first evening after Donna and I arrived. "We just want to sit around this table and read the Bible. If anyone has anything to say about a passage, they speak. If they don't have anything to say, we just move on."

Week after week, Donna and I would sit and listen as they read one verse at a time and then talked about what the passage meant to them. In the quiet rhythm of lives intersecting holy text, I came to realize how these friends brought their lives into the Word.

One evening in February, Donna and I drove through the darkness to the Homeland Park church expecting to see exactly who would be in Bible study this week. We had come to recognize the participants by their vehicles and knew before we exited our car who would be waiting for us to arrive.

This evening we saw the entire parking lot and the lawn connecting the church to the parsonage full of cars.

"What are all these cars doing here?" Donna said in confusion. "Are they having some sort of community meeting? Did we miss something? What's going on?"

Instead of answering her, I stared at the cars. I began to wonder if this meant my first appointment had reached a tragic end.

Doubt screamed in my ear. As though awaiting the best time to pounce, fear came rushing to the forefront and gushed out all the anxieties I had been carefully avoiding in the first half year of pastoring.

"They have found you out!" a voice yelled in my mind. "They know you don't know what you are doing. They realize your calling is not real! They are here to tell you just how horrible you are and what terrible damage you are doing to this beloved church. They don't want to work through the proper channels of the church, they just want you to leave…tonight!"

The voice relished this rare moment when I gave it full permission to speak. As though contained too long, it flooded my mind with paranoia.

Donna seemed excited at what was happening and continued to ask questions and ponder aloud what must be taking place.

The voice became a shrill siren within my mind as I tried to maintain a calm expression so as not to alarm Donna.

"I hope nothing is wrong," I stated quietly as I opened the car door.

Donna turned to me. Instead of excitement and curiosity, she spoke with a calm and caring voice.

"I'm sure everything is fine," she said with a smile as we held hands and walked across the parking lot to the back door.

As soon as we opened the door, the crowd in the fellowship hall shouted: "Surprise! Happy Birthday!"

As they all began to sing, I realized this massive party was for me.

Morning

Turning twenty-nine is not ordinarily celebrated to excess, but it was their pastor's birthday. Even though they might not be the biggest and most accomplished of all churches, they knew they could make sure I realized just how much Donna and I were appreciated.

As people rushed forward to hug us both and laugh with us at our surprise, I caught Donna's quick glance in my direction.

Her eyes stared directly at the source of the doubting voice. She smiled at me as someone began to hug her and pull her attention away from the moment. Without a doubt, I knew she had seen the hidden place of my worst fears. For a second, she gained access to all of my self-doubts. Perhaps for the first time, she understood my need for her strength.

Her green eyes filled with sympathy followed immediately with a look of gentle, accepting resolve. I knew she understood that even though I might be surrounded by boundless love and acceptance, the voice would always be waiting for its moment.

Chapter 11
Adoption

"I DON'T THINK ANY MORE TESTS ARE REQUIRED," the doctor said in an extremely comforting tone displaying his competence with great kindness and compassion. In the pause between phrases, I remember thinking and hoping his next words would be positive. I even went so far as to dream, for just a second, that he would tell us the surprising news of Donna's long-awaited pregnancy.

"There is no reason for any further tests," the doctor said to us in the privacy of his office, "Donna cannot possibly bear a child."

Pain ran up my shins; my toes curled tightly in my shoes. I weakly smiled at the doctor and gently squeezed the hand of my precious Donna. Silent tears ran down her face.

"It's OK," I stated in as cheerful a tone as I could muster, "we will be happy to adopt a child."

I wondered how many times husbands and wives had comforted themselves with the same words in similar situations in countless doctor's offices around the world.

"And let me speak plainly to you," the gentle doctor said as though he had not already given us the plain and simple truth.

"You should not get excited if you do become pregnant because you would not be able to successfully give birth to the child."

Words of certainty and truth. Words putting an end to questions and wonder and fascination. Words that changed our course and direction as completely as an unexpected detour.

Donna and I made appointments with the county officials who oversaw all the processes of adoption. While knowing we would continue on this course, we needed to be instructed how to proceed.

Months later, state and county mandated classes were completed. During a home inspection visit, we sat in the den of the parsonage with our assigned social worker, Cathy. While working with her through all the necessary certifications, we found great assurance in her knowledge and experience in her field of work. After completing all of the necessities, we were finally finished. Certified by the state as potentially good and caring parents, every legal requirement had been met.

Donna and I thought this meeting with Cathy would be one in which she went over the paperwork one more time to make sure all was in order. We came to realize how this meeting formed a crucial part of the puzzle as she helped us make important decisions.

Sitting in the den, Cathy quietly looked over our file one more time. Donna and I were confident this house would pass any inspection as an acceptable residence for a child. The well-built brick ranch style parsonage would be a very comfortable home in which to start our new family.

The Homeland Park parsonage had been built with great care by a contractor still new in the profession. By the time we lived there, the builder had gained the reputation of being the premier general contractor of the finest homes in the area. His "touches" were noted by those who could afford the very best. I would silently chuckle as I heard those construction details noted by others. Crown molding, built-in bookcases, large fireplace with ash chute, and a bathroom ceiling composed entirely of opaque tiles hiding the many fluorescent light bulbs were just a few of his trademark features.

The large kitchen created a welcoming point in the house. With windows looking out to the side and back of the house, the roomy kitchen became the place to gather. Its walls were painted a bright and sunny yellow.

"What sort of child would you like to adopt?" Cathy said with a smile as she looked up from her paperwork. She efficiently tore through any preliminary niceties and got right to the point.

Slightly stunned by the question, I started pondering the meaning of "sort of child". Donna and I never discussed adopting children of different ages, races, conditions, and situations who might be available for adoption. I began to panic as I realized our desperate need for more preparation.

"Any child," Donna said putting an end to the emerging train wreck in my mind.

"Race, age, or special need makes no difference to us whatsoever."

I looked at her with great pride. She always possessed the gift of clarity of purpose and mind which I sometimes lacked. She simply stepped around all of the confounding issues and made a stand.

Cathy smiled and looked down at her paperwork. I almost expected her to say she already had a child in mind for us.

"I think since this will be your first child you should go for what would be the normal course of events in your life at this time." Her words were kind but strong. She obviously wanted us to hear and heed what her experience had taught her.

"The normal course of events in your life would be for you to have an infant. I would suggest we proceed with this in mind and for this result. Later, you can always adopt other children as you see fit."

Donna and I glanced at each other knowing this one decision would change a lot of things for us. I wanted to question Cathy as to exactly how any of this appeared in the least bit "normal". I also wanted to dive into a discussion of normal and how we or anyone else could define what would be normal for us.

Donna and I looked at each other for a fraction of a moment. Her green eyes locked with mine and we communicated the philosophy of the question completely without saying a word. We analytically reasoned and prayed and held late night debates with a look in each other's eyes. Before the clock ticked again, I knew we had reached our decision. Donna blinked and then turned back to Cathy. The instantaneous unspoken discussion came down to doing as the expert advised.

"Since this is your course of action, I need to tell you the state agencies do not have an infant for you now or in the foreseeable future. You will need to proceed with a private adoption. The good news is with all the work you have completed, you are now ready to begin your search."

Over the next few weeks, we selected an attorney who had been involved in successful private adoptions. Without fully understanding it, Donna and I became part of the private adoptions world with the connections existing between other adoption attorneys in our region of the state.

"Did I say you needed a boy's name?" the kind attorney of an old and extremely reputable law firm in Greenville asked as he sat in his elegant office in an historic downtown building, "I meant to say the young lady is expecting a girl."

He had sent us to lunch to come back with a boy's name. This turn of events had come in a rush. Our young niece and nephew were spending the weekend with us when a call came from our attorney telling us to go to Greenville to meet with this attorney. We hastily called Donna's aunt who lived in the area to come over and spend the day with the children.

To make the lunch meeting even more frantic, the attorney had asked if, when we returned in an hour to his office, we could not only have a boy's name but also three thousand five hundred dollars for the legal fees. Mom agreed to quickly drop everything she was doing and meet us at a downtown restaurant with the cash in hand. Our small savings account held only enough for the next seminary tuition payment.

Before we left his office, we had paid for everything, signed everything, and given him our chosen name for the unborn child. That evening as we were finishing up a fun dinner at home with our delightful niece and nephew, Donna and I kept looking at each other. With smiles expressing unspoken thoughts, we relished in the hope of our home being filled with the laughter of our own child.

The phone rang. I thought it might be another family member congratulating us and asking joyous questions about how everything had happened so fast.

To my surprise, the attorney from Greenville was on the phone. With great care, he explained that the expectant young mother had changed her mind about the adoption and had decided to keep her child.

"I'll give you a complete refund of your fees," he said as a parting expression of his sympathy for our bitter disappointment. "I'll also keep you in mind should I hear of any other possible adoption."

With a click on the other end of the line, our lives returned to the task of waiting.

Surprisingly soon, another chance arrived. As if to make the whole situation seem as surreal as possible, this expectant young lady contacted our attorney with her desire to meet with the prospective adoptive parents before making her final decision.

As we walked into the attorney's board room, we met a young lady who was obviously in the last months of her pregnancy. We also met her mother. Amazingly, none of us seemed very nervous about the meeting.

"It's much more important than the clothes we wear or the smiles on our faces," Donna said during the early morning hours before dawn when we realized neither one of us was sleeping. She leaned over to me and put her head on my shoulder. Her mahogany brown hair tickled my ear as she quietly spoke.

"Our words and manners will be judged, but hopefully she and her mother will be much more interested in getting to know us than just to come to a decision based on superficiality. I think we should just be ourselves. If she doesn't like us or feels somehow it is wrong, then it's probably not the right thing for her and the baby."

Her words brought to mind the truly important points and ended my cluttered thoughts. As I hugged her in gratitude for her ability to see clearly and speak with certainty, I wondered at her gift of deciphering life events and giving them meaning and purpose beyond our frail needs and desires.

The early glow of another sunrise began to lighten our bedroom window. The sun's rays came over the horizon from the direction of the church. I knew one of the things now becoming visible in the outside would be the small steeple of our church just across the lawn from this side of the house. As the sunrise began, Donna's strength of faith seemed so much greater than my own. I knew it provided us with a peace beyond the unfolding events.

The interview went very well. We left the attorney's office after about an hour and drove home silent. Neither one of us felt like examining our thoughts about the mother and her daughter. Later we would marvel at how much they reminded us of ourselves. In our meeting, we connected as families maneuvering through difficult turns while trying to be true to ourselves in the face of the reality of events shaping everything.

The attorney called us not long after we arrived at home. He congratulated us on the fact they had decided we would indeed be the parents of the soon expected daughter. They made no demands upon us other than the hope we would surround her with our love.

Over the next week, they brought to the attorney's office some of the items they had already purchased for the baby. The attorney laughed as he explained how his back office now looked like a nursery with crib, car seat, blankets, baby clothing, and a changing table. Donna and I decided we would move our items out of our already prepared nursery so the baby would have the furnishings her biological family wished her to have.

About a month later, we were informed of the healthy delivery of the baby. We had learned from Cathy and our attorney how many times just after the birth the biological mother decided to keep the baby. While understanding the weight of the emotions present at just those moments, we prayed for whatever was best for everyone involved. Later, the attorney notified us the new mother still wished for us to adopt the child. For the time being, our work was finished as the legal proceedings moved forward.

Another morning arrived. Donna and I stood at the kitchen door making sure we had everything we needed. We were leaving to go to the attorney's office to receive our new daughter. We would then proceed to the family court where a hearing before a judge had been scheduled. Covering every potential turn of events, our attorney and our case worker made it clear to us that even though every part of the law had been followed, the biological mother would legally have plenty of time to change her mind and reclaim the baby.

"Actually," Cathy had pointed out, "the biological mother has years to make sure this is the best decision for her. It would be very difficult for a judge to deny the biological mother's claim for perhaps even as long as seven years. It takes that long for the adoptive parents to have a solid legal claim for the child."

The claim could also come from the biological father. In our case, the father had been notified. He had responded to our attorney's request and had

Morning

signed the necessary papers to allow us to adopt the baby. A change of mind coming from him could also alter everything for years to come.

At one point, my fears and uncertainty began to crowd out the possible joy of having a child. I never verbally expressed my doubts, but Donna could tell the prospect of waiting years to know if the child would really, finally, and truly be ours haunted me.

I wondered how we would react to such a situation if the child had lived with us as our own for three or four years. Even though rare, someday we might have to stand before a judge to hear a decision rendered as to whether or not this child would remain as our child.

Out of my desire to shield Donna from such thoughts, I never spoke about those things. Even though I knew she could handle anything, I still desired to shelter her from pain.

Ironically, Donna knew my weaknesses better than I knew them myself. She understood and accepted my desire to protect her. Even though she saw it as completely archaic and unnecessary, she accepted it as a part of our relationship.

"If it's right for us to adopt a particular child," she said one evening as we finished our dinner and sat at the kitchen table, "then it will happen."

"I believe God wants us to have a child," she said in words confirming the joy of her smile. "God will provide the child who will never be removed from us by a court. We just have to be patient and see what God has in store."

In the midst of my middle year of seminary where everything about faith and doctrine is torn apart so it can be constructed again in a stronger format, a part of me immediately thought of many theological arguments to her simple faith. The power of her faith made such an argument seem profane.

Donna started looking through her pocketbook as we stood at the kitchen door. We had been ready to leave the house for an hour but knew arriving too early would not be wise. Now the time was right for us to depart. I opened the door as Donna took the first step outside and I stood ready to follow. We would go on our short trip beginning a new lifetime journey of fulfilling one of our dreams.

The phone rang.

Looking quickly at my watch I had just checked two seconds before, I verified we needed to be leaving. Instinctively, I grabbed the receiver off the kitchen wall prepared to tell the caller I really could not talk at the moment.

"Dan, don't come to the office," our attorney said without greeting as soon as he heard my voice. I could tell by the tone of his voice the next words would be difficult for him to say. "She's changed her mind. She is not giving the baby up for adoption."

Dan Batson

I hung up the phone and Donna stepped back inside. I closed the kitchen door and repeated the short bitter message. Standing at the closed door, we held each other and wept in the sunny yellow kitchen of our home.

Chapter 12
Tyler

"WHAT IF I CAN'T REALLY LOVE SOMEONE ELSE'S CHILD?"

Dark, unspoken thoughts reflected my worst fears. Forbidden emotions from the very moment of their inception kept step with the thrilling anticipation of what might be.

In the midst of all the efforts and preparations for a child to be brought into our lives, this one thought kept finding its voice. Doubt of my ability to fully love an adopted child became the nagging fear I refused to state aloud.

I wondered if Donna felt the same way but realized she did not waste much time on doubts. I knew she had fears and confusions from time to time, but she had the capacity to move quickly beyond them. While mine lingered and forced me to sort them out and deal with them over and over until finally settled, she confronted her fears quickly and victoriously marched through them. Her gentle smile hid a strong determination that even though worries always present themselves, they could not be the focus of living.

"This time it's real," Beverly's voice sparkled with enthusiasm over the phone. Being a wonderful friend and church member, she and her sister, Vicky, had walked beside us as we went through one disappointment after another in failed adoptions.

"There is no doubt about it!" she exclaimed as I waited for an explanation.

"Let me tell you what just happened," she said through her laughter. "You are not going to believe it! One of our employees came to see me today to talk about her health insurance benefits and the coverage she has for her daughter."

I knew Beverly worked at one of the large textile manufacturing plants in Anderson as a benefits coordinator. She often spoke about the pressures of her job and the frustrations of corporate audits and of making sure the employees received everything they deserved. Like her faith, her work also received her best energy and efforts.

"This employee's daughter is expecting a child, and they were checking on health insurance coverage. During our meeting, she mentioned giving the child up for adoption."

I felt another surge of optimism about the possibility of adoption. At the same time, I also experienced a slight shudder at the thought of this one, like all the rest, ending in failure.

"Perhaps it's God's way of letting you know you are not worthy of receiving a child you cannot love," the voice whispered in my mind. I physically shook my head in an effort to dislodge it while continuing to listen to Beverly.

"Her daughter is thirteen and pregnant. She just broke up with her boyfriend and has no interest in starting a family with him. She wants to continue in school so she can become a nurse," Beverly's excitement made her voice almost breathless.

"The employee's daughter and her son were adopted," Beverly exclaimed with zeal. "They have had a wonderful life and have thought about raising this grandchild for their daughter. But since she and her husband are in their sixties, they don't feel prepared to start over with an infant."

Beverly paused as though gathering her strength to continue telling the story.

"I told her our young pastor and his wife can't have children and are trying to adopt a child. She seemed pleased about the two of you getting the baby, and said she would speak to her daughter about it. She then said she was certain they would want you to have the baby!"

"It's amazing," I exclaimed with laughter as she stopped to catch her breath. "With all of the attorneys, doctors, and social workers working on this adoption, I never thought you would find us a baby! I can't wait to tell Donna!"

"But there's even more," Beverly exclaimed. "This adoption is guaranteed and straight from God! There's no doubt about it at all. Just wait until you hear! You're not going to believe it. So, the mother assured me her daughter would agree and that as far as she was concerned you and Donna could have the child. She said a friend had taken her daughter to see a doctor and as soon as they were finished with the appointment, she would speak to her daughter about it. After she left my office, Vicky called me before I had a chance to call you."

Beverly's sister, Vicky, demonstrated great faithfulness and dedication. Her work at the church meant a great deal to me and others.

"The first thing she said to me was she had a baby for the two of you!" Beverly's laughter now combined with mine as, for a moment, the conversation stopped. I immediately began to think through the details of how we could modify everything for two infants. Even though it sounded strange, I knew we could make it happen.

Morning

"Vicky and I laughed about it and then decided it would be fine and you would probably be more than willing to take advantage of this great opportunity."

"Yes!" I exclaimed.

"Well, you haven't heard the best part yet," Beverly stated with more laughter. "You know Vicky works at the doctor's office. She told me this morning a young lady came in for an appointment to see him. She also told the doctor she wanted to give the child up for adoption."

"Vicky told the doctor about the two of you and he stated he had a young pharmacist and his wife who were also seeking to adopt an infant. He said he would have to call them first to see if they might be interested. When he returned from his office, he told Vicky you and Donna could have the child because the pharmacist felt things were not right for them to adopt at this time."

"Wonderful!" I shouted into the phone. "That's amazing!"

"No, the amazing thing about it," Beverly stated in a tone still filled with excitement and joy but now also mingled with obvious tears, "the amazing thing about it is we now know this adoption is 100% guaranteed by God." Beverly stopped speaking as though to make sure I heard clearly her next words.

"As Vicky and I continued to talk about the young lady, we suddenly realized we were talking about the same young lady and the same child. At exactly the same time her mother was in my office saying you and Donna could have the child, the young lady was in the doctor's office saying the same thing!"

I could not speak as a sense of calm washed over my fears. Relief relaxed my shoulders and brow and I became physically aware of this moment of grace vanquishing my forebodings of yet another failed attempt.

This was much more than just a coincidence.

"God has it all planned out," Beverly stated as though she had just returned from the heavenly courts where a meeting had been held about our future. "You have nothing to worry about now!"

My fingers ran over the incredibly soft white faux fur of a cute and cuddly stuffed polar bear. Holding the plush toy in my hands, I rocked back and forth in the same smooth wooden rocking chair where I had spent many hours studying in high school. Mom had given the rocker to us for the nursery.

Donna stood in the doorway silhouetted by the light shining behind her. I could tell she was smiling at me as I rocked back and forth holding the polar bear. Light from the hallway made the colors of the nursery visible.

"We should use strong, primary colors in the nursery," Donna had stated with authority as we had planned the nursery a few months ago. "Everyone thought gentle colors were better for infants but now it seems primary colors are better at stimulating them and getting their minds ready to learn."

I could tell by her careful choice of words she envisioned many opportunities to help this child learn all about our world. Unlike the limited and precious time she could spend with her students at school, Donna would have abundant time to shape our child's mind with the fascination and wonder of all things.

The room became a celebration of primary colors in keeping with the theme of Noah's ark. Animals, rainbows, clouds, and sunshine flooded the room. Donna wanted each waking moment to be one where our child would be given opportunities to be delighted with the diversity of our great world.

"Our child is on the way!" I said to the polar bear. The bear seemed to nod his head in agreement as I rocked with enthusiasm.

I stared into the black bead eyes of the bear. They seemed to look back at me as though in the shimmer of the hall light they came to life. The eyes flickered for a moment in perfect agreement. Soon our nursery would be truly complete.

Early on a Sunday morning, the phone rang. Waking from sleep, I reached for the receiver and heard the voice of our attorney.

"Dan, the baby was born this morning," he stated. "The mother held the child for a while after he was born but said she knew the best thing would be for him to have the two of you as his parents."

Sunday's child was born for us. A son. A son to be loved and cherished. A son to learn from us and to experience life and love with us.

I turned to Donna who had tears of joy streaming down her face. She could not have heard the conversation but could tell the good news from my expression.

"What is the nursery rhyme about Sunday's child?" I asked as I took her in my arms and hugged her tightly. As the sun once again began to rise over the same beautiful steeple of the church, she said: "But the child who is born on the Sabbath day is fair and wise and good in every way."

Donna recited the words as though she had prepared them for this particular morning. We laughed together as we realized even though both churches were in prayerful anticipation of this birth, our attorney reminded us nothing could be said for a few days.

After three years of serving my first appointment, another anticipated appointment had been arranged for us by the bishop. This Sunday, both churches were coming together to have a farewell dinner after morning worship.

"They might not understand why we both appear so happy about everything," Donna said as she held me tight. "I don't think I can stop smiling all day!"

On Tuesday, we stood before a Family Court judge who reviewed all of the documents and legal preparations. We faced the judge with our attorney and two other attorneys we had retained. The state required the child had his own attorney whose interest would be for the child. The state also required the mother, since she was a minor, be represented by an attorney.

Donna and I each had to take the witness stand and answer questions from the attorneys and the judge. They pointed out concerns over Donna's desire to continue teaching. After questioning her about this plan, they also questioned me. I explained my mother was a teacher, and I had never felt neglected by her career. After all was said and done, everyone seemed to be convinced of our resolve to provide the very best home for this child.

"Do you fully understand that in adopting this newborn you take complete responsibility for him?" the judge asked as we stood before him.

"He is to be treated as your very own child, in the same standing as any biological child you might have."

"The judge will see through your lack of love," the voice stated within my mind. "In all of his experience with other couples who have stood before him, he will know how false you are!"

While the judge spoke, he looked down at the documents before him. I feared if he examined my eyes he could see the fraud taking place in his courtroom.

"This child must be seen by the two of you as completely yours with full right of inheritance. Do you completely accept this responsibility?"

The judge looked up from his paperwork and focused on us. Relieved that he spoke of responsibility instead of love, I knew I could answer with complete honesty. Responsibility had always been easy for me.

"We do, your honor," Donna and I stated in unison.

"The adoption is granted," the judge declared as though everything was completed even though we knew everything had only just begun.

Tyler Martin Batson came into our lives.

Tyler's attorney went with us to the hospital. I didn't know if he just wanted to make sure we knew what we were doing or if he thought there could be some legal questions from the hospital he would need to answer.

We waited outside the hospital nursery before being told that the doctor never released a newborn until three full days after delivery.

"No problem," the attorney stated obviously realizing it would be futile to argue with the doctor's decision. "But the Batson's would like to see the baby."

The nurse looked concerned and then said it was against hospital policy.

"All adoptive babies are kept concealed from the public and all family members until we release the child to the adoptive parents," she said while trying to show some compassion for us.

"I'm afraid I can't allow you to see the child today."

"I understand completely," Tyler's attorney said without missing a beat. "But I'm not the adoptive parent. I'm the legal representative of the child through the family court. I would like to see the child."

The nurse thought for a moment and then looked at the attorney's confident and no-nonsense expression and agreed.

She told him to come to the nursery window and she would bring the child there. After she walked away, the attorney quickly turned to us and said, "Follow me."

We followed him to the nursery window.

"They might say you aren't allowed to see your son," he said with a defiant smile, "but they can't say you can't stand beside me as I see my client."

We watched as the nurse went to a screen separating one of the acrylic cribs from the rest. As a reminder to all the nurses, a note had been pinned on the screen that read, "I'm special."

The nurse brought the baby to the window and then unceremoniously held him up so his feet dangled beneath him. Completely healthy and longer than any newborn I had ever seen, he looked beautiful. Donna and I hugged each other as the attorney nodded in approval to the nurse who returned our smiles of joy.

The next morning, we agreed to meet the same attorney at 10 a.m. at the hospital. The nursery worker presented Tyler to us and placed him in Donna's arms.

Without crying she bent her head as though in prayer, locked her eyes in his, and then gently kissed his forehead.

"I don't want him to see me for the first time while I'm crying," she said. "I want him to see how much I love him."

Morning

    I knew Donna would have found peace and completeness even without a child. Her strength and faith did not allow her to define herself through a husband, a family, or a child. Even though she knew how to live contented in every situation, I could see her unspeakable joy in holding our son in her arms.

    I stared at her as she held Tyler and marveled at her ability to move beyond all questions and express her love to the fullest without hesitation.

    "Here, Daddy," she said with one of the biggest smiles I had ever seen on her face. She moved closer to me and gently held Tyler out to me.

    "This is Daddy," she said to him as though he had asked. His eyes were now closed and he appeared to be asleep. "He loves you very much."

    I wondered as I reached for him if she was talking to me or to him. Even though he had been behind a screen in the hospital nursery, blocked off from everyone else, he had never been in the absence of love. His biological parents had loved him enough to want the very best for him. His mother, now fourteen, realized the completion of her love for him by granting us the privilege of loving him beyond measure.

    I took the sleeping newborn, our Tyler, into my arms. I ran my other hand and forearm up his delicate back to fully embrace him. He did not stir. His eyes did not open. He was completely at ease with me.

    Looking into his sleeping face, I realized I held our child. As the weight of his tender young body settled into my arms, I knew the amazing wonder of receiving such a gift from God.

    Without contemplation, without thoughts, without fears, and without doubts, love exclaimed its simple and eternal presence and its absolute truth. Right then and forever, I completely—and without any hesitation—loved my son.

Chapter 13
Sandy Springs & Zion

TWO BOSTON TERRIERS EXAMINED ME. Each one stood with their front paws on the bottom half of an open Dutch door at my office. Two sets of these doors opened into a beautiful courtyard next to the sanctuary.

I stared back at the dogs and thought of my Aunt Helen's faithful companion, a Boston terrier with a bright smile. The energetic dogs gazed at me and perked their ears as though to hear what I might say. This country church provided land for them to roam and play. I wondered which neighbor had released them to romp in the fields.

Looking at first as though they would like to jump into the office through the open door, they finally settled down.

"Why are you here?" they seemed to ask simultaneously.

Both dogs cocked their heads to the side. My amusement at their friendly faces turned to discomfort. They looked as though they understood me much better than I understood myself. They silently assessed my strengths and skills.

"What are you doing?" they asked with their piercing black eyes.

Posing those questions without a bark or a whimper, they looked at each other in great satisfaction and ran out of the courtyard as quickly as they had appeared.

They didn't wait for an answer. They almost seemed to know, in their great terrier wisdom, that some time would have to pass before I knew the answer to those questions.

Earlier in the day, I sat in a small old country farmhouse resting inconspicuously in a little field beside a busy two-lane road. The importance of these vanishing family farms consisted mainly of the ever-increasing demand for subdivisions. I listened to an old gentlewoman relate her grief to me over the death of her much beloved husband. A well-respected member of this community and of the church I now pastored, this farmer was grieved by many.

Even though faith assured us his life and work continued in Christ, we all understood his death represented the fading memories of older times. With

Morning

each passing of an old farmer, the collective experiences of everyone seemed a little less clear.

This wonderfully faithful and quiet lady dressed in her casual cotton dress told me she would continue to live in the little house as long as she could. She changed from speaking about the pain of her recent loss and started relating to me the things she needed to accomplish.

"I need to get out there and gather the ripe figs," she said in obvious frustration.

I had seen the fig tree outside her kitchen window. It reminded me of the one outside my grandmother's kitchen. The teardrop shaped figs would ripen from green to dark brown at different times and would quickly rot if not gathered each day.

"I'll give most of them away," she said with sadness over the futility of her daily tasks since her husband was gone. "I don't have much use for figs anymore."

"Do you make fig preserves?" I asked hoping to help her see her life could be filled with meaningful activities benefitting her family and friends.

"I used to," she said as she glanced out the kitchen window at how many ripe figs awaited her attention.

"I don't think I will make any this year."

We continued to talk. I knew I could not eliminate her fears of uselessness. I also understood my words would not lessen her growing concerns about her ability to care for herself in the future. More by her attitude than her words, she conveyed to me a rather bleak vision of what awaited.

I knew I could state words of our shared faith. I could remind her of God's shepherding care for her in this and every situation. I could give her encouragement and reassurance of God's presence being seen and felt by her now and in the future. I wanted her to feel some joyful and hopeful anticipation of the future where she would discover God already waiting.

All of those words crowded into my mind, but as I started to speak them in full confidence of their ability to bring comfort, I found myself asking about her childhood.

"Did you grow up near here?" I asked while looking out the window past the fig tree and across the field to the pine trees surrounding the property.

She smiled and began to tell me about herself. I found her story to be very familiar and yet peculiarly her own. Through the tone of her voice, I sensed she relished an opportunity to share some of her stories as though revealing secrets about herself. I knew she might have shared these stories many times in the past and to some people they might seem as old and as tired as she appeared. But to me, she came to life through these stories. It was easy for me to become more than just engaged in her stories. I experienced them with fresh eyes. For this moment, I became a companion with her in those precious memories.

"My father always thought I should be a very proper young girl," she said with a devilish grin temporarily wiping away the years and the grief.

"He did not like to see me playing with any of the boys who were my age from the other farms. The only problem was our neighbors didn't have any little girls my age. So I would finish my chores and go down to the woods next to the creek where I knew the boys would be playing."

She chuckled and tilted her head back as though surprised she remembered all of the details.

"My mother would notice how dirty my dress was and would scold me for playing near the creek, but I didn't care. I couldn't play alone and the boys didn't care how dirty they got, so I got dirty with them."

"One day the boys decided to swing from the tops of the young pine trees growing near the creek. I had never seen anything like it, and it looked like so much fun!"

She brushed aside a gray curl of hair. "One of the boys climbed a young pine tree and then kept going up and up until he was at the very top. The tree began to sway one way and then the other," she said as she began to slowly move from side to side in a swinging motion in her old wooden rocking chair. She opened her eyes widely as though watching him again. "It looked like the top of the tall pine tree would break right in two, but the boy just kept getting the tree to sway more and more and more until it looked like something crazy. He pushed and pulled on the tree and looked like he was having the ride of his life."

"After he finished, all of the boys took a turn climbing up that tree and swaying until they were almost too dizzy to climb back down. When I told them I wanted to do the same thing, they didn't try to stop me. I guess they knew I was going to do exactly what they had done. They helped me get started and soon I was at the top swaying even more than they had."

"After we finished, one of the boys had the idea if several of them climbed the tree at once they could manage to bend it enough so the top would touch the ground." She continued as her voice became more and more childlike.

"They brought the top all the way to the ground. Then Sam, who was always the first one to do anything daring, said he was going to take a ride on the tree. He held onto the top of the tree and then told the other boys to let go of the trunk. That pine tree shot him right up into the air and then continued to bend one way and then the other." She laughed as she held up her hands and feet in the air as though going through the wild motions herself.

"It bent so far it went clear across the creek to the other side and back," she said while laughing. "After he did it, we all had to do it. I would fly over that creek holding onto the top of the tree and feeling as though I would soar forever. We found other young pine trees all along the creek bank and soon we were flying from one side of the creek to the other faster than you could imagine."

She stopped and looked at me as though inviting me to take her place at the top of the tree and experience it for myself.

"Riding the tops of the trees became our favorite thing to do, until someone saw what we were doing," she stopped and stared at me and continued in a quiet tone.

"That night, my father told me I was never to ride the tops of the trees again. He said it was not becoming to have a young girl in a dress swaying up high in the air."

Leaning closer to me with a sly smile, she whispered, "I told my father I would never do such a thing!"

She leaned back in her rocker obviously proud of herself for this misdeed.

"The next day we were all in the woods riding the tops of the trees as fast and as far as we could. It was great! Just as I got on the best of the trees and the boys let go of the trunk and I went flying through the air, I looked down… and there was father, far below, looking right up at me."

Our shared laughter filled the old house.

"Why are you here?"
"What are you doing?"

Intersections of lives and faith continued at a much more rapid pace than I had imagined possible. I wanted to make a verifiable impact on the world or at least upon the church and community where I served as pastor. I wanted to be able to measure the difference I made each day and see my ministry bearing fruit with every effort and action. As I went through the ordination process, I awaited the time when the bishop's hands would be placed on my head as he called upon God to pour out the power of the Holy Spirit anointing me with strength to accomplish the building of the Kingdom.

During this time of preparation, I prayed that the Lord would prevent me from being ordained if it was not in God's plan.

As planned, the bishop ordained me as an Elder. I embraced the ordination with trust in God's gentle grace becoming evident through my frail efforts.

☙

"Why are you here?"
"What are you doing?"

A wife shared with me her frustrations over the fact her husband needed daily exercises in order to recover from a recent stroke. The therapist had demonstrated to her how to walk him around the outside of the house while holding onto the belt at his waist to stabilize him.

"I told the therapist I was too weak to hold onto him," she said while shaking her head. "She just said maybe I could find someone who could help me."

She frowned and looked down. Her husband, Wallace, looked disturbed. A rough man who had welded on many different construction sites around the nation, he was used to being able to handle himself in any situation. His pride rested in the fact he had always provided for his wife. Now he looked completely lost in being dependent on others.

I could tell by his glance at me he could never accept his situation. For him it was more than just a matter of pride, it was just who he had always been and would always be. Dependence meant more than just change, it meant a destruction of self beyond his ability to comprehend.

"I'll run by here four times a week and walk Wallace," I said reassuringly. "I'll be happy to do it."

Most days we would speak for a few minutes about how things were going and then I would help Wallace up from his recliner. While holding his belt, I would get him to the front door and then down the ramp as we began our walk around the house.

The first day we almost didn't make it completely around the house. By the time we got to the backyard, I found I was nearly carrying him. His only way to move his right leg was to do a little jump with his left leg. His left arm would be around my shoulders while his right arm remained uselessly bent across his midsection.

At first this jumping motion would completely exhaust him. We would struggle to get back to the ramp at the front of the house and then to his recliner. I worried about the effects of working him too much, but Wallace told me he was used to working on the tops of skyscrapers until he was too tired to move. His determination to get well outweighed how he felt in the process.

After a few weeks, we finished one time around the house with ease.

"Let's go around again," he said with great pride just as I was thinking he should stop and enjoy this accomplishment.

Each time we would go around the house, he would tell me stories of his travels and the amazing ways he did his work. Realizing I knew nothing about this kind of life, he enjoyed giving me details of how the beams would be brought together to create the framework of a giant structure.

"We never stayed on a worksite long enough to see it finished," he said with great satisfaction. "They always needed me to go to the next project in another state to get things done there."

Over time, he became more comfortable in talking with me as though I had become the child he and his wife never had. Using me for physical support, he gave me spiritual support and encouragement interspersed with words I could never use from the pulpit.

Our walks continued over a two-year period, and I found myself looking forward to the time spent with someone who was as different from me as anyone could be.

One day I arrived to find the driveway full of cars. When I entered the house, Wallace's chair was empty. His wife, Ruby, met me with tears and a hug.

"He had an aneurism that busted," she said through her tears. "I got an ambulance here, but they couldn't do anything for him. He died before they could even get him to the hospital. It all happened so fast. I don't think he knew what was happening."

As I prepared my thoughts for his eulogy, I became obsessed with making sure everyone at the funeral realized Wallace was someone important, significant, and cherished. People knew him only as the rough guy who welded. I wanted them to know much more about him. I was going to make sure they knew his great worth as a person of strength.

I started the eulogy with simple words.

"I had a friend named Wallace..."

I couldn't finish the statement as sobs choked my voice.

"Why are you here?"
"What are you doing?"

I loved Anna Laura. I loved the fact she corrected me the first time I called her, "Anna".

"My name is Anna Laura," she said with a smile. "Not just Anna."

I loved her because she introduced me to the wonders of the savory dishes of aspic and oyster pie. I loved the way she spoke and laughed. I loved to listen to her play the old organ at the Sandy Springs Church. I loved her very old house and her extremely educated mind.

I loved the fact she always continued to read and learn and gave herself tirelessly to every good work and cause in our little community. I admired how she knew all the history of everything. I marveled in the fact she became the Post Mistress of our little Post Office and also taught school. Her daughter, Ann, lived next door to Anna Laura's old house. Ann became alarmed one day because Anna Laura did not return from a trip to town. Her daughter met her when Anna Laura decided to return home and scolded her for failing to leave a note on the kitchen table detailing exactly where she would be going and when she could be expected to return.

"You're ninety-two!" Ann told her mother. "It's time you acted your age!"

Anna Laura gave her daughter every assurance she would comply with her daughter's wishes. The next morning Ann saw Anna Laura drive out of her driveway. Using her own key, the daughter went straight to the kitchen table to see if her demands for a detailed itinerary had been met.

"There on the kitchen table was the note from Mama, just as I had asked her to do," Ann later told me. "Mama had written it out in her wonderfully good handwriting and had carefully detailed exactly where she was going and who she would be seeing and exactly what time she would be returning. Or at least that's what I figured the note said, since the entire thing was written in French!"

The daughter looked at me in exasperation made worse by my laughter.

"Even though she loves French, she knows I don't know any French!"

I loved Anna Laura and her clarity in seeing how things generally work out one way or another.

I commented one day to her about the scrapes on some wide concrete steps outside the church near the parking lot.

"Oh, Mary and I made those scrapes when she drove me to the church to look for her teeth," Anna Laura said as though no other explanation was necessary. "She put her car in drive instead of reverse and the front end of

Morning

her big old Cadillac went down the first step. She put the car in reverse, but it couldn't pull itself out. So I told her to just put it in drive and see if it would go down the steps. The car bounced down the steps all the way to the bottom. It did leave a few scrapes, but I don't think anyone hardly notices them."

"Do I know Mary?" I said with a smile. "And why were you at the church looking for her teeth?"

Anna Laura smiled and then said, "Mary always sat with me at church and one Sunday her false teeth really started hurting her. I think she had not had them very long and they didn't fit very well, so she took out her handkerchief from her pocketbook and without drawing too much attention put the handkerchief up to her mouth and took out the new teeth. She then very discreetly put the handkerchief with the teeth back down into her pocketbook."

"When she got home, she reached into her pocketbook to get her teeth so she could eat her lunch only to discover her teeth were missing." Anna Laura covered her mouth as she laughed at her remembrance of her toothless friend.

"She came by and got me because she knew I had a key to the church, but when we searched the pew where we had been sitting, we could not find the missing teeth."

"We looked all around the church and knew we were among the last to leave so if anyone had found the teeth, they would have mentioned it."

I nodded in agreement since I knew she was probably talking about the same faithful fifteen members who showed up every Sunday morning for worship.

"When we were leaving, we ended up going down these wide steps in the courtyard," she said as though finished with the story.

"But what about her teeth?" I said unhappy with the lack of a better ending to the tale.

"Oh, it was the funniest thing!" Annie Laura said with a laugh. "About two years after Mary had died, I was getting ready to go to church one morning and decided to bring one of my Sunday pocketbooks I had not taken to church in a long time."

I knew what she meant by "Sunday pocketbook" because my mother, aunts, and grandmothers had the same type of pocketbook. Only used on Sundays, it rarely contained anything more than a handkerchief.

"I got it from the back of one of my closets in the guest bedroom and opened it to make sure it had a handkerchief in it," she said while opening the imaginary pocketbook in her hands.

"When I reached down into it, I found Mary's teeth wrapped in her own handkerchief in my pocketbook!" Anna Laura exclaimed in laughter.

"She had been dead a couple of years by then, and there I stood holding her teeth! She must have slipped them in my pocketbook by accident and never realized her mistake."

*

"Why are you here?"
"What are you doing?"

The man on the phone seemed concerned about whether or not I would know who he was talking about.

"It's George and Elizabeth," he said slowly. "They're brother and sister. They live not far from your church. I run the country store at the crossroads."

He paused as I told him I knew them very well.

"They came by my store and they're very upset and said I should call you right now," the man stopped for a moment as though trying to make sure I knew the importance of this situation.

"They sounded like they needed you to come out to their house right away," he said in an exhausted sounding voice. "They said you were the only one who could help."

I assured the neighborly store keeper I would leave immediately and check on them.

As I drove, I wondered what might be wrong. George and Elizabeth lived in one of the oldest farm houses in the countryside surrounding my church. With two high gables on the front of the house, the charm of the place was only diminished by the extreme neglect this once prominent home suffered.

George and Elizabeth had mental challenges from birth which would have probably forced them to live in a place where they would have been cared for by others. Living in their old familiar house in the country surrounded by neighbors who watched out for them and a brother who resided not far away changed their destiny. They lived out their lives in their childhood home in their own world.

Now they faced a challenge. They needed me. I drove a little bit faster than usual to their house wondering all the way what must have happened.

Without a word, George opened the back kitchen door and then brought me through several dark and cluttered rooms. Old walls scarred with faded paint or ancient wallpaper whose colors and patterns could hardly be seen surrounded broken furniture from the earlier part of the century. He took me into a larger room in the middle of the house where Elizabeth sat on a couch while holding her face in her hands.

"Oh, I'm so glad to see you," she said holding out her hands to me. The room was strangely dark even though it was a sunny afternoon.

I sat on the old tattered couch near her.

"What happened?" I said calmly. "What can I do to help?"

She paused to collect her thoughts about the details of the calamity.

"The last time I saw him," she said with deep dread, "he went under the couch."

I felt myself lifting my feet off the floor and wondering who exactly was under the very couch upon which we sat.

"Who," I said quickly, "Who is under the couch?"

I started to stand up and look under the couch wondering if I would be able to see anything in the darkness of the room.

Elizabeth put her hand on my leg to stop me from leaving her side. I began to get a little uneasy with the whole situation as though I had seen something like this in a scary movie.

"The last time I saw him," her voice became more ominous, "he went under the couch. I don't know where he is now!"

"I don't know where HE is either, but I'm getting out of here!" I wanted to say, but instead I quietly asked her again who was under the couch.

Elizabeth looked at me and frowned.

From across the room, George answered my question.

"The biggest black snake I've ever seen!"

I felt momentary relief since we were not sitting on something from another realm, but realized we were possibly sitting on a snake. I started to stand up, but Elizabeth grabbed my hand and pulled me down.

"I couldn't think of anyone else to call," she said in a pitifully desperate tone. "I didn't think anyone else would be willing to help us. But I knew you would."

I assured her I would. I also explained they did not have to be afraid of the black snake since he was only interested in seeing if they had any mice in the house. I told them the snake was probably just as frightened of them as they were of it.

"But we have to check every room of the house," she said with tears starting in her eyes.

I patted her hand and told her I would check every room and make sure the snake had departed.

She seemed completely relieved and then told George to take me to the back bedroom to start the search.

As he took me down the wide hallway, he gave some quick instructions.

"This is where we keep all the stuff people keep bringing us. We both think he is hiding in there. We want all this stuff taken out of the house so he can't hide in there anymore."

George opened the door to the large room and pointed. From one end to the other, the room was filled with very large and very full black garbage bags.

"People keep bringing us things," George said while looking at the bags filled with clothes, blankets, and other household items. "We don't know what to do with all the stuff, so we just put them in here."

From the condition of the bags, I could tell the collection started a long time ago. Very few of the bags had even been opened.

I assured George I would take care of everything. He left the room and I started to work. With each bag I lifted, I expected to find Mr. Black Snake looking back at me. I smiled to myself thinking the snake might be surprised at what would happen with such an encounter.

Far from being a "snake handling preacher", I nevertheless had some experience in handling my brother's pet snakes he kept in aquariums in our basement. He even had a large black snake. I knew how to grab them right behind the head paying no attention to the thrashing and coiling of the rest of their bodies and slowly bring them under control. I also knew a black snake could bite and bring blood but it had no poisonous fangs.

As I pulled out each bag and watched as different varieties of roaches scurried for cover, I marveled at how God had obviously put me together with George and Elizabeth. I wondered how they knew I could help.

During the long afternoon, I cleared out the room and was able to get some church members to help move the many bags of clothing to the thrift store in town. Soon the room was completely cleared with no sign of the snake.

I left Elizabeth and George with the repeated assurances that the snake had left. I also left them knowing I was just a phone call away.

"Why are you here?"
"What are you doing?"

Last minute check. Saturday night. Sunday morning approaches.

On this Saturday night, I was not ready for the service the next morning. I had intended to get everything done during the day, but somehow the time

Morning

got away from me. Now it was dark, and I realized if I wanted a peaceful night's rest, my tasks would have to be finished.

"I'm running over to Zion," I told Donna rather quickly. "I won't be long, but I have to go."

Donna smiled. She did not have to ask questions. She did not have to go into her teacher mode and instruct me on the proper use of my time during the week. All she had to do was to look at me and smile.

I accepted her point without question and knew she expected me to make improvements in my time management in the weeks ahead.

Tyler, now age five, made it clear he would not be happy unless I took him with me. Since it was not yet his bedtime, Donna agreed he could ride the few miles to the church.

Once inside my office at the church, Tyler busied himself with looking at the variety of things around the room. On Sunday morning my office became one of the ladies' Sunday School rooms. The arrangements worked out well since the room was large enough for a circle of about a dozen chairs and my desk and work tables.

Tyler started playing around the chairs and then stopped and looked out into the courtyard through the windows of the office.

As I was just about ready to complete my tasks, he asked a question.

"What does S-H-I… spell?"

I stopped and wondered if I had heard him correctly.

"What did you say?" as I got up from my desk and started walking across the room.

"What does S-H-I…" I interrupted him before he finished and turned him away from the window.

The lights from my office illuminated enough of the courtyard so I could see what he had seen.

Black spray paint had been used to express someone's great displeasure of our congregation. The beige walls of the courtyard were now decorated in hate-filled messages about how we were all sinners who were going to our judgment.

I tried to remain calm as I reached for the phone on my desk and called the parsonage. I explained my situation to Donna and asked her advice.

"The sanctuary windows look directly out to the courtyard," I said in great dismay. "Should we hang sheets over the windows? Should I call for some of the Trustees to come at once and see what can be done before the morning? Should I try to get some spray paint and paint over the words? What can I do?"

Donna suggested the first thing I might do would be to calm down.

"Schools deal with graffiti all the time," she said in a matter-of-fact voice. "I don't think anyone who comes to church will not have seen something similar before. They may be shocked someone would do this to our church, but they will understand there was nothing to be done about it on a Saturday night."

"Call someone and let them know what you found," she said calmly. "I think they will agree with me. Worship will happen tomorrow and everyone will understand."

Of course, everything turned out exactly as Donna stated. An explanation was given, a police report was filed, and we worshipped as normal.

I used the courtyard messages, especially the one stating we were all sinners, to say to the children during the children's sermon the next day that our perpetrator got one statement right.

"We are all sinners," I said with a smile to the children. "That's why we come to church! We need to be forgiven by our loving Lord."

On Monday, Donna suggested I go to the janitorial supply company and see about some cleaner her school custodian had used on graffiti. Within a few hours, Donna and I had successfully cleaned all the walls. We sprayed the wonderful cleaner and wiped one long wall to the next, one ugly letter at a time. The spray miraculously dissolved the black paint and restored the walls to their original color.

After several hours, we stood side by side and looked at the courtyard walls in amazement. It looked as though nothing evil had ever touched them.

Why are you here?
What are you doing?

Advent in the country. In the midst of many holiday preparations, I asked Donna if she would mind having a Christmas drop-in for the churches at the parsonage on a Sunday afternoon. My mother volunteered to help with a very large sampling of her many favorite Christmas goodies.

From the lawns and porches to the laundry room, everything was finally ready. On Sunday morning we gave the house one final examination. The large dining room table was covered with shining sterling silver trays waiting to be filled with delicious and tempting festive treats. Everything looked perfect except one decoration needed a new light bulb. I told Donna I would get one right after church before the guests arrived.

Morning

As I normally did, I drove my small pickup truck to church that morning. Donna taught the youth Sunday School class every week at the larger of the two churches on my pastoral charge. I preached at the smaller of the churches first and then drove over for the worship service at the larger church.

As soon as both church services were finished, I got in my truck to run to the store to buy the light bulb. Tyler wanted to go with me, but since I was just on this short errand, Donna decided it would be better for him to go with her and get his lunch.

As I drove down the two-lane country highway, I was excited about the fun time we would have at the drop-in and how great it would be to have everyone come to the parsonage to share in our favorite Christmas treats.

On the last straight section of the highway, just before I reached my destination, I noticed a car coming up very fast behind me. It was traveling at such a high rate of speed I braced myself for what I thought would be a very hard impact. At the last possible second, the car veered over into the other lane. I checked to make sure another car was not approaching from the other direction. A sense of relief came over me as I realized the speeding driver had avoided hitting both me and another car.

Just as he got even to my door, he turned sharply into my truck.

Hit at such a high rate of speed, my small truck immediately left the road and rolled down a steep bank. The jolt of the hit stunned me so much I didn't know exactly what was happening. All the glass in the truck cab cracked so finely I couldn't see anything as I continued rolling down the embankment faster and faster.

I only had one thought: *Where is the tree?*

I had driven past this location for years and knew that down the steep hill stood a row of trees. I knew I had to be headed right for one.

All I could do was wait for what I thought would be the last sound I would ever hear.

Everything stopped. All was quiet. My truck rested at the bottom of the hill as though I had parked it there. The cab looked strangely open. Every piece of glass was completely gone.

I also noticed I could not turn my head.

Reaching up, I felt rubber wrapped all around my neck. As I slowly unwound it, I saw that it was the rubber gasket which originally held the rear window in place.

The gasket had somehow wrapped itself completely around my neck like a very protective brace. Not so tight as to restrict my breathing, the gasket did its job perfectly.

"Praise God! You're alive! You're alive!"

A man stood at the driver's door shouting and looking at me as I unwound the gasket.

"Are you alright? Are you bleeding? An ambulance is on the way! My wife and I saw the wreck, we saw your truck roll down the hill! I told my wife you had to be dead! Praise God! Praise God! You're alive!"

I knew I was not harmed and, as far as I could tell, did not even have a scratch. I began to climb through the completely shattered front window, I still only had one thought: *Where is the tree?*

My truck sat between the trees. In all the expanse of the highway with all of the trees lining the highway, one small section, about the size of a small pickup truck, had no trees.

My truck, smashed and broken, sat in the small section which had been prepared for me.

On my last day in the office, I sat looking at the empty desk and the cheerful classroom I would not see anymore. In keeping with our traditions of an intenerate ministry, our bishop had decided it was time for me to take another pastoral charge.

The Dutch doors looking out into the courtyard stood half open as they did most nice days when I was there.

Suddenly I heard the familiar sound of scampering claws on the concrete, and the two Boston Terriers jumped up and put their front paws on the door edge and looked at me with their perpetual smiles.

"Why are you here?"
"What are you doing?"

Looking at them, I finally had an answer to their inquisitive stares.

"I am the extremely unworthy one who survived," I said aloud to them. "Now I am saddled with the task of discovering why."

Chapter 14
Hickory Lane Extension

DONNA, TYLER, AND I RODE DOWN HICKORY Lane Extension. This little thoroughfare ran from one small country road to a tiny street. I never found Hickory Lane itself, only this extension. No homes existed here. The old road resembled a light gray path instead of a road paved with asphalt. After many years of tractors and trucks, the sun-bleached tar seemed to barely keep the white gravel in place.

We traveled down Hickory Lane Extension after leaving a New Year's Eve party. Amy had hosted a small gathering of friends at her beautiful country home to watch the old year end and celebrate the arrival of the future.

We ate her famous spaghetti noodle baked cheese pie and feasted on her fluffy biscuits. We sang songs around the piano as she played every tune we could imagine. We laughed and toasted in the New Year with sparkling cider. After hugs and well-wishes, we got into our cars to go home to our comfortable beds.

As we made our way down the lane, with no other cars following us, I took my time driving the short distance from Amy's house. Tyler immediately went to sleep, and Donna settled quietly in the seat next to mine as though already thinking about how nice our warm bed would feel.

Wooded areas, fields, and pastures lined both sides of Hickory Lane Extension. I could have driven up the road with my eyes closed. Many days after lunch, I walked this lane before returning to work. Situated near the parsonage, this rarely used road became the perfect spot for some quick afternoon exercise in the fresh country air. Most days the postal delivery woman in her little jeep would be the only person I would encounter.

I loved watching the countryside of the lane go through the changes of each season. The hay fields would turn from green and lush to harvested and brown and then slowly back to green again. Sometimes in the winter months I would detour from the main road and walk down one of the dirt roads running between the fields and the woods. On a section of one of the field roads, large round bales of hay waited for their final destination. Placed in a neat row, they formed a barrier between the cultivated fields and the wooded areas.

One day as I walked down Hickory Lane Extension, an odd sight caught my eye. In the middle of the forest, an ordinary bare oak tree had become illuminated. Singled out from the rest, this one tree was somehow highlighted by a ray of sunshine.

The day was rather overcast but not rainy. A ray of sunlight had momentarily burst through the cloud cover and found its target on the gray bark of the oak. Nothing else about the tree seemed in the least bit outstanding, but now the bark glowed with a radiating passion. I smiled and thought it was somehow humorously interesting one tree would be highlighted in such an odd fashion. I stopped walking as I realized the tree represented me. With a certainty requiring no further explanation, I knew this tree exposed my future. In complete loneliness, surrounded by other trees but still in utter solitude, this startling and unwelcome vision destroyed the peace and beauty of the day.

One day I would be completely alone.

I turned away with a shudder and shook my head in defiance of what I had seen and hoping to get the image out of my mind. Immediately rationalizing how a ray of sun might illuminate tree trunks all the time in this particular spot of the forest, I looked back to verify my new assumption. The tree no longer shimmered in the light. Everything had returned to normal as though nothing had occurred.

As I drove down Hickory Lane Extension on New Year's night, I wondered if I might be able to see the same oak tree in the darkness. It was not until then I noticed the night was very clear and almost bright. Realizing a full moon must be illuminating the sky, I looked up through the front windshield to see if I could find the moon.

I stopped the car and got out.

"What on earth are you doing?" Donna questioned as I walked a few steps away from the car. "What's going on?"

"Look!" I said in excitement.

Donna stepped out of the car and held her coat close to herself against the chill of the evening. She looked up and smiled.

"I've never seen anything like it," she said as she walked around the car and hugged me. We stood in our embrace and looked up from the little country road and relished the moment of magnificence God had created.

In the heavens, the full moon brilliantly reflected the glory of the hidden sun. Completely encircling the moon, a perfect rainbow gloriously eclipsed the beauty of the night and the stars.

I quickly said a prayer as I looked at this display of the birth of a new year. I thanked God for the covenant of the rainbow but also made a quick plea for a year of peace and renewal. Even with the grace-filled beauty of the

Morning

celestial manifestation, I prayed against this moment becoming a foretelling of tragedy and despair.

I looked away from the glorious heavens and gazed at Donna's upturned face. The bright moonlight enchanted her smile. Her peace hushed my fears. Her joy changed the visions of Hickory Lane Extension from dreaded moments of what might happen to the simple and unmistakable assurance that no matter what, she would always be with me.

She sensed I was no longer watching the heavenly show and looked at me.

"I love you," she whispered in the complete and still silence of the midnight hour.

Chapter 15
Dad

LIGHT FROM THE LARGE PICTURE WINDOW in the dining room awakened me. I would have preferred to have remained asleep. Donna did not stir. Tyler made no sound from his room. Only the golden light of the dawn made the house seem any different than it had been when we went to bed late in the night.

The light grew stronger, and I knew I had to face this day and make a decision. A question from the previous evening still ran through my mind.

"Do I want to speak at Dad's funeral?"

Drowsiness fell away from my mind and body as I searched for the answer. I knew I could simply do nothing and let others handle the funeral service and eulogy, but I felt compelled to do more.

Dad lived a simple and uncomplicated life filled with constant work. He worked from early in the morning until past the time most people went to bed. He found ways to work on different projects even on the coldest of winter nights. He worked six days and nights every week. On Sunday he worked at the church doing whatever needed to be done while also worshipping God. He simply never stopped working.

His interaction with his three sons revolved around the business, yardwork, and farm chores. I never saw him pitch a ball or play any sort of game. Even though he never taught us how to fish or play golf, he taught us one very important thing about life.

"Your Dad is not lazy," Mom told us one day when we were complaining about the many chores he required of us. "You should learn from him. Never let anyone think you are lazy."

I knew I could not stay in bed on this morning. I needed to witness the dawn whose golden rays seemed to be at their peak right then. I quietly walked through the house to the large picture window of the dining room facing east. On the other side of the front lawn, I could see the ever intensifying light over the tree tops of the woods across the road.

My mind could not accept the beauty of this sight as I stood in the quiet of the house. Standing there I remembered another time of mourning I had experienced in this same room.

"Why is everyone here?" I whispered to Don as he leaned over to me. Dad effortlessly carried the two of us, one in each arm, as we moved through the house full of people. I knew this house, the home of my grandparents. I

Morning

knew the laughter of my grandfather and his wonderful smile. I had seen love and admiration in his eyes when he spoke to me.

Now Dad carried the two of us through a throng of people. We could not get down to walk because there was simply no space. We stood in the dining room and looked at our grandfather in what appeared to be a small strange bed against the wall.

"Is he asleep?" I asked Don. He did not have to answer; it was obvious neither one of us knew. People kept making their way to us and pinching our cheeks and smiling and laughing at us as though they were happy to be in the house.

Dad held us securely in his arms as we held onto his shoulders. It felt like we were floating over a lake full of people who understood why we were all there.

Dad took us to one of the bedrooms and opened the door. Unlike the rest of the house, this room was empty except for one person.

"Mother!"

She walked across the room as though almost still asleep. A long white nightgown covered her from neck to ankles. Her brown hair hung loose on her shoulders, and it appeared she was just getting ready to go to bed. She reached out one hand and put it first on Don's cheek and then mine.

I knew we both wanted to ask her what was happening. We wanted her to explain everything as she normally did whenever we were confused. I wanted her to speak with soothing tones so we would know everything was alright.

She smiled at us and then turned and walked toward the bed. Dad spoke to her and then left the room.

As we drove out the circular driveway, I saw more parked cars all around the house than I had ever seen in my life.

On this golden morning, I stood in the same dining room. Dad no longer carried us into this room to have another encounter with death. With his strong arms and hands, he had cradled us close to him. Even though we could not fully understand what was happening, we did not have to be afraid. He had prepared the way for his children.

This house was now my house. Passed down to my mother and then to me, the Homeplace came complete with my grandparents' furniture and endless memories.

"I loved my little duck," Grandmother told me one Saturday morning. "I don't think I had ever become so attached to one of the animals on the farm before. But for some reason, I fell in love with this one baby duck."

At her kitchen table, she told me this story and many more about growing up on a farm near Abbeville. She had been born in 1895 and had lived all of her life in the country. She spent most of her childhood picking cotton, and now she enjoyed telling me how things used to be.

"My little baby duck loved me, too," she said with her calm voice. Her still and quiet tone captivated my attention and took away all other thoughts except listening to everything she said.

"He knew when I got out the hoe he was going to get some worms!"

She laughed as she talked. I could tell by her words she was back on the farm, and I wanted to see what she was seeing. I wanted to live in the world of those days, but all I could do was simply listen and learn.

"My pet duck knew I would pick out the best spot near the barn where there was plenty of manure to dig for worms. He knew I would do the digging and all he had to do was the eating!"

"I started digging through rich black dirt and then uncovered a bed of worms. I reached up with my hoe to dig the hole a little deeper. Just as I swung the hoe down, my little duck jumped in the hole."

Grandmother stopped talking and looked at me making sure I was old enough to hear the next words. Her eyes penetrated through my childhood innocence and my weakness. As one capable of understanding who I was and who I would become, she evaluated me. I must not have come up lacking because she finished the story.

"I killed my precious little pet duck with one stroke from my hoe before I could stop myself," she paused and then looked out the kitchen window. I knew the intensity of her emotions surprised her. I felt what she must have felt.

"I learned something very valuable right then," she said as she turned from the window and looked at me. Again, I sensed a searching from her eyes to mine to see if I was worthy enough to receive her wisdom.

I knew she would find me to be a willing student. I knew she understood how I longed to be taught about life, family, and faith by her. She knew how happy it made me to listen to everything she had to say.

"Just remember this," Grandmother said with a serious tone while I leaned closer to her as though to feel the weight of the wisdom of her breath upon me.

"Always have someone else hold your baby duck when you dig for worms."

It was not exactly the great words of wisdom for which I had hoped, but I came to understand and truly appreciate her lessons of life. Grandmother's wisdom came from her stories of how she lived and how she allowed her many encounters with others to shape her.

Now I stood in her dining room surrounded by her furniture, her china, her crystal, and her silver remembering her stories. In the midst of thinking about all of her wonderful experiences, I wondered how I could ever write something about Dad. How could I capture anything about him truly honoring who he was and what he had given not only to his sons and his family but to everyone?

What could I possibly say about this man of ceaseless work? How could my words become a fitting statement to honor him while also giving glory to God?

I looked across the lawn once again to the tops of the leafless trees on the other side of the highway. The branches looked triumphant in the golden morning. No longer gray and frail, they resembled mad slashes of life reaching out from the earth and claiming their position in the light.

Oak trees reaching up for the light as they have for centuries, I thought.

I knew they were oak trees because Dad taught us the trees. In the golden light while I stood in this house full of memories, I realized I wanted everyone at his funeral to know he would be remembered, in part, for teaching us to name the trees.

On Sunday afternoons in the late autumn and early winter, Dad would take us on walks in the woods. We would start at the old farmhouse and visit for a while with his sister and his mother who lived there. We would then set off down to the old barn. Dad would open the corn crib next to the barn, and the cows would start to gather from across the fields. If they happened to be down at the river or over at the creek near the river, Dad would call them to come for this once-a-week afternoon treat.

"Come hep!" he would call. His strong voice would resonate across the pastures and through the woods. "Come hep!"

The cows would answer from the riverbank and the creek. Their mooing sounded mournful as though asking for forgiveness at being tardy. They seemed to be saying he should wait for them; they were on their way.

The small herd knew to gather in a neat row at the corn crib. They would lower their heads through the opening in the side of the building and wait patiently for the hearty food to be given. Built at the right height for cattle, the trough, which could be accessed from inside and outside the corn crib, would be filled from one end to the other with the heads of the white-faced Hereford cows and bulls.

We would crowd into the small corn crib to watch as Dad removed the lid from the large wooden barrel standing in the rear corner of the room.

Once opened, a wonderful aroma infused with sweetness flowed from the barrel. Even though the building had been built with slits between each narrow slat in the wall to allow for proper ventilation, the sweet aroma lingered and teased the cattle.

Peering inside the barrel, we would marvel at the mixture of corn and grains making up what Dad always called "sweet feed". The cattle would start to get restless as they smelled the variety of grains mixed with dark molasses.

Dad would reach deep into the barrel with a large wooden scoop and pour the grains into the trough. He would also allow each of us to pour one scoop to the grateful herd. With their heads bowed as though in prayer, they would begin their contented munching.

After the Sunday afternoon sweet feed treat, the cattle would ignore us. Dad would close up the crib and then we would walk up a hill behind the old log barn. A well-worn trail used by the herd started at the side of the hill. We would follow Dad as though expecting some sort of sweet feed treat, but he was simply leading us through the woods and by the river to the pasture on the other side.

We had no purpose in making the journey other than to simply do it. As we walked along, Dad would comment on just about everything we saw. He told us about the poisonous wild cherries which were so dark purple they looked the color of shiny coal. He pointed out the rabbit tobacco and the broom sage growing on the edges of the pasture.

We would always stop at the locust tree and gather a few of the prune colored long pods. He would show us how to peel away the outer husk of the pod and lick on the sweet golden paste surrounding the seeds.

As we entered the forest, he would look at the base of a tree and find a little brown jug plant. Kneeling on one knee, Dad gently pushed aside the rotting leaf litter to reveal a small white or brown jug at the bottom of the plant. After we marveled at how much it looked like a jug made of clay, he would cover the delicate jug once again leaving only the arrow shaped leaf exposed to the light.

He taught us to listen to the honey bees residing in one old hollow tree. We would put our ears tightly against the worn smooth surface of the tree and hear the hum from inside. Like a mighty army of tiny engines, the constant humming verified their presence. By looking up at a hole in the tree trunk, we could witness the arrivals and departures of these amazing insects.

Moving further into the woods, we would finally come to the top of the hill where it began to gently slope down to the creek bordering this side of the farm. Standing at this particular spot with Dad, I felt we could see forever.

Morning

The forest around and below us always appeared completely devoid of undergrowth as though the herd spent most of their time not only keeping the grass of the pastures neatly trimmed but also the forest clean and clear of tangling vines and bushes.

From here, we could look back and see a young forest of tall pines and a part of the pastures. On the edge of the pasture stood the small farmhouse with the tractor shed and smokehouse. Dad would stand on the hill surveying all he could see. As the eldest son, he took personal responsibility for the entire family and especially the family farm. On days such as these with his three sons at his side, he would pause and then—with great care—begin to name the trees.

"That's a poplar," he would say slowly as though giving us a very treasured gift. "You can tell by how straight and tall the trunk is."

We would look in the indicated direction and marvel at the tall strong tree as though seeing it for the first time.

"There are the sweet gum trees," he would say pointing from the ridge to another direction. "Your mother will want us to get some of the sweet gum balls off the ground to make Christmas ornaments."

My brothers and I would remain quiet while he stood there teaching us about the trees. He would slowly point out each tree and tell us something about them so we could remember their characteristics.

In naming the trees, we learned about the enduring strength of the locust trees whose wood made great fence posts. We experienced the aroma of the cedar trees whose lumber he had used to line our closets. We spotted each of the squirrels' nests in the tallest of the red oaks.

We came to love the persimmon tree and looked for its fruit to turn from the bitterest green to soft, golden, and edible after the first frost. We would be amazed at the bountiful harvest available from the hickory nut trees and the black walnut trees growing in abundance in these woods.

As though in the midst of a rare moment of teaching us about the most valuable lessons of life, Dad would stand on the hill on many Sunday afternoons and share his knowledge. Without realizing it, he instilled in us a great love for the intricate beauty of an ordinary forest.

We would slowly make our way down to the creek and then to the river. Walking up the shore, we would reach the highest ridge on the farm. Covered in leaves and wood ferns, the ridge seemed to go straight up and looked like a forbidden wall protecting the rest of the forest from the spring floods of the Saluda.

My brothers would run to the ridge and begin climbing with all of their might to get to the top. Dad and I would join them and begin the arduous task. They would be laughing and talking as they went up and then sideways and then up some more before getting to the very top. From there they would start running up the old logging road leading to the unused hog pen and the side pasture.

I would still be struggling on the ridge. Left in the middle of the climb, I would begin to wonder how I would ever make it to the top. I knew I could go back down and take the longer way around the ridge, but I also knew they would be on the pasture running and playing before I would ever get there. In my frustration, I would start climbing harder only to find my feet constantly slipping on the leaves. The small scattered trees offered little help in giving a handhold.

Dad simply walked up the ridge. Without bending or stooping, he made the trek look as simple as walking up a sidewalk. His large boots conquered each step and held perfectly as he reached an impossibly long distance with his other boot. With great ease he would finish the climb and then watch me in the midst of my struggles. Without a word of frustration over my lack of climbing abilities, he would stand on the top of the ridge and keep his eye on me. I sensed he didn't want to tell me how to do it since it would be better for me to figure it out on my own.

At the same time, he would not leave me in the middle of the ridge. When he realized I simply could not struggle anymore, he would walk down the ridge, plant his feet firmly in the soil and reach out his hand to me.

Several months after Dad's funeral, I decided I would take Tyler on a walk in the forest of the farm. Since at this point Tyler was still very young, he did not seem to fully appreciate the way I would stop and talk about each item of the forest. He delighted in tasting the locust pods and in romping through the old trails which had almost disappeared. To my dismay, the honey bee tree was now just pieces of rotting wood on the ground. The herd no longer kept the forest free of undergrowth, but from the hill overlooking the creek, the trees could still be clearly seen and differentiated. I stood there and took my son in my arms and named the trees.

We walked along the creek as though no years had passed. We came to the river, and I allowed him to throw sticks into the currents and watch them float away. We even went down the bank to the spots where I had fished in my childhood. As we made our way closer to the side pasture, I saw the high ridge.

Smiling to myself, I wondered what Tyler would think about this formidable natural formation. I started to tell him about it when I realized he was running for it as fast as he could. Laughing, I ran behind him and watched as he began to climb the ridge.

Using his feet and hands, he began to quickly ascend. As though he was on the greatest piece of playground equipment ever, he smiled and laughed and pushed aside the wood ferns and made amazing progress.

I stood at the base of the ridge thinking he would tire quickly and come back down. Without stopping, he zoomed past the mid-point and began to make his way to the top.

"Wait up!" I shouted to him not sure he would stop running once he finished the climb. We were still fairly deep in the forest, and I suddenly became uneasy thinking he might wander away.

Now filled with fatherly responsibility for my son, I began my climb using sure and steady steps. All too soon my climb became the same slow and uncertain progression of slipping feet and tumbles. Looking up, I saw Tyler nearing the top. Deciding it was time for me to go into four-wheel drive like he had done, I hunched over and used my hands along with my feet to make better progress.

If I could have climbed with only my hands, I probably would have succeeded, but my feet kept sliding through the damp leaves. After landing flat on the ground several times, I stood again and began reaching for trees. Finding one after another, I pulled on them for support.

Hearing Tyler laugh, I glanced up and saw he was at the top looking down.

"Stay right there!" I said as loudly as I could in the midst of struggling for breath. "Don't go anywhere! Daddy will be there in just a few moments."

Pulling myself to another tree, I suddenly realized how much I missed my Dad. I thought about how wonderful it would be to see him tall and strong standing there with me in the midst of my struggles.

I gasped as I realized I would never again feel the confidence of his hand in mine pulling me to the top of the ridge. I bowed to the ground and realized I would have to give up my vain efforts to climb this mountain alone.

Hearing small footsteps in the leaves, I peered up through my tear-filled eyes to see Tyler standing just above me. With a confident grin, he spread his little feet and stomped each one into the slope to get a sure footing.

He smiled and reached out his hand to me.

Chapter 16
Mom

"Maybe I should wait to have this surgery," Mom had said a few days prior.

"It's only been two weeks since your father died," she added. "It just doesn't feel right to be having surgery so soon after the funeral. It almost seems disrespectful."

"No, no," I said trying to reassure her. "No one is going to think you should postpone the surgery. It's been scheduled for a long time. The doctor said you need to take care of it."

The surgery in question was simple. One day in the hospital at most. Simple removal of a cyst. She would be back on her feet in no time.

"I still have so many things to do here," she said while trying to convince herself to delay the procedure. "I need to work more on the probate."

I knew Mom liked to stay ahead of all her responsibilities. I also knew she did not want to burden us with business matters she could handle.

"Mom," I said almost sounding like a teenager, "all the other stuff can wait. You need to get this done, especially since it's already scheduled. You don't want to have to go through setting up the surgery all over again. Let them take care of it. The sooner the better. Then you can get back to handling everything without having this surgery hanging over your head."

She reluctantly agreed.

My older brother, Jim, and I stood in the hall of the hospital waiting on the doctor. A nurse had just told us the doctor was on his way to see us.

I spotted him walking down the hall and realized immediately something was terribly wrong.

"We need a private consulting room," the young doctor stated while looking uncomfortable.

He walked down the hall and then motioned for Jim and me to follow him.

"This was supposed to be a very simple surgery," the doctor said quickly after we were seated in the room. "We had no indication anything else was wrong."

He paused for a moment and looked at us. I wondered if he thought we might get angry at his next words.

"But when we went in," he said quietly, "we discovered a lot of ovarian cancer."

My head jerked back in surprise almost as fast as Jim's. The shock on our faces mirrored the dismay of the doctor.

"We had no indication any cancer was present," the doctor said while obviously trying not to sound too defensive. "But there it was, nonetheless."

"What does this mean?" I hoped he could give us some assurance about treatment options.

"This cancer does not generally spread," he said regaining his professional tone of voice, "but it doesn't have to. It will cause her to slowly starve."

I waited for him to say, "to death", but then realized he didn't have to add those words. It was written all over his face.

"We will try treatments, and there have been advancements made in treating ovarian cancer, but…it's probably just a long shot at best. There is too much already present."

I held her hand while Jim and Don watched her as she tried to deal with this unexpected news.

We stood beside her hospital bed as she cried and the nurse administered pain medicine. This shock had come too soon after the surgery. Mom needed calm and peace to recover from the surgery so she could begin to deal with the cancer.

"Jesus, Jesus," she said softly.

I couldn't tell if she was beginning to pray or simply calling out his name.

"Jesus, Jesus."

I recognized the tone in her voice as I gently squeezed her hand to let her know we were all there with her. Her voice resonated with regret and remorse.

She's praying for forgiveness, I thought. *She's seeking reassurance of mercy.*

I leaned closer to her. She did not open her eyes.

"It's OK," I whispered in her ear. "Everything is going to be OK."

"Jesus, Jesus," she responded.

"It's OK," I repeated softly.

She seemed to settle down some.

"Everything is going to be OK," I repeated as though the untruthful, empty words needed to be emphasized again.

When Mom held me as a child and said those words to quiet my fears, I knew she was speaking the truth. The world seemed to obey her wishes, and security from all harm was indeed absolute.

In the face of the absoluteness of suffering and death, I could only offer empty promises of false hope. Even though Mom could make everything alright, even though she could make sure the world did not harm me or my brothers, even though she could put an end to any fear and any suffering I might face, I knew I was powerless to do the same for her.

In this situation, I offered her the only truth I knew.

"God is with you; God loves you," I said with assurance.

Chapter 17

Spartanburg

I SAT DOWN IN THE LARGE EMPTY SANCTUARY on the pew next to her. Neither one of us said a word. I smiled at her as I tried to genuinely express my admiration and love for this remarkable older lady. She did not look at me.

She wore a light pink suit that fit her small frame perfectly. On her left shoulder a delicate brooch displayed colorful gemstone Easter eggs filling a golden basket with a shiny gold wire bow.

On her lap, she held her black patent leather handbag matching her shoes. Without looking up, she quietly spoke.

"This isn't Easter, is it?" She was not asking a question. She was stating the obvious.

"No, Evelyn," I said softly. "It isn't Easter."

I took her hand in mine as we welcomed the silence between us.

"What day is it?" she asked while still refusing to look at me.

"Evelyn, today is Tuesday," I said in as gentle a way as I could possibly muster. "But it's always wonderful to see you."

She looked up and smiled at me, a faint reminder of the strong and wise woman I had met and learned to love just a few years ago.

"These things happen sometimes, Evelyn," I said while still holding her hand. The secretary had alerted me when Evelyn had arrived and gone into the sanctuary. She also told me Evelyn appeared to be dressed not only for Sunday morning worship but also for Easter.

"I love your Easter dress," I said with a smile. I wondered if I should tell her she would still have to wait almost a month to wear it again.

This woman had welcomed us to our new church. Strong and capable, she provided great leadership to the church and city in which we now lived. Her father had owned a large business, and Evelyn had not only inherited the business but succeeded in making it even more prosperous. All of this she had accomplished in the 1960's.

Her kindness and insight into the functioning of the church continued to be highly valued by the members. Just recently, it became obvious things were starting to change for her. We tried to think it was minor. With the events of this Tuesday morning, I knew I would have to tell her family she needed closer attention.

My hand in hers, I would gladly sit with her all day in the sanctuary if it would give her comfort.

Much like Evelyn, her church had a great and glorious past. Duncan Memorial United Methodist Church in Spartanburg had been named for a much beloved bishop of another time. When Tyler saw Bishop Duncan's large and impressive portrait in the narthex of the church, he made a proclamation to Donna.

"He must have been very bad. He was so bad they even put his picture in the foyer."

Being only seven years old at the time, Tyler did not understand that the narthex of the church was not the place of punishment. In his world, when he misbehaved, he was sent to the foyer of the parsonage to sit in a little chair in the corner until told he could leave.

Duncan Memorial claimed at least two books written about its past. One told the story of the junior college started by a pastor for the young textile mill workers of the community. The other book stated the many times the church had been blessed.

The latter book started with the story of the survival of the church when most of the mill village was destroyed by a devastating fire. Miraculously, the flames did not consume the church but came so close the paint on its walls melted.

The community and the mill village era had passed, but they claimed this part of history for their own. The many members who worshipped at Duncan Memorial dearly loved their church. They would completely fill the many pews of the sanctuary every Sunday. Most of them were at least in their seventies. They loved being together, worshiping together, and fellowshipping together. They maintained the old rambling building in near perfect shape and would generously respond with ample funds to any need of their spiritual home.

Every Sunday felt like a family reunion, and even though they knew it could not last, they thoroughly enjoyed their church of family and old acquaintances to the end.

The other church on my pastoral charge was St. Mark. Situated between Spartanburg and the historic little town of Cowpens, this congregation had merged with another congregation and built a new sanctuary a few decades before. Now situated on a main highway, they remained poised for growth.

St. Mark so completely immersed itself into the community it became difficult at times to distinguish between the two. Church events became community events and community events and neighboring church events became St. Mark events as well. They thrived by being connected with everything and every family.

Evelyn turned to me. I could tell her mind had cleared completely. She carefully wiped her eyes and looked at me.

"When I was a little girl," she said after a few minutes of silence, "my father always had a routine on Sunday mornings."

"He would come into my room and sit on the edge of my bed and take my hand," she squeezed my hand as she continued. "Then he would very gently say, 'Evelyn! Evelyn! It's time to wake up! It's time to go to the Lord's house!'"

"Even though he said it with a whisper, I could tell he was so excited about going to the Lord's house with me." I felt her shudder with joy as she remembered this precious moment of her childhood.

"I loved it when he would wake me up on Sunday mornings," she said lifting her head and closing her eyes. "I would be so happy to get ready and go to church with him. He made it sound like the best place to be in all of the world…and it was!"

She stopped talking and then took my hand in both of her hands.

"I wish he would wake me up on a bright Sunday morning one more time and tell me to come with him to the Lord's house. I would be so excited to see him again. I would be so happy to go with him. I'm ready! I'm ready!"

Chapter 18
Kidney Transplant

DONNA CAME TO THE BACK PORCH AND ASKED me to come inside. I made a quick check on Tyler and several of his friends as they played outside and felt confident they would be fine. Even better than the fence that kept the boys in the yard, a warning from one of the neighborhood grandmothers stopped the boys from wandering into the wooded area behind the large subdivision.

"That's the Girl Scout Camp," Mrs. Bullis stated to the boys one day when she found they had left her yard and gone venturing into the woods. Her grandchildren and several other boys, all of the same age, had decided the woods contained wonderful things to be explored and had climbed the fence to start on their journey when they were caught.

"Those Girl Scouts have cameras hidden in the trees," she said as though rehearsing for a Halloween production. "They watch to see if little boys come from our neighborhood and go into their woods."

She paused and stared at the five young boys to make sure each one listened carefully.

"Do you know what happens if they see a little boy coming into the woods?"

"They send the Girl Scouts out into the woods from the camp to get you!" she exclaimed with great enthusiasm to demonstrate that this would be the worst thing imaginable.

Donna and I tried not to laugh as Mrs. Bullis demanded from each boy an assurance they would remain in our yards and not go to the forbidden territory.

On the strength and impact of past warnings, I went into the house leaving the boys to play.

Donna sat on the couch in the living room at the large bay window looking out on the centipede grass lawn shaded by giant white oak trees.

"The doctor said I'm ready for a kidney transplant," she said simply and without elaboration as I sat down on the couch beside her. In the shock of hearing those words, I found myself having difficulty understanding what she was saying.

Since the very first time the situation with her kidneys was diagnosed as a child, she and everyone involved had worked carefully to insure her one good kidney would last for her lifetime. I knew she would take this news as a defeat of all her efforts.

Once again, I imagined the young child Donna running down the hospital hallway defiantly daring the doctor to catch her as he watched her mahogany brown ponytail waving farewell to him.

"He's been monitoring the situation very carefully for the past few years as things have begun to change. He said very soon I would have to start dialysis since my good kidney is now in failure. He does not want me to start dialysis and feels the only option is to begin the process of getting a kidney transplant."

Her calmness in stating these words amazed but did not surprise me. With an enduring tolerance for every tempest, Donna resolutely captained her life.

I reached out to embrace her. She settled in my arms and breathed heavily while remaining silent. I felt motion as she quickly wiped away a tear. I wanted to cry with her but knew she would prefer me to remain calmly strong for her.

I tried to give her the strength of my embrace even as I realized my enfolding arms reached out for her soothing presence which always hushed my fears.

I had received several letters from the Navy stating they were currently seeking young pastors to serve as chaplains. I would read each letter several times. Surprisingly, I began to realize this would be an exciting new way to experience and fulfill my calling. I cherished my time in the local churches, but I also knew I could be an effective pastor to those who served our country.

After reading one letter after another and praying over the decision I needed to make, something kept telling me to wait. Something also kept telling me to keep the letters to myself and not share them with Donna even though I normally shared everything with her.

Now in her arms, I knew I would have to end that notion in order to make sure I would always be present to take care of her needs as they might arise. This small sacrifice on my part seemed like nothing compared to her health and wholeness. I gladly kept the secret and smiled as I put it to rest forever.

"I knew the doctor had been getting increasingly concerned over my blood chemistry levels," she said quietly as she hugged me tighter. "I just didn't know the transplant would come so quickly."

"That amazing kidney you and the doctors have pampered and nurtured since you were a child has lasted all these years," I said as cheerfully as I could. "I don't think we could have asked it to do any better. Now we just have to get you a new one to last just as long and even longer."

She smiled as she pulled away and looked into my eyes. I understood she sought verification of the truth and sincerity of my words. I could sense her sadness and frustration of the futility of years of painful surgeries and even more excruciating recoveries as she carefully followed every bit of advice and instruction from her doctors.

I knew my words could not fulfill her yearning that this major life effort on her part had been worth the effort. I looked into her eyes knowing she would see my admiration for all she had done and everything she had steadfastly accomplished.

"Let's do this," she said wiping another tear. "I'm ready to get this behind me and get on with life!"

The next few months passed with great efficiency. As though all things had been prepared for the eventuality of the transplant, the gears moved in quick and synchronized fashion.

The doctors informed us we would not have to travel very far for the procedure since the Medical University of South Carolina at Charleston ranked among the best kidney transplant hospitals in the nation. The next step would be to find a kidney.

We met with the kidney transplant team in Greenville. They flew from Charleston for the day to meet with potential patients and go over all of the steps involved. The team included a transplant doctor, a pharmacist, a nutritionist, a financial advisor, and a nurse.

Donna and I sat in an examination room as each team member came in to meet with us and explained everything in great detail.

"After all of the paperwork is completed and you have been approved, we will have to obtain a donor kidney," the doctor stated quietly.

"I will donate a kidney," I said emphatically. "I have an identical twin brother. If I ever need another kidney, I'm sure he would donate one for me."

"It's sort of like I already have a spare one," I said with a smile.

"It probably will not be a match," the doctor said in a kind voice. "It would be very rare if it were. We will have to start with Donna's closest blood relatives, if they are willing to donate?"

"Well, I have been offered twelve kidneys," Donna said while laughing. "Of course they are not all relatives, but my two brothers have said they are willing to donate."

"Good," the doctor said while taking notes. "We will start with them. Our last option will be a cadaver kidney, but we will start with your relatives and see where it goes from there."

Morning

Continuing at a remarkable pace, everything fell into place. Updates occurred daily as we realized this would happen even sooner than we had anticipated. Arrangements were made for Wayne, Donna's older brother, to be tested at a hospital in Nashville where he lived.

"Both of your brothers are matches for you and can be donors," the doctor said happily on our next visit with him. "But the outstanding news is your older brother is a six-antigen match. This is extremely rare. His kidney is what we would classify as a perfect match. This means your chances of rejection are very low, so low you will probably not have to take the regular steroid treatment for very long and will have the lowest possible dosage for the other anti-rejection medications."

The doctor smiled. "It makes all the difference in the success of your transplant."

The doctor doesn't realize how comforting his words are to Donna, I thought. *He could never realize the depth of the relationship Donna has with her older brother.*

I knew in her no-nonsense approach to life, Donna would have been very grateful for any kidney to accomplish what was needed. But to have this kidney, her brother's perfect match, meant more to her than she would ever be able to put into words.

All the plans were made and we waited for the day of the surgery when her kidney problems would be gone for the first time in her entire life.

The next day, Donna stood before me and spoke in a monotone voice.

"The insurance company has denied coverage for the transplant. They are refusing to pay. The case worker at Charleston told me the insurance company stated I would have to be on dialysis for a while before they would even consider covering the cost of the transplant. The doctor is very upset along with everyone else. They said I should call any person of influence in the government we know and have each one of them put pressure on the insurance company. The case worker said I have to act quickly because my condition is getting worse and soon, I will have to be on dialysis."

Donna stood before me saying all of this without taking a breath. She had just gotten off the phone and had come into the den to share the news.

Once again, her resolve took control of her emotions. I could see she wanted to cry, but at the same time she knew much had to be done.

"I'll feel sorry for myself later," she said quickly wiping away one stray tear. "Right now we need to get on the phone. Who do we call?"

Family, friends, and church members came to our aid. Anyone who knew anyone in local, state, or national government volunteered to call or write requesting assistance. Soon we were receiving calls from our local and state officials and from our U.S. Senator's office obtaining information from us in order to help.

"I know someone in the governor's office," Donna's stepfather, Smokey, stated right at the beginning of the ordeal. "I'll give them a call and see if we can get the governor involved."

About a week later, I heard Donna laughing over the phone and wondered if we had achieved victory. She saw my hopefulness and shook her head while continuing her conversation with the other person on the phone.

"Well, you said I should contact everyone we knew in government, so we did," she said while laughing.

"OK, well, thank you. But we are going to continue to work on it," she said with unwavering conviction.

Hanging up the phone, Donna turned to me and smiled.

"That was one of the transplant team members from Charleston," she said. "He asked us to please call off the dogs. The hospital is being bombarded with phone calls from many officials and today they received a phone call from the governor's office demanding an explanation."

"They said they had no idea we would get so many people to respond so quickly," she said with a look of defiance on her face. "The bad thing is the whole situation is not really Charleston's fault at all. Charleston is hoping the government officials are also giving the insurance company grief as well."

As it turned out, the insurance company was immune to political pressure. While thankful for the immediate and strong response received, we were nevertheless confronted with the fact that Donna would have to get sicker before the procedure would be approved.

One of my older church ladies called one evening after hearing the insurance company would still not pay for the transplant. She expressed her sorrow for us and assured me of her prayers.

"I just can't believe this is happening to you," she said with a broken voice.

I tried to console her with the fact that we had not given up hope.

"I know as long as God is involved there is hope," she said as strength returned to her voice. "Let me pray with you right now."

"Please do," I answered emphatically. "We certainly need all of the prayers we can get."

She prayed a sweet prayer of one who talked often with her Lord. Her words carried the gentle experience of a long-standing and deep relationship with the Shepherd. It amazed me how much I needed to hear her prayer. Her conversation with God calmed me.

Morning

Her voice began to quaver as she spoke to the Maker about the insurance company. Expressing her concern and then her anger over the plights of others, she asked God to get the attention of those in control of the decision.

"God, I humbly ask you to make them realize how much dear Donna needs the kidney," she pleaded. "And, dear Lord, if they don't hear what you have to say to them...then Lord, I pray you will shake them...SHAKE THEM OVER HELL! Just until You get their attention and they get the message. Thank you, dear Lord. Amen."

Luckily, I kept my laugher in check and was able to thank her for her very uniquely powerful prayer.

"I will make whatever financial arrangements I have to make for the transplant to happen," I said on a phone call to the case worker in Charleston.

"If I have to pay for this for the rest of my life, I will do it. I will not see her get sicker and sicker before anything is done."

"I appreciate what you are saying, Dan," the case worker replied, "but the reality is our medical center would never approve it. It's not just the surgery. The aftercare is also extremely expensive. Even though she will probably be on the lowest dosage possible for the anti-rejection medication, the medication bill alone would run over three thousand dollars a month. It simply would not be approved as a private pay situation. It will never work."

In desperation, I called the person in charge of our insurance benefits for the state's United Methodist pastors. He knew of the situation, but I wanted to let him know how everything we had done had failed to make a difference.

"I don't know what to tell you, Dan," he said, "but I'm flying to Chicago tomorrow to meet with the person who is over the insurance benefits for all of the United Methodist Churches in the country. Actually, I'm having dinner with her. I'll talk it over with her and see if she can help us convince the insurance company to comply. I'll let you know."

A day after the dinner in Chicago, we received a phone call stating the transplant had been approved.

A week later, I was asked to preach at the state-wide gathering of the United Methodist Women. They were meeting at our Assembly Grounds at Lake Junaluska in North Carolina. I preached about this situation and how, because of God's goodness and blessings, victory had been achieved. Bishop McCleskey and his wife, Margaret, were in attendance and ate lunch with us as we continued to celebrate our good God.

When we were driving home that evening, Donna said in a calm voice, "Everything is turning out very well. It's good to celebrate what God has done, but what about the people who don't have a voice? What about the people who never get to celebrate the goodness of the Lord? What do we say to them? I can't tell them God loves me more than God loves them. How do I explain what happened? How can I tell them God allowed a chance encounter with the right person to take place so I am blessed?"

She sat in the car with a very concerned look upon her face. I wanted to make her feel better, but I also knew I admired her all the more for asking the hard questions.

"All I know is this," I said softly. "God means for us to be together forever."

"It is a big beautiful kidney," the doctor proclaimed loudly to everyone who had gathered in Donna's hospital room in Charleston to await the outcome of the surgery. "Everything went perfectly. She is going to be fine. A big, beautiful kidney!"

We all laughed and thanked him. In just a few minutes, Donna was brought into the room on her bed. She was peacefully sleeping. Her expression looked as though she were dreaming of a place far away filled with beauty and peace. I hoped she would sleep a while longer, but as they positioned the bed, her eyes opened and she looked at me.

"Everything is finished," I said while leaning close to her so she could hear my whisper. "You are going to be fine. The doctor is thrilled with your new kidney."

As though giving me assurance of how she felt, she closed her eyes and smiled.

Everyone in the room laughed quietly. Her smile remained even as she drifted back to sleep. Her confidence, her smile, and her peace made everything complete. All was well. All would be well.

Chapter 19

Courage

A MAN, CALLED BY GOD TO PREACH THE WORD, ordained by the church in response to the obvious gifts and graces evident in his life and proven through the manner in which he lived and worked, spoke to us on the shores of Lake Greenwood. The pastors of the district I served sat on picnic benches after our lunch. Now retired, the pastor spoke about his past challenges and the trials we would inevitably face.

Everyone listened intently, partially because of his reputation of many excellent and selfless years of powerful leadership, but mainly because we loved him.

"I remember that night very well," he said with a gentle smile. "I thought it would be my last night on earth."

"On Sunday I preached on the evils of segregation," he said quietly. "I knew it would be a hard sermon to preach since there would be many in the congregation who would be extremely upset with me. But I knew it had to be done."

"South Carolina and the church faced the decision we could no longer be 'separate but equal'. The courts, including our church court, had spoken. Many of us were very pleased to see this much needed change take place. But of course, there were those who felt it would mean the end of everything."

He lowered and shook his head as though remembering the trauma of those days. He then lifted his head and smiled a gentle but victorious smile.

"I knew I couldn't stay quiet. The message had to come from the pulpit that this change must be embraced and quickly carried out for the betterment of everyone involved."

"My church members took the sermon rather well," he paused and smiled broadly. "They knew me well enough to know exactly what I thought about the whole situation. I don't think they were surprised or shocked, and many of them probably agreed with me. But there were those in my church and in the community who could not believe I had preached such a sermon."

His face took on a look of seriousness as he weighed the next words carefully.

"They didn't want me to leave," he stated simply. "They wanted to put an end to me. I think they decided I would be an example to other radical preachers in the area. If they got me, the other preachers would keep their mouths shut."

"That evening at the parsonage, I received the first threatening phone call. The caller sounded very angry but also calmly determined. He said they were going to come and get me and my family and burn the parsonage to the ground."

As I sat and listened to him speak about the ordeal, I wondered how I would have handled the situation. Now it was easy to speak openly about the evils of segregation. My church members would probably be in complete agreement with me, but in those days, desegregation meant many people felt only fear and anger. Would I have been as brave as him to face the hatred of church members and the community? Would I have remained cowardly silent and hoped everything would soon be back to normal?

The questions I faced in hearing him speak of that time made me realize how much I tended to try to please my congregation. I wondered if my faith would have been sufficient to meet the challenge. I also realized he spoke these words to us not just to tell of a difficult time but also to show us that the necessary path is many times the hardest path of all.

More than a point of historical importance, his words challenged us to grow and be prepared.

"I really didn't know what to do about the phone call," he continued. "It was already pretty late when the call came, and I didn't want to alarm anyone. The voice was one of the most evil and sinister I had ever heard in my life. The person sounded as though they were completely determined to do exactly what they stated. My wife assured me it was a prank call and we should just ignore it."

"'They just don't want you to sleep tonight,' she said to me. 'You'll have to show them you are not afraid.'"

"Of course I stayed awake all night making sure everything was alright," he said with a laugh. "My wife told me since I couldn't sleep, they had won. In the light of morning, it all began to look like an empty threat."

"Before we could eat breakfast, the phone rang again."

"I know you didn't sleep any last night," the caller said, "We wanted to make sure you sweated a while, but we'll be back tonight to finish everything."

"I called some church members and told them what was happening and asked if my wife and the children could stay with them," he said calmly. "Even though my wife objected, I told her I had to stay at the parsonage or they might come looking for me. I didn't want anyone else to be hurt. I also didn't want them to burn the parsonage."

"The sheriff's office couldn't do much with just a threat," he said as though in defense of their position. "They said a deputy would ride by several times during the night, and I asked them if they would call the fire department if they saw the house going up in flames."

We all laughed uncomfortably.

"After sending my family away," he continued, "I realized other than prayer, there was nothing else to do. The back yard had no neighbors for miles and no lights of any sort."

I imagined him standing there looking out the window while wondering what might happen in the darkness. As he continued to speak, I wondered if his refusal to leave was based, at least partially, on his determination that no one would make him run away. I could not imagine how his wife must have felt leaving him in the house alone.

Donna would never have left, I thought. *She would have been very upset with me for refusing to leave. She would've taken Tyler to someone's house and then stayed with me.*

I wondered if it would have forced me to leave and almost chuckled as I realized she probably would have stayed just to make sure I didn't.

"I knew," he continued, "I didn't want them approaching the house from the darkness of the woods and bushes in the back yard. I rigged up an electrical cord from the house and hung one light bulb on the limb of a tree. I told myself at least I would see them coming."

"That night I stationed myself in a chair overlooking the back yard since I felt they would probably come from that direction. I kept looking at the light bulb and found myself wondering if that solitary light might scare them away."

"Just then I saw movement behind one of the trees," his voice took on a tone of defeat as though even then he realized the whole confrontation was inevitable.

"I kept looking and then noticed several people standing in the shadows behind trees and bushes. I could not tell if they were armed but thought they must have been. I decided I wouldn't wait to find out if they would set the parsonage on fire."

He took on a look of determination and sadness as he took a slow breath and continued recounting the events of that evening.

"I walked out of the house and down to the light bulb hanging in the tree so those people hiding could clearly see me."

"'You don't have to hide anymore,' I said with a loud voice so all of them could hear me. 'I know you are here and I know why you are here. Do what you want to with me, just don't burn down the parsonage.'"

"Slowly," he continued, "one person and then another came out from behind the bushes and trees. When they got close enough to the light, I realized they were my church members."

"'We heard what was supposed to happen tonight,' one of them said to me as they all began to form a circle around me. 'We knew they were serious about their threats, but we decided if they were going to get to you, they would have to get through us, first!'"

He stopped speaking as we all sighed in relief and then began to laugh and clap.

He did not have to expound on the reason behind telling us this story. Most of us were still fresh into the fulfilling of our calling. Without preaching at us, he skillfully taught us our churches were and would always be filled with some of the best people in the world. He also gave us an unshakable hope in their ability to stand beside us in the worst of times.

Chapter 20
Andros Island

I PUT MY ARMS AROUND TYLER AND TRIED TO DIG my fingernails into the wooden deck of the sailboat to secure us from being thrown into the raging sea. Praying for safety, I wondered how we had ever gotten ourselves into this situation.

Just an hour or so before, our boat with twenty-three youth, seven adult leaders and two captains sailed away from Miami. The amazing sight of the tall well-lit buildings of the city helped make up for the unsteady reception we experienced at the dock.

Ronnie, our youth director, first came up with the idea of taking our youth group from Broad Street United Methodist Church in Clinton to Andros Island in the Bahamas on a mission trip. My first reaction was a mixture of humor and scoff.

"A mission trip to the Bahamas?" I said to him in disbelief. "Won't most people say we should call it a vacation trip to the Bahamas? I'm not sure anyone will take this seriously."

"This captain makes numerous trips to Andros with youth groups who are willing to spend a week helping the churches there," Ronnie had prepared a speech for my objections.

"Andros is the largest of the Bahama Islands, but it's also the poorest," he continued. "Their main source of income is exporting fresh water to the other islands. They also make a type of cloth, or they dye cloth or something like that, but most of the people are unemployed. As a matter of fact, they have 80% unemployment. One of the United Methodist churches there is trying to build a large Sunday School classroom onto their building, but they keep running out of supplies and money. Captain Steve and his wife, Captain Barbara, are committed to helping with this situation. Our boat will not only take us to Andros but will also carry all the necessary supplies to finish the addition to the church."

"How do you know about all of this?" I asked in disbelief.

"Other church youth groups have been on these mission trips with Captain Steve and Captain Barbara. They told me about the wonderful experiences they had. One group from Camden is willing to speak to our youth group and their parents and answer any questions."

The group from Camden came and spoke at a Wednesday night fellowship meal at Broad Street. Just as Ronnie had told me, they represented the trip as one of great and meaningful work as well as adventure.

Soon our church busied itself with fundraising for the trip. We had no problem in getting enough youth to sign up, and before too long, our entire community knew of the project. Car washes, hotdog sales, auctions, bake sales and other activities helped the group fund this ambitious mission.

Endless planning sessions demonstrated the commitment of the youth and the team of leaders. As the time of departure approached, it became increasingly clear nothing else could be done on our part to make this a successful event.

The church sent us forth with prayers for God's blessings and the hope that our faith and efforts would truly make a difference on Andros.

After our flight to Miami and the bus trip to the docks, the group anxiously waited to see the sailboat that would be our home for the next ten days. As we neared it, everyone stared at what could only be described as one of the plainest looking boats we had ever seen.

"This can't be right," one of the youth parents said to me. "It's too small. We won't all fit."

"Where are the sails?" another parent asked while staring up at the one, rather short mast. "I thought we were supposed to sail to Andros."

"Maybe there's more to it than meets the eye," another parent said as we continued to walk down the dock. "It must have more room on the lower deck."

Much to our dismay, it was just as small and cramped as it appeared. We each had one large duffle bag to hold everything we had been told by the captains to bring. Four men, including myself were to sleep in the forward cabin. Our four duffle bags barely fit in the space. We quickly realized we would have to share one small triangle of floor space in our cabin that was only big enough for one person at a time to change clothes.

"Where are we going to sleep?" Ronnie nervously asked Captain Steve as the parents began to discuss whether or not this boat could get us to Andros.

Captain Steve, thin and tan with long blonde hair pulled back into a ponytail and an unkempt beard complete with braids, shrugged his shoulders. "No one really sleeps in the bunks. Everyone loves to sleep on the deck," he said with a slight smile. "It's great at night. You'll see."

Since we had no other choice, the decision was made to continue. As we navigated past the giant cruise ships to the open sea, I marveled at the view while wondering why we were sailing as the sun was setting.

Morning

The sky quickly turned from bright sunlight to darkness. I felt some comfort by keeping my eyes on the shoreline of Miami and telling myself we could make it back to the shore if we had to. The tall buildings formed an impressive wall of gleaming towers reflecting upon the ocean. Trying to capture every moment of beauty, I realized we had turned and now faced not only the darkness but also the increasingly rough open sea.

Just as we lost sight of the gleaming shoreline, the waves hit.

I had never seen waves like those. They towered almost as high as our solitary mast. One after another they came up from the black depths of the sea to stop our foolhardy journey. Each wave seemed capable of completely swallowing our little boat. Amazed at what was happening, I hardly had time to become frightened as our situation turned from pleasant and adventurous to catastrophic. Somehow the boat floated above every wave. Most of the youth went down to the galley as the waves appeared to worsen. I stood behind the two captains watching as they piloted the boat. The sail was brought down and the engine pushed the boat through the waves as though more determined than us to get to our destination.

After several of the youth became seasick, I wondered if some action should be taken to stop this misadventure.

"Do you think we should head back to the shore?" I said to Captain Steve as he held onto the wheel. He looked completely at ease. I saw his wife, Captain Barbara, look away from the compass to her husband.

"I think this is pretty bad," I said sternly, letting him know I was beginning to lose all patience with anything jeopardizing my flock.

"It's not bad at all," Captain Steve stated with a calm voice. Captain Barbara looked back to the compass which glowed with the red light of the night setting. She did not speak and showed no expression on her face.

"This is nothing at all, nothing to be alarmed about. We haven't taken on any water. There's no reason to turn back because the boat is secure and we are well. These waves will soon end. Then you'll see just how beautiful the ocean is at night."

His calmness quelled my anger and my fears. I realized even though I had never experienced waves like this, that to a sailor, these waves must not be very alarming. I settled down on the deck behind the two captains who casually talked to one another.

Holding my twelve-year-old son as securely as I could onto the wooden deck, I tried to be as calm as the captains.

"This really isn't as bad as it might seem," I told Tyler while wondering why my fingernails could not dig out a secure holding spot in the deck.

"Captain Steve and Captain Barbara know what they are doing. They don't seem the least bit afraid or concerned. It's going to be just fine. He said the waves would end soon."

"But what's keeping the boat from turning over?" Tyler asked. His tone fully expressed his fear.

"Oh," I said with a cheerful voice, "I thought you knew about the keel."

He shook his head, and buried his face in my arm as we climbed another wave.

"Sailboats have a keel," I said in a matter-of-fact voice. "Keels are on the bottom of the hull and are sort of like a fin on a fish. The keel goes down deep into the water and keeps the boat from flipping over. It would be very hard for the boat to flip because of all of the pressure of the water on either side of the keel."

"That's smart," Tyler said with a yawn.

"It's going to be alright," I told him.

I knew my definition of a keel was probably not entirely correct, but it sounded so good, it even comforted me.

In a few minutes, he was asleep. I knew I would not sleep until the waves disappeared. I doubted if I would sleep then.

"The battering waves, the safety of the boat, the keel underneath us to safeguard our journey. That'll preach!" I thought to myself.

One of my fellow seminarians would shout that declaration in class whenever a professor gave a particularly interesting point. It became everyone's favorite expression and one the professors seemed to enjoy.

While thinking about those days of the past, I drifted to sleep still holding Tyler tight in my arms.

The next morning we arrived at one of the outlying cays of the Bahamas. Captain Steve met with the officials to make sure we would be legally accepted with our crew and supplies bound for Andros. While the meeting took place, he encouraged us to swim around the boat while it was anchored in the clear blue waters near the brilliant white sands of the shore.

Donning my facemask, I decided to see what I could on the bottom of the ocean near the boat. The first thing I noticed was a barracuda not very far from me in the amazingly calm and clear water. Even more alarming, I noticed our boat had a completely flat bottom.

"That'll preach too," I thought to myself as I made my way back to the boat to avoid being bitten by the many teeth of the barracuda. "False Hope the World Offers," I mused.

"I need a better title," I muttered to myself as I climbed onboard.

Chapter 21
Navigating

LATE INTO THE MOONLESS NIGHT, WE SAILED underneath a bowl of stars. Upon the deep black waters, we seemed to glide through the reaches of endless galaxies. I steered the boat while most of the others slept in their life vests on the deck.

The captains slept in their not-very-stately stateroom while Tyler and a few others slept in the galley. Tasked with the responsibility of cleaning the galley after each meal, the youth had quickly learned to accomplish this work in accordance to the captains' very demanding specifications. After the first night of rough seas, Tyler and most of the other youth had decided the galley offered the best chance of a good night's rest.

On this night, a very capable and amiable young teacher became my navigator. She watched the ever-glowing compass while I took the wheel. We chatted some but fell silent under the spell of the massive display of heavenly wonders above us.

"I've never seen so many stars," I whispered to her. "I almost want to wake up everyone so they can see this."

No clouds obscured our view of the night sky. More importantly, no artificial lights dimmed the radiance displayed through the heavens. During our watch, we did not see a shoreline or even a passing ship.

"I never realized this many stars could even be seen from our planet," I said in disbelief.

"Slightly to port," my navigator stated quietly. I knew she was keeping us on the course setting Captain Steve said must be maintained. As though he understood we would not be capable of keeping the course exactly on mark, he gave us a range on the compass to allow for the fact it would be the first time either of us had ever piloted a sailboat.

"That's good," she said as I made the correction.

Even though she was extremely capable in every way, making the adjustments to the ship wheel did not seem to suit her.

"I'll tell you when you are off course," she told me earlier as we switched seats, "and you make the corrections."

She let me know the moment the boat veered from the course. I would then make the correction on the wheel. Then she would tell me to make an adjustment to make up for my overcompensation. Then she would tell me to compensate for the overcompensation of the adjustment for the overcompensation.

It did not take us long to realize we were enjoying the beauty of the sky and sea at night in a giant zigzag course.

After a few more corrections, a method began to appear. If I kept the top point of the mast directly on one bright star, we could maintain the correct heading. Every time the mast ventured away from the star, a simple turn of the wheel toward the star would bring us back on course.

After the better part of an hour, my navigator realized she had not needed to give me a compass correction.

"You're really getting the hang of it," she said sounding rather astonished. "What are you doing differently?"

"I'm following a star," I explained trying not to sound like a wise guy.

The night breeze did not stir the waves into a frenzy but gave us just enough push on the solitary sail so the diesel engine became unnecessary. The sail filled magnificently. The gentle movement of the boat and the soothing sound of the water breaking away from our hull gave assurance we were making slow but steady, and straight, progress toward our destination.

Seeing she no longer had to worry about the compass, my navigator began telling me about her small part in an upcoming movie.

"They're filming most of it in Charlotte," she said quietly. "A friend of mine who is working on the film told them about me. They were looking for a women's basketball coach for a segment of the comedy. I interviewed for the part and got it even though I haven't had any acting experience."

She went on to tell me about the part and her frustration in the slow filming process. Her school had decided she could have some extra days off from teaching to do the movie, but then the filming schedule changed.

"All of a sudden, they said I would have to be there for several more weeks," she said with a smile. "I knew I couldn't do that and keep my regular job, so I told them they would just have to use the parts I had filmed because I had to leave."

"When will it be out, so we can all see it?" I asked excitedly.

"The movie will be released later this year, but I won't be in it," she said with a laugh. "After all those days missed from my job, they told me the segment including me would probably end up on the editing room floor. Since I couldn't finish my part, they would just eliminate it entirely."

She laughed and I thought how wonderful it was she had not gotten herself so wrapped up in this amazing opportunity she forgot her calling to teach.

"I'm glad I did it," she said with satisfaction. "It was amazing to see what goes into a big production like that. It takes a tremendous amount of work and money to make it all happen. I especially enjoyed getting to know more about the other extras."

"But you weren't considered an extra, were you?"

"I really don't know what they considered me to be," she said with a carefree laugh. "Even though I had a speaking part, the people in charge didn't seem to know how to classify me. So I just stayed with the extras."

"Did they get most of them in Charlotte?"

"That's the funny part," she said showing fascination over what she had learned through this experience. "When I got to know them, I realized many of them traveled from place to place around the country to be extras in movies."

"How many people are we talking about?"

"Well, more than you would think. Since the comedy centered on basketball, they needed a crowd scene for the arena. I watched as they had the extras sit in a certain section of the arena and cheer and make various reactions to an imaginary game. The film people would then take this one section of spectators and multiply that image all over the arena to make it look like a packed house."

"So it ended up being an arena full of the same people, the same extras," I said while laughing. "That makes perfect sense. What a clever way to do it."

"The extras told me the money wasn't good, but they just enjoyed being there while a big movie was being made. They liked all the excitement and the potential of meeting some big movie stars."

"It's amazing people do it for a living," I said while thinking it would be a challenging but perhaps fun way to live.

"But they all agreed even though the money was not very good, the food was always great."

"They provided food for the extras?" I asked in amazement.

"They provided food for everyone. And it was always a big spread of great food. I guess they knew if they weren't going to pay the extras very well, they had to at least give them wonderful buffets."

While we talked, I kept my eyes on the star and made the minor corrections as necessary. The boat, the wheel, the compass, the sail, the ocean, all seemed to be in harmony. I wondered if the sailors of old had felt this triumphant in a successful run through the nighttime currents.

A loud bang ended my piloting career as the boat came to a complete stop. I knew we did not hit anything because the boat did not lurch. The sail flattened and the peaceful sound of the hull making its way through the water ceased.

I still felt the breeze, but now it came from a different direction. The sail fluttered uselessly.

The point of the mast no longer pointed at the star which all of a sudden seemed to disappear into the mass of other stars overhead.

"Why aren't we moving? What was that noise? What's happening?" she said quietly. "What was that bang? We're going off course even though we aren't moving. Why is the sail flat?"

"I think the bang came when the sail hit the mast," I said quietly hoping no one would wake up and ask how I had managed to break the boat.

"But I don't know what I did to make the sail flatten," I said growing even more embarrassed.

"What should we do?" she asked. "I don't think we should just sit here in the ocean with no forward motion. We're going to get way off course!"

I could tell she wanted to be upset but was trying to remain calm.

"I think it is time for Captain Steve to take control," I said quickly. "I don't know what I did wrong, but I'm sure he will know."

I left my navigator to stay by the now useless compass and wheel and went down below to the small closed stateroom door.

"Captain," I said to the closed-door hoping Barbara would answer and Steve would stay asleep.

"What's going on?" Captain Steve said quickly as he opened the door, "why aren't we moving?"

He quickly sprang up the steps to the deck realizing I did not have any answers.

When I got back to the deck, he was sitting in front of the wheel.

"You ran into a crosswind," he said in a calm voice. "It happens sometimes."

"We were going along so smoothly and then the sail went flat and everything stopped," I said trying to convince myself it wasn't actually my fault.

"Did I do anything wrong?" I asked.

"No," he said calmly, "the easiest way to get around this is to take the sail down and just run the engine until morning."

Captain Steve took down the sail and then started the engine and steered the boat for the rest of the night.

Feeling rather useless, I sat on the deck behind the navigator and captain. My night of wonder had come to an end with the unexpected.

Morning

    A crosswind swept over the ocean and shattered all my illusions of being the pilot of the course set out in front of me.

Chapter 22
Red Stone Cliffs

THE SAND MUST HAVE BEEN REFLECTING THE FULL brilliance of the sun, or maybe it was just the fact that the bright blue waters made the sand appear dazzling white. Actually, it was more than just dazzling, it was blinding. We anchored near the shore and jumped into the crystal blue water with instructions to be on the lookout for barracuda and stingrays while swimming to the beach.

Captain Barbara told us the inhabitants of this cay had long ago departed and now it was just an abandoned place full of white sand, an inland river and rocky cliffs. I was hoping we would have time to go from one end to the other in exploration, but soon realized this place had barriers I could never have imagined.

The beach itself turned out to be some sort of amazing sand trap. Perhaps it was the lack of constant parading feet, or perhaps it was just a trick of the ocean, but the sand gave way under our weight. Down and down through the hot sand our feet would go until we were almost up to our knees in the stuff. Each and every step turned out to be a slow and humorous agony. After a little bit of walking, I longed for a pair of snowshoes.

Exhausted and hot, we continued across the beach to get to the only river running through the heart of the cay. Hoping each step would somehow reach the point of solid ground, we continued to trudge forward until we saw our first little treasure. Actually, it wasn't so little and it certainly wasn't a treasure, but to me it was a delight. Across the river and up the steep rock walls of a cliff, we noticed the old remains of a house on the precipice.

I guess it had been a house. Perhaps it had only been some sort of old outpost sitting on top of the highest cliff on the side of the island overlooking the beach and the sea, but it looked like a dwelling place from long ago. With the roof completely gone, the house had almost reverted to nothingness. The stones for the walls had obviously been chiseled from the reddish-brown rock of the cliff itself. Had it not been for the stone walls, nothing would have survived.

From the bottom of the cliff, the climb seemed daunting but overwhelmingly interesting. Actually, the solid feel of the rocks was such a welcome relief from the sinking sands that the climb seemed almost easy. Once we reached the top, I could not stop looking at the view long enough to fully look at the ruins of the dwelling. From the top of this cliff, I noticed

Morning

the cay was much bigger than I had thought and realized there would not be enough time on our little excursion to get around even a small section of the shoreline. Above everything else, the view was spectacular. Whether the inhabitations had selected this spot for the sake of safety or beauty, it was well chosen.

But who were they? Where did they come from? How long did they live here and why?

All of my questions went unanswered. The sea wind had swept the place clean many decades ago. Then our time came to an end. The captain rang the bell on the boat signaling us to make our slow return across the uncompromising sand to our refreshing swim back to the boat.

As the others began to make their descent to the shore, I stopped and looked around one more time. The tall coconut trees grew in abundance on either side of the river and then to the clear blue waters of the ocean. Even from this height, I could see the sea floor for what appeared to be many miles.

Immediately, I longed to be standing on this amazing spot of great beauty with Donna. I wanted her to see it and experience the wonder of trying to discover who had lived on this cliff and what their lives had become.

I wanted to look into her clear green eyes as she looked out to the horizon and beyond.

"I'll come back here, one day," I said quietly to myself. "I'll bring her here, to this very spot, and we will see all of this together."

Chapter 23
Uncle Charlie's Blue Hole

EARLY THE NEXT MORNING, WE LEFT OUR BOAT in the main harbor on Andros as Captain Steve drove us in an old yellow school bus to the church where we would be doing construction work. Before we left the boat, we bathed in the waters of the harbor and rinsed ourselves with fresh water on deck. We then ate a great breakfast cooked in our own galley. By this time in our adventure, we had come to appreciate the Captains' amazing meals.

Our scenic trip to the church did not take long. Just like our boat, the bus obviously had been built by people who never heard of air conditioning, but the open windows, like the open deck, made us all feel closer and more connected with the entire experience. Riding along dirt roads and through forests and open fields, I began to understand the sense of adventure the group from Camden had told us to expect. Soon we were standing beside a small red brick church at the top of a hill overlooking a beautiful undisturbed semicircular bay. Warmly greeted by the church members, the service soon started. The lay leader of the congregation preached to our group as we worshipped. In worshipping our God together, we became brothers and sisters in Christ accomplishing, for this brief moment, the joy of celebrating our Savior as one.

After the service, the lay leader took us to the back of the sanctuary and showed us the incomplete work on the Sunday School room.

"What a beautiful place to work this week," I said to our group as we stood on the hill overlooking the bay.

"But you can't work on it this week," the lay leader said as though surprised that we would even think of such a thing. "This week we celebrate our independence. This week no one works because of the big regatta in the main harbor."

He smiled as though we should have already understood. This man, who worked as the principal at the local school, obviously knew the local customs. All eyes turned to Captain Steve.

"I don't know why I didn't know about this," he blurted out quickly. "We'll have to find something else to do. It won't be hard. I'll let you know."

On the way back to the boat, the captains conferred with one another for a while. Then Captain Barbara explained since we could not work on the construction of the Sunday School room, the materials we had purchased for the work would be left at the church for another construction crew at a later

Morning

date. We would be spending our week at the Red Bays School conducting Bible classes for the many children there.

"Red Bays is about twenty miles inland so we will have to make a bus trip every day, but it will give you a chance to really see Andros."

The smiling faces of the inhabitants greeted us as we rode past small communities each morning. No one seemed to be involved in a morning rush to get to work. As they walked along the roads, they looked perfectly at peace on their island. Their clothing, relaxed lifestyle, and constant smiles gave the impression they fully appreciated living in their tropical paradise.

"That's the bank," Captain Steve yelled to us while driving. "It's the only one on the entire island. And it's only open on Wednesday mornings."

As we drove along the narrow roads taking us deeper and deeper into the island, one site became increasingly familiar. In the midst of tall overgrown weeds stood small rows of gray concrete blocks. Some blocks formed walls four or five feet in height while others sites would have rows of only one or two blocks high. None of the partial structures seemed to be connected to another, and all the sites looked totally deserted.

"What are the unfinished concrete block structures we keep seeing?" I asked Captain Steve as we drove to Red Bays one morning. "Why are they all deserted?"

"Those are future homes," Steve said without looking back at me as he drove the bus down his familiar roads.

"Since most of the islanders don't have any sort of regular work, they can't possibly borrow money to build a house. They buy a concrete block whenever they can and start building their homes one block at a time. It can take many years for the small house to be completed, but when they finish it, they don't owe anything to anyone!"

We knew we had arrived at our destination when we saw beautiful mango trees heavily laden with ripened fruit and tall coconut trees surrounding a small school next to an even smaller church. Each day we were greeted by over a hundred children with constant smiles and beautiful accents. The parents seemed just as excited as the children to see us coming up the road in our old yellow school bus.

The children spoke to us freely and seemed eager to tell us everything about this place and their lives. None of them seemed in the least bit shy, withdrawn, or hesitant. Even though they spoke the same beautifully accented English of their parents, their accents seemed much more pronounced. Combined with the rapidity with which they spoke, we had trouble understanding the children. Fortunately, we grew accustomed to their accents and began to understand and love their enthusiastic voices. Gracious and warm, they welcomed us to Red Bays each morning as though we were long lost friends.

I never knew where these children lived since it didn't appear there were more than a dozen or so completed houses in the whole area. The children arrived each morning ready for Bible school and the breakfast which we brought for them from the galley of our sailboat. They were also ready to hear what we had to say about the faith.

At the first class I held with my group, I stood before them in the little school room of the mostly white concrete building and told them I was going to teach them about Moses.

Immediately, the entire class began reciting the Ten Commandments in the correct order and in perfect rhythm.

Realizing they obviously knew more about the Bible than I imagined, I quickly changed the direction of the lesson and made it more of a discussion suitable for young Bible scholars.

"I had no idea all of these children would know the Bible so very well," I told the pastor of the small church beside the school. We spoke underneath one of the mango trees growing next to the Poinciana trees filled with vibrant red blossoms.

"I feel sort of foolish trying to teach them anything about the Bible," I said trying not to frown.

"They are taught Bible in the public school," he said with a look of surprise that our group did not know this fact.

"It's wonderful," I said trying to let him know this was not a problem. "They obviously take their lessons very seriously. I think I could ask them anything in the Bible and they would know it. It's really amazing, but at the same time it makes me…sort of…wonder why we made this journey to be here?"

I hoped my words would not offend him but felt I had to express some of my dismay. I felt funny complaining about the children knowing so much about the Bible, but at the same time, I knew the others in our group would be wondering the same thing. So far the purpose of our trip had been changed from one of construction to instruction and now it seemed as though we were instructing a group who knew more about the Bible than most children in America their same age. I was beginning to think our amazing adventure would soon be classified as a farce. I also feared this very dedicated pastor might think we didn't appreciate just what a great job he was doing at Red Bays.

Morning

"They are taught the Bible," he said clearly understanding my growing fear that our trip had no lasting purpose, "but they need to see Christians at work."

"They need to encounter and interact with Christians to know you exist in other places," he said quietly but firmly. "Here they are taught the Bible and they see people living the faith, but other things seem much more appealing to them. We are surrounded by the old religions. Voodoo is still practiced by many. The children must see there are Christians who don't believe in voodoo so I can keep them from leaving their Christianity."

The seriousness with which he spoke made me realize the importance of what we had to accomplish. Much like the work we tried to do at home, our words carried only as much weight as our actions. Seeing us live out our Christianity became much more important than anything we might say to the children or their parents.

As we finished for the day, I told my group of students that our group from the boat would be going to see a famous Androsian landmark, Uncle Charlie's Blue Hole. The children's smiles disappeared and they became silent.

"We're going swimming in the blue hole!" I said with great excitement thinking how wonderful it would be to swim in cool fresh water. Our saltwater baths tended to leave us feeling dirty rather than clean.

There were frowns from the group as Chris, one of the little boys who always had a smile, turned to me and said,

"That's a bad place. That's where people drown."

Chris followed me out of the school building and stood on the step of the bus blocking my way. He deepened his frown and told me again that the blue hole was a bad place.

"Why is it such a bad place?" I asked. I knew he would probably not be able to change our minds as to our excursion, but I wanted to let him know I was taking his concern seriously.

"People go through the forest and jump off the cliffs into the hole," he said with fear in his eyes. "They forget to make sure the wooden steps are still intact on the side of the cliffs. They cry out for help, but no one is there for them. They do their best to climb out or to keep swimming, but after a day or so, they drown."

His look of sadness made me think he probably knew some of the victims. His expression then changed from grief to determination as though he was angry we would take such a risk.

"It's a bad place," he emphasized. "People are not the same even if they don't die. Bad things happen there. You should not go."

"Thank you for telling me this," I said trying to make sure he understood how much I appreciated his concern. "I assure you I will check the wooden steps to make sure they are in very good shape before we start jumping off the cliff!"

As the bus pulled away from the school, I could still see his frown through the dust flying up from the unpaved road.

We knew that Uncle Charlie's Blue Hole was famous. It had been proven through underwater exploration that the submerged caves of the blue hole went through the island to the sea.

Our bus ride took us further into the heart of this large island where suddenly the blue hole unceremoniously appeared as a large crater in the middle of the jungle forest. We drove up to one side of it and got out of the bus and walked over to the edge. The dark blue water down below looked like it covered about two acres. Steep rock walls measuring about twenty feet or more in height went straight down to the surface of the water. On one end of the crater I spied the only way out of the hole. As I had promised Chris, I studied the old rickety wooden steps. Somehow, they had been attached to the rock cliffs, and even though they did not look new, they did look substantial enough for our group.

I had never jumped from a high rock cliff into a bottomless pool, but the lure of cool fresh water overcame my hesitations. The jump was quick and painless and the reward was greater than I could have imagined. I alternated between floating and slowly doing backstrokes. The rest of our group was in the water and enjoying every moment. Even though I relished in this refreshing experience, one thought kept coming to my mind.

What's beneath me?

The thought would not leave me alone. I kept telling myself to think of something else, but all I could think about was what sort of creatures might inhabit those deep waters filling miles of cavernous mazes to the depths of the ocean. I found myself trying to look through the water to see if I could spot a fish or maybe something else.

Even though I could not see a thing, I reluctantly started swimming toward the wooden steps. I smiled to myself as I remembered Chris' very serious frown. The temptation of the beautiful waters had been too great for me even though I should have listened to the wisdom of my young student.

As I swam over to the side, I motioned for Tyler to follow me. I knew no one else would understand or agree with my groundless fears about the potential habitants of the unknown depths so I did not sound a general alarm.

Morning

Surprisingly, Tyler seemed more than ready to leave the clear blue waters of the hole and return to the edge of the cliff.

I could hear the soothing voice of the Scriptures reminding me the everlasting arms of God were always underneath me. I took great comfort in those words, but instead of just being afraid of unknown sea creatures, something else troubled me greatly.

I should have been calmed by the waters. Its clarity and azure tones not only reflected the sun but also absorbed the light. As I swam to the steps, my hands broke through the surface and light burst forth from every drop falling off my fingers as the water freed itself from the confines of the depths. Then, in exhilaration, these blue topaz liquid gems would capture more clear light before falling into the deep once again.

This pool shimmered with possibility and the grandeur of life. As I continued to swim toward my destination, I realized the source of my discomfort. These waters reminded me of the azure waters that reflected the light of the lantern in the cavern river we had visited years ago. On those waters, Donna and I had been spectators as we peered into the image of the mysterious azure moon from the side of the gondola. We did as our guide instructed and looked into the glow of the lantern on the surface to see if it told our future.

No longer a spectator, I now swam in the azure waters. More than just a casual participant, I had been submerged and rejoiced in the depths even as I was terrified by them. I moved through this forbidden pool into the future we could not then clearly see. Somehow, these bottomless water filled caverns gave its azure clarity that those unseen events were upon us.

I remembered seeing Donna's face as the reflection of the azure moon filled her features with wonder. I heard her voice echoing across those waters and these.

"What does it mean?"

Even in the midst of the beauty of the day, I felt tears welling up in my eyes as I longed to hold my love in my arms.

Chapter 24

Lancaster

"COTTONWOOD TREES," I SAID AS WE DROVE DOWN the road searching for our new home. "We didn't have those in Clinton."

Donna appeared to ignore my comments on the flora of the area as she intently looked for the names on the street signs. The fluffy cottonwood seeds filled the air like an out-of-season snowstorm. Amused with the display, I felt as though a ticker tape parade of nature welcomed us to our new neighborhood.

"They're everywhere," Donna said with a small laugh. She surprised me with the fact she was indeed enjoying the gently floating white cottony puffs.

I took her hand in mine and squeezed it with gentle excitement.

"A new adventure awaits us," I said softly as she pointed for me to turn right. "That's one thing about being a pastor, no matter where you go and no matter what church you serve, you're always going to meet some amazing and faithful people."

Donna silently nodded in agreement with this statement she had heard me say on many occasions.

We had already heard a great deal about the church and parsonage. Everything sounded wonderful, especially since my district superintendent spoke so highly of the congregation.

"They have always had a great appreciation for their pastors," he told me in the meeting at his office when he revealed my next appointment. "I served near there several years ago and heard how well they treated their staff. I think this appointment will suit you very nicely."

The current pastor in charge called me the same day.

"Have you heard about this parsonage?" he asked as if I should have heard about it. "It's simply amazing. A generous church member bought it for the church. He realized such a large house required a great deal of maintenance so he also provided a substantial endowment for its upkeep."

"How very thoughtful of him," I said. "I've never heard of a parsonage with its own endowment."

"He didn't want his gift to become a drain on the church's finances," he continued, "so he made sure it never would be. The parsonage is probably around thirty-six hundred square feet with four bedrooms, four bathrooms, three staircases, three fireplaces, and a double car garage. It's on a large wooded lot not far from the church."

Morning

"That's unbelievable," I said as I truly had a hard time believing what he was saying.

"It has a wonderful sunroom looking onto a beautiful backyard, aged heart-of-pine flooring and salvaged wooden exposed beams from old low country tobacco barns. I can't wait for you to see it. It's simply amazing."

"It sounds like my wife, son, and I will be lost in it," I said with a laugh.

"Well, tell your wife she need not worry about cleaning the whole thing," he said with a chuckle. I started to let him know we shared all of the household tasks, but he continued too quickly.

"The endowment pays for the church sexton to clean the house every other week from top to bottom."

"I've never heard of a parsonage with an endowment paying for cleaning and maintenance," I said while repeating his chuckle. "How very nice of them to think about every detail."

"They've really thought of everything when it comes to this house."

To his credit, the pastor also spent a great deal of time telling me about the congregation. It was obvious he greatly admired the members. He and his wife had moved to Lancaster from Myrtle Beach when he started this appointment.

"I found the people here to be very supportive and appreciative," he said as though he knew what the district superintendent had told me.

As we drove up East Edgemont Drive, we both searched for the first sight of the parsonage. We came to the end of the street and realized we must have driven past it. Turning the car around, we drove more slowly the second time.

"I see why we missed it," I said pointing at a large wooded area. An impressive roofline was barely visible through many trees.

We turned into the driveway and made our way around the display of azaleas, Japanese Maples, daylilies, and other flowering bushes. As we stopped at the house, Donna seemed troubled.

"I can't be the pastor's wife living in a house like this," she said in a startled and sad tone of voice. "They will expect me to entertain here regularly. I'm sure all of the former pastor's wives have hosted big dinner parties and fancy teas here. I'm not that sort of person. I don't know how to do all those things. I just stay busy teaching."

Her doubts in her abilities did not surface very often. I knew better than try to casually dispel her ungrounded fears, but at the same time, I knew she could handle anything.

"I don't think they would expect you to do a lot of hosting while you are teaching," I said calmly and reached for her hand.

"I don't want to live in a great house," she said quietly. "I'm not a great house kind of girl."

I smiled at her and squeezed her hand tightly.

"They're going to love you," I said confidently. "Every church has loved and cherished you because of who you are and the work you do. The other churches realized how dedicated you were to them. This church won't care if you don't throw elaborate dinner parties and teas. They will love you because of your heart."

She smiled. I loved to watch her overcome her doubts. She possessed an amazing way of quietly confronting her fears, embracing them, and then gently allowing them to dissolve into nothingness. I didn't know if she accepted my words as true or just as encouragement. Either way, Donna always had a way of facing challenges in a straightforward fashion.

"If something can't be avoided," she would say, "then you just have to do whatever must be done."

She regained her calm expression, and I knew her quiet resolve had pushed itself to the forefront.

"Anyway," I said with a quick smile, "I bet you could throw the best dinner party this house has ever seen!"

A member of the committee took us through the house and enthusiastically answered all our questions. She also provided a good account of general information about the furnishings and appliances.

As we walked into the master bedroom on the second story, the pale blue carpet and the lightly stained antique fireplace seemed to relax us just as they were designed to do. Beside the fireplace, a solid white upholstered chair radiated quiet comfort. I eagerly anticipated the evenings we would spend in this room with a cozy fire in the fireplace while reading a favorite book from the bookshelves in one corner of the room. Across from the fireplace, a box window with a window-seat allowed for a view of the front entrance of the house. I would later see how this box window provided an interesting architectural flair above the mahogany and beveled leaded glass front door on the Chippendale style brick stoop. A master bath with three sections provided ample dressing space.

Stepping through double doors, we walked out onto the loft of the master bedroom overlooking the living room. Giant wooden beams ran to the highest pinnacle of the open arched ceiling and intensified the warmth of the fireplace covered with round river stones from floor to ceiling. Windows filled the walls above the rows of French doors which opened onto a wrap-around deck where one could view the naturally forested front property of

Morning

the house. A dry creek bed filled with large rocks ran the length of the house and completed the beauty of the scene.

In the back corner of the loft, a beautiful iron and wood spiral staircase gave access to the formal dining room. Even with the massive wooden ceiling and the dark old beams, outside light filled these rooms as the many large windows opened out to the woods and the landscaped areas of the property.

"The master bedroom carpet is a little worn," the committee lady said with a smile. "We are planning on replacing it but thought we would ask you what color you would prefer. After you have moved in, you can let me know your preference."

Donna told me later she did not want the carpet replaced.

"It's really not bad," she said seriously. "I don't think it looks to be in terrible shape. I don't want to have new carpet. If I get something on this carpet, they won't care because they feel it needs replacing anyway." I smiled at her practicality and agreed.

"As soon as you are ready," the committee woman stated, "I would like to take you to visit Mr. Bradley. He is looking forward to meeting you."

In the quick trip in her car to Mr. Bradley's office, she told us about him.

"Mr. Bradley is the chair of the parsonage committee and has done a great job with the financial arrangements we have for the house. Because of his handling of the endowment, we have plenty of money for repairs and for updating the furnishings from time to time. This arrangement means the regular church budget is used for ministry and missions instead of keeping up the parsonage."

"Mr. Bradley retired after a great career in banking and corporate finance," she said in a quietly excited tone. She mentioned the multinational company very well known in our state. In its day, it had the largest textile plant in the world in the city of Lancaster.

"After retiring, he continues to work even though he's in his nineties! He is now the chairman of the board of the real estate company for the corporation. Here's their building now."

We drove up to a modern white building near the downtown area. Even though we arrived after regular office hours, a receptionist greeted us and ushered us into the main office.

Mr. Bradley stood as we entered and introduced himself. His large desk was covered in papers and letters; his work never stopped. He asked us to sit and then proceeded to get to know Donna and me.

At first I wondered about the purpose of this private meeting. Normally, I met the committee members together in a regular meeting with the district superintendent present. I started to get slightly amused when I realized this interview might be a test for whether or not I would be introduced to the committee or if the Bishop and the Cabinet might have to rethink my anticipated appointment.

I knew Donna probably understood what was happening. Through experience, we had seen churches handle things in very different ways.

"I'm not worried about where you are appointed and where we will live," she told me on several occasions. "I know God will have us go exactly where God wants us to go. The pastors have been praying about the change, and the congregations of each church affected by each move have been praying about the move, too. And I'm sure," she said emphatically, "the Bishop and the Cabinet have been praying about each move. With all of these people praying about this situation, the last thing we need to do is question whether or not God is involved."

As we continued to be questioned, I began to realize I had, perhaps, misjudged Mr. Bradley's intentions. As we spoke, he praised other pastors who had served the church. His tone of voice and manner convinced me he was sincerely interested in getting to know his new parsonage family so he could better meet our needs.

I left feeling even better about our new appointment, and I could tell Donna seemed much more at ease.

"Our immediate past governor worked for Mr. Bradley," the committee woman told us as we drove away from our meeting. "The governor's parents sing in our choir," she continued. "I know you will enjoy getting to know them."

Years later I stood in the sunroom of Mr. Bradley's spacious home. Instead of a receptionist, a nurse had ushered me through the house to the sunroom which now served as a hospital room.

"Dan!" Mr. Bradley said with his usual friendly and direct manner of speaking. "I wanted to go over a few things with you."

Everyone, including Mr. Bradley, knew he was dying. No one could imagine Lancaster without him. Some people had expressed alarm not only over the future of our church but also over the community. To many, Mr. Bradley simply kept everything running. Even though things always changed, Mr. Bradley's continued presence meant all was well.

I greatly admired Mr. Bradley. During our first meeting I sensed a sincere love of others in this man who had undoubtedly witnessed the best and the worst in people over his many years of business affairs. Instead of being jaded by almost a century of living and his years of multimillion-dollar dealings, I could tell he had accomplished something much more important than accumulating wealth and power.

His greatest achievement towered over everything else. I truly believe it was the secret to his great success. Somehow, he always saw the potential in people and helped them realize and claim their best. I came to understand this in watching him interact and describe others.

Without exaggeration, he would describe someone not by their profession or by their achievements but by their abilities. Over time I realized he saw everyone as gifted in one way or another.

He embraced the world by those terms and continued to be optimistically joyful in all things.

As I sat next to his hospital bed in his sunroom, I hoped he could see the beauty surrounding him. Birds sang from the tree branches, and flowers bloomed just outside his open windows. The sunlight gave reassurance of healing and happiness. He seemed very much at ease as he spoke about some of his final wishes.

"Dan, I'm not going to have a whole lot of speakers at my funeral," he said calmly. "If I started letting one of them speak, then all of them would want to speak," he said with his characteristic smile.

I knew he served on many boards around the state and had been on the Board of Trustees for the University of South Carolina for over thirty years. I also knew the family members who owned the large corporation would want to speak as well.

"You'll just have to let them all know we aren't going to have a lot of speakers," Mr. Bradley said with a smile. He knew he was asking a tall favor and seemed to enjoy the predicament in which he placed me.

"I know you'll smooth it over with everyone so no one gets their feelings hurt," he said with a mischievous grin.

After going over some more of the details for the funeral service, I could tell he was getting tired.

"Let me have a word of prayer with you," I said hoping my voice could convey my great admiration for this remarkable man.

"I want you to start praying," Mr. Bradley said in a serious tone. "Then let me pray for a little while, and then you close in prayer."

I started praying, and then paused. Mr. Bradley began to pray. I wondered at first if he wanted me to hear his prayer on his deathbed as a confession of past mistakes. I pondered if he might pray for the business he loved very much. I also thought he might pray for the continued success of the church and community.

Instead of these prayers, Mr. Bradley prayed for others. As the sun shone through the windows and the birds sang, Mr. Bradley quietly prayed for his family and friends, each person by name.

He prayed for their strength and their health. He prayed for happiness and for faithfulness. He prayed for hope and grace. He prayed God's blessings on countless people as I sat beside his bed and held his hand.

Chapter 25
Amelia Island

THE LADIES OF LANCASTER, MOTIVATED BY A NEED to make the season of Lent a memorable one, dedicated themselves to building an experience of spirituality for the community. In the large fellowship hall of our church, they constructed a passage. The passage took each individual through a journey from one elaborately decorated tent to another. Each themed tent contained unique visual, auditory, olfactory, and tactile encounters designed to focus on the continuing development of our relationship with God. The participants were invited to remain in each tent as long as they desired.

Teams of women were assigned to each tent to make sure every encounter would be not only amazingly beautiful but also extremely spiritual. The purpose of the event did not center on anything as commonplace as entertainment but rather on changing the perspectives of our Lenten pilgrimages.

One tent haunted me. There the ladies placed many clay containers of various sizes. Simple green plants and soft lights accentuated the earthenware jars and urns encircling an altar made of old weathered wood. A cross stood on the center of the altar. The dark wood of the simple cross showed signs of wear as though the wood had been used for many different, harsh purposes. The sturdy thickness of the old dark timbers demonstrated that even though it had been sawn, hammered, cut, and scarred, its strength remained.

A solitary wooden chair sat in front of a small table. The table and chair looked as though they had been used in a garden shed. A large wooden bowl rested on the center of the table. Carefully written and framed instructions explained how the contents of the tent could be used to deepen the experience. One by one, the participants were encouraged to sit at the table and select a small clay pot from the many in the tent. A prayer of illumination was to be prayed as the person contemplated their life and the process and progress of their spiritual journey to this point.

After a period of prayer and meditation, the participant used a marker to write their sins and regrets on their clay pot. The words on the pot would be their own private thoughts and confessions.

The words did not have to make sense to anyone but the writer. They could represent continuing sins or new mistakes. Lost hopes and forgotten dreams, constant fears and bitter disappointments, relentless anguish and unrelenting sorrow could all be written on the pots. Words on the clay composed a unique montage for each individual.

After writing and lingering over the meaning of each word, the pilgrim placed the pot inside the wooden bowl and covered it with a simple cotton cloth. An old rubber mallet sitting on the floor of the tent next to the table was then to be used to shatter the clay pot into broken and smashed pieces.

The instructions invited the pilgrim to take the shattered pieces of earthenware and pour them from the wooden bowl into one of the large clay urns in front of the altar. In the moment of offering to God the hidden and unspoken, hope for renewal existed.

This tent held great significance to those who walked the passage. They stayed in this tent and meditated over their words written on clay pots. The sound of shattering tended to move from tentative to passionate.

Even though the other tents contained moments of calm renewal and the ability to help the participants expand their passion for the work of Christ, the tent of the clay pots held special meaning for me. The whole concept of shattering and then pouring out those pieces before the altar fascinated me.

My fascination grew in the following weeks as I could hear the sound of shattering all over the church. No matter where I was in the building, the sound would find me. With each strike of the mallet, I knew someone had confronted the worst and most painful part of themselves. Even as sad as the sound of shattering seemed to be, I knew the person found at least the beginning of redemption in presenting those fragments as a unique and precious offering to God.

As I sat in the tent and held the small perfect clay pot in my hands, I wondered at the words I would write. Mistakes and failures crowded to the forefront of my mind demanding to be written. I almost laughed as I realized how many clay pots it would take to pen my sins.

My hands grasped the slightly rough texture of the smooth clay and I began to think not only of my mistakes but also the unaccomplished. As though opening a great hidden chasm reaching down much further into the depths than I wished to go, I realized the immensity of those things not done. My actions and accomplishments paled in comparison to all I should have completed.

I sat in the beautifully serene tent next to urns containing many shattered pieces. I had heard the shattering, and now those echoes spoke more clearly to me than the peace of the tent and the reminder of God's graceful presence. Instead of meditating in calmness, I sensed a call to action. I panicked as I wondered where to start to make amends for all the hurt my incorrect actions and my selfish inactions had caused. Before I could plan out how to make amends for all things, a sinking feeling of futility overcame me. I understood the complete uselessness of even trying to recapture moments lost as the hopelessness of the forever undone became a reality.

Carelessly, I dropped my clay pot of unwritten words on the hard tile floor of the tent and watched as it shattered loudly.

Slowly, I began the tedious task of picking up each shattered fragment and placing it in the urns of the altar.

The following evening, a candle held in an earthenware sculpture was lit as a part of a study group consisting of four ladies. We met in an upper room in the oldest section of our church building. The row of windows in the room gave a view of the massive roof of the sanctuary and the ring of ornate columns supporting the large copper covered steeple.

We gathered in this room every Tuesday evening to participate in a study designed to enhance our spiritual journey of our continuing understanding of Christ. The study quietly led us through scriptural readings and discussions. Even though I was initially disappointed with the small number of participants, a blessing of enhanced companionship became evident as we shared our faith journeys.

 In the time allowed for the study, we each felt free to express our frailties of faith while encouraging one another in continued growth.

The study also gave suggested activities to enhance the experiences of being together.

On one such evening, I brought a shallow box filled with white sand. Our readings for the week centered on Christ's encounter with the woman accused of adultery. The imagery of the writing in the sand by the Son of God and Son of Man became even more confronting through our discussions and insights of the texts used to enhance our understanding of the Biblical event.

Following the instructions of the study, each participant went to one corner of the large room and prayerfully wrote in the sand anything they desired. After prayer and meditation, they were to smooth out the sand, forever erasing the physical manifestation of their thoughts.

As the rest of us quietly talked about our discussion questions for the week, I watched as one after another would go into the corner and write in the sand. Some took longer than others. I wondered if they were writing about things we had discussed, or if perhaps, they were writing about grief and pain. Even though I knew these disciples very well, I had no clue about the words or images being drawn.

I couldn't help but notice the facial expressions of each lady as she smoothed the sands. A definite look of sadness, a brief note of triumph, a fleeting appearance of wonder, a dark shadow of concern. Undeniably, each face captured the meaning of what had just transpired.

After they were finished, I walked over to the sand and bent down. After a prayer, I wrote: "Thank you." For some reason I felt obliged to follow those words with a large question mark slowly written in the sand. I paused and looked with disbelief at the large punctuation mark. Ashamed that somehow my gratitude would be followed by such an act of defiance and doubt, I quickly erased what I now considered to be a mistake. The image of the question mark stayed in my mind as though the smooth sand still revealed my heresy. I looked at the white sand as my mind immediately went to the many moments of suffering and anguish I had witnessed. The images of the tears of others marked those sands more clearly and distinctly with heavy lines of pain than anything my fingers had been able to accomplish. Slowly I realized my faith gave hope, love, and gratitude, but the tears of sorrow still needed to be wiped away.

Reluctantly, I left the sand as I had found it and wondered if the others had seen the look of confusion and sadness on my face through my ordeal.

The next afternoon as I sat in my office getting ready to return home, I wondered about the clay pot with the unwritten, unfinished words. I winced as I thought about my sand writing hoping God would understand my desire to be comforted in my weakness.

My moments of contemplation came to a sudden end. I heard a loud crash and knew it came from the front doors of the church. Running through the hall and out the main doors of the narthex, I discovered a large black SUV slowly sliding down one of the four massive stone columns at the front steps of the church.

I stood there in astonishment as the vehicle gently slid down the column and landed. A well-dressed businesswoman stepped out of the driver's door and stood looking in disbelief at what had happened.

"I totally lost control," she said without the least bit of panic in her voice. "All of a sudden, I was coming right at the church. I remember hitting the steps and then the front end of the car went straight up. I couldn't even tell what was happening. It was like someone had lifted me straight up to the sky."

"The next thing I knew the whole car just started slowly moving back down and then came to a quiet stop. It was very calm."

"Are you alright?" I asked. She nodded in complete amazement.

Morning

A policeman arrived and helped with the traffic as people slowed and even stopped to look. Since her SUV was undamaged, she only needed to put it in reverse and back down the short flight of steps and onto the street.

I took a moment to look at the stone column her vehicle had somewhat successfully scaled. I hoped the column had not been knocked off its foundation or damaged. After a careful examination, I discovered it did not have a single scrape or mark. The foundation and the top looked to be exactly as it had been for a very long time. Sturdy, strong, reliable. From what I could see, not even the steps were damaged.

"I really don't know what to say," the lady said to me. "I can't believe I'm not more upset about the whole thing," she said calmly. "It all happened so fast, but it was somehow so easy. I'm not even shaking."

She held out her hands as though she needed to verify her lack of fear.

"I'm just so glad you aren't harmed," I said. "Also, just so you know, the column and the steps would appear to be undamaged. I think you can just drive away and pretend it never even happened."

The policeman started speaking with her as I walked back to the narthex doors and stood there wondering if I would need to give the officer any information. While I waited, I admired the row of stone columns. I knew they symbolized strength and continuity going all the way back to the columns of the ancient Greek temples. In silent affirmation of the old style of architecture, these columns continued to speak the message of those times.

"I'm more than just a column," they appeared to state as they stood there in magnificent strength. "I represent the truth and power given to this place. I stand here in witness to the presence of the Spirit receiving everyone at their most vulnerable and bringing peace and ultimate security out of the chaos of life."

I patted the old massive column and turned to go back into the sanctuary.

"Well done," I told it as it continued in its task.

Donna came out of the old house sided with dark brown cedar shingles situated very close to the ocean on Amelia Island. She held keys in her hands.

"Go up this main road for about one mile," she said with a grin.

"What did the realtor say?" I asked as I backed the car out of the sandy parking lot. "Do they have something? Are we going to be able to find someplace to stay?"

"Just keep driving," she said with a laugh. "I'll tell you when to stop."

I could tell she was up to something, but I couldn't guess enough to ask questions as I drove the car up the street.

"Slow down," she said as she leaned forward and peered over the dash. "There it is!" she exclaimed while pointing to the ocean side of the street. "Pull in there."

To my utter astonishment, we pulled up to a small replica of the large Amelia Island lighthouse we had just passed moments ago. Situated between two beach houses, the lighthouse stood at least four stories high and looked as though it had been built right on the sand dunes. Wild sea oaks surrounded the structure completing the too perfect picture.

"How in the world did you find this?" I asked in amazement.

At the same time Tyler shouted in excitement, "We're going to stay here?"

"This is really a house?" I asked still amazed we would be staying in a lighthouse.

"Before we go in," Donna said quickly, "let me tell you a few things about the place. I saw it when we were driving by and noticed you didn't see it. I also saw the rental sign and thought I would at least ask about it."

"The nice ladies at the realty company said it was originally rented out for this week, but at the last minute the renters had to cancel. It's a miniature replica of the lighthouse on the island and has a lookout around the top. The rental company also provides a breakfast in the morning delivered to us in a picnic basket. She gave me a menu and said we should order lots of stuff since it's included in the price. They will also bring a thermos of coffee and a newspaper. All we need to do is call in our order and tell them what time to deliver."

Donna stopped talking and beamed a smile at me.

"They said to make sure we order plenty because the breakfast items are made by a local chef. They insisted we try his famous cheese crepes and blueberry muffins!"

The only entrance of the lighthouse opened into a large round room with a terra cotta tile circular floor. A curving staircase hugged one wall of the room. A pair of narrow deep set windows faced out to the sea catching a continuing view of the sand dunes covered in sea oaks and the dark orange blossoms of straw flowers.

On the other side of the room a doorway opened into the bathroom with small tan tiles on the floor, walls, and ceiling, and a sunken shower stall.

"We have to walk down those steps to get in there and take a shower?" Tyler asked with astonishment.

Morning

"They said it was a combination shower and bathtub," Donna said. "If you want to use it as a bath, you simply fill the whole thing with water."

"What?" Tyler shouted stepping down the four tiled steps into the tub. "This is a swimming pool!"

We walked up the stairs while marveling at the odd sensation of how the walls and steps quickly began to curve into the interior of the structure.

"This is weird," I said as we carefully walked up the stairs to the next level. "I knew it would have to get smaller as it went up, but I had no idea it would be this dramatic a change from one level to the next."

"I guess you don't notice it as much in a full-sized lighthouse because the whole thing is so massive," Donna said while smiling. "I'm so excited it's actually as amazing and beautiful as I hoped it would be. It costs more than I thought we should spend, but I knew you would love it!"

I leaned over and kissed her on the stairs as we heard Tyler exclaiming with joy from the next level up.

"It's got at TV!"

The next level contained not only a TV but also a small kitchen and one cleverly designed couch suspended by chains from the ceiling.

"I guess they were saving space," I said sitting on the couch.

From the suspended couch, the windows of the room gave a great view of the ocean. From the windows, the panoramic scene seemed to be from a greater height than just the second level.

"We still have two levels to go," Donna said with glee as she started up the staircase. These steps curved even more sharply as the walls appeared to be coming into the center even faster with each step upward.

At the next level, a bedroom with a double bed and one tiny closet took up all of the available space. On the other side of the bed, a portal looked out to the ocean. We all climbed on the bed and marveled at the view from this small window which opened easily and captured the breeze.

"I think this is the best view in the lighthouse," Tyler said with excitement. He scampered off the bed and then began climbing up the steps leading to the top of the lighthouse.

"Wait on us!" Donna cried out. "Don't go outside without us!"

She began to climb the incredibly small steps which curved in so drastically they were almost impossible to maneuver. Quickly she began to climb using her hands and feet.

We reached the lantern room to find Tyler sitting on one of the curved benches surrounding a slowly rotating light in the center of the small space. Glass walls surrounded the benches and beautiful exposed wooden beams formed the ceiling. From the center rafters hung an antique light fixture which looked as if it had been salvaged from an old ship.

The amazing view stretched out before us on every side showing the complete shoreline of our island retreat. A glass door beckoned us to step outside to the wrought iron walkway circling the very top of the lighthouse.

"I think this walkway is called the gallery. I hope it's safe," I said to Donna as we ventured out to walk all around the outside of the lantern room.

Our fears could not compete with the view, the ocean breeze, and the sound of the waves crashing on the beach.

"Look at all the surfers," Tyler exclaimed. "These waves are incredible!"

I hugged Donna as we stood at the top of the lighthouse and felt the warmth of the breeze and of our happiness together.

"Thank you, Darling," I said as I hugged her tightly. "You knew exactly what we needed. You made all of this happen. You still surprise me!"

I closed my eyes as Donna gently laughed in contentment. I prayed a prayer of gratitude to God for our endless blessings.

Tyler decided to sleep on the couch on the second level while we slept in the bedroom on the third level.

"Open the portal so we can hear the waves as we go to sleep," Donna said in a small sleepy voice.

Following Donna's lead, I quickly fell asleep while looking forward to the basket of great breakfast foods arriving early in the morning.

Something awakened me in the middle of the night. I realized I had been hearing a particular sound for a while. It now seemed like a distant memory, perhaps a part of a forgotten dream.

I peered through the open portal to the waves below and saw the high tide. Looking out to the sea, I saw the lights of distant ships along the horizon. In an instant I was brought back to the first house in which I lived. At the top of the attic stairs of that old house, a small window built into a beadboard arch let sunlight into a little landing on the flight of steps. I remembered standing there as a little boy looking out the window. From this point in the house, I thought I could see the whole world. The view filled me with excitement. Everything seemed possible. The world invited me to come, see, and enjoy.

In the small bed in the lighthouse, I experienced the same joy and excitement of my much younger self. Looking out to those waves and to the dark ocean filled with the reflections of the shimmering night sky lights, I realized blessings of joy and peace.

Morning

The waves crashed with even more intensity below the open portal as I settled back down to the comfort of the pillow. I put my arm over Donna who continued to sleep, and then I heard the sound again.

Faint and yet unmistakable. Almost the sound of crashing waves but different. I wondered if I had fallen asleep again and now continued in my dream.

What was the sound?

It didn't startle me as though something to bring concern. It seemed to be more like a sound surrounding only me.

As though coming out of slumber, I recognized the sound as it continued in my mind. I knew it was the sound of something remembered. I wondered why it came to me during this first night in this enchanted lighthouse on our island getaway.

I closed my eyes. Above the gentle sound of my peacefully sleeping wife and the smoothing sound of waves coming ashore, I clearly heard it.

The sound of shattering.

The shattering of the little clay pot as it fell from my hands and smashed against the hard tile floor still haunted me. Through closed eyes, I saw the pieces flying up and out as they bounced off the floor. The unwritten words would not leave me even in this idyllic place. Instead of the incredible scenes of the night surrounding me, the incomplete words of hopes and dreams disappearing into fragments obsessed me.

The sound of shattering rang more clearly in my mind than the first time I heard it. The bed no longer held comfort. Sleep now forgotten, I rose and climbed the narrow twisting steps up to the lantern room and went out onto the gallery.

The strong summer breeze made me shiver as I peered out to the ocean seeking an answer.

Why the shattering? I thought. *What is shattering? Why am I hearing the pieces breaking?*

I knew all things could come to end in an instant. I understood how, even though we are people of faith, we prepare ourselves as best we can for anything this world might throw at us.

But why now? What is it about this place that brings to mind the sound of shattering of all that is forever undone?

Just thinking those thoughts made me feel as though I was falling, and I instinctively looked down. Even at night, the white walls of the lighthouse could be clearly seen through the iron bars forming the open flooring of the gallery. From this angle, the steep walls seemed to rush down from a great height to the dunes far below. The dizzying view began to make me feel unsteady as though the entire structure now shook in the wind.

I held more tightly to the railing and looked out to the ocean to regain my bearings. Then I looked up. Even as the sound of shattering continued in my head, I tried to restore calm by thinking of the Shepherd.

Before I could begin to pray, a sharp unexpected wind pushed me closer to the edge of the railing.

I turned to retreat to the safety of the lantern room and saw Donna sitting on one of the benches right inside. She looked at me and smiled a wonderfully sleepy and contented smile.

"Why are you up?" I asked her as I opened the glass door and sat down beside her.

"I knew you went up here and wondered if anything was bothering you?"

"No," I lied. "I just needed to think about some things and clear my head."

I put my arms around her and drew her close to me. I kissed her as the sound of shattering began to fade into the memory of our first kiss years ago.

Chapter 26

Duluth

I STOOD ON A BLACK BOULDER LOOKING OUT to magnificent waves cresting in the wild winds as far as I could see. The massive wet rock upon which I stood did not move as the breakers crashed against it as though in war with this immovable object that halted the waters' assault against the shore.

Mesmerized by what I witnessed, I gave no care to the spray of the angry white waves covering me. Even though the cold wind never diminished, I could not believe I was witnessing this powerful scene in this distant and remote place.

The long road trip to Duluth, Minnesota in the early part of July became necessary because of Tyler's new summer job. On the last afternoon before returning home, Donna and I decided we would travel up the North Shore Drive at Lake Superior while Tyler began his work.

As it turned out, Tyler, now eighteen, played the drums rather well. He belonged to the Lancaster High School drumline and enjoyed it so much he began playing the drums on his own. We knew he relished any opportunity to see local bands play in the area. We soon found out he also craved the chance to play in a professional band.

"Dad, Dad!" Tyler shouted one day running through the house in search of me. "They want me to join their band!" he said breathlessly when he finally found me. "I have to be in Duluth in one week. Their tour starts then. They lost their drummer and asked for people to audition. I did and they liked me and we will be touring all around and even play in New York City!!"

"We have to get ready and go!" He stopped all of his excited shouting and looked at me as though I would get in the car with him right then and leave.

"Duluth," I said while smiling and trying to look somewhat excited about the whole thing. I knew it was a big deal to him, but I had to have more information. I tried to look pleased for him even though I didn't understand.

"Well, Duluth is not very far away," I said while smiling. "How did you hear about this band from Georgia?"

"Daaaad," Tyler looked at me like I had lost my mind. "Duluth's in Minnesota! We've got to get there next week. We've got to get everything ready to go! I'll need my car and my drum kit. We'll have to take two cars. Where is Mom? We need to get packing!"

Duluth, Georgia, near Atlanta, sounded like a much more reasonable destination, but Tyler's enthusiasm led Donna and me to come to the conclusion that this was an important opportunity for him to experience playing for a moderately successful band.

"He's got to see for himself what it means to travel and play with a band," Donna said to me one evening as we privately discussed the situation.

"If we stop him from going now," she added, "he'll just find another band some other place."

She paused and looked away for a moment. I knew she was fighting tears, and just the thought of her crying made me start as well.

"I'm afraid," she said using her no-nonsense voice which always meant she had decided her reason would have to win out over her emotions, "if we don't let him go…if we don't let him have this big chance…he will always think we held him back."

She turned away from me as though ashamed of herself for starting to cry.

"We've always wanted him to dream big, and we taught him he could do anything he put his mind to doing," she managed to say without sobbing. "I don't know how we can tell him at this point he needs to stop dreaming and become practical."

"And look at it this way," I said through my own tears as I walked over and hugged her. "I can't help but be proud of how he did this on his own. He wanted it, and he made it happen. That's something all by itself."

"I'm not ready for him to stop being our little boy," Donna said wiping away the last tear. "And mother thinks we have both completely lost our minds for even considering letting him go!"

One week later, two cars left our driveway carrying one large drum kit, two fearful parents, and one ecstatic young man bound on a northern adventure.

Everything turned out much better than we could have anticipated. The two young men leading the band turned out to be brothers who lived with their parents. The whole family had experience in the music business. The tour came as a result of the newest CD they had produced using a large private professional recording studio in the basement of their home. One of the songs they had written and recorded was gaining a lot of attention. A summer tour could help them get a bigger musical career started.

While Tyler did some preliminary work with the band, Donna and I decided to drive around the city. Built into the side of a mountain coming straight out of the lake, the steep streets of the city seemed more like San

Morning

Francisco than Minnesota. We drove around admiring the views and ended up on the top ridge of the city.

Overlooking the city and the lake, we found a large United Methodist Church. I pulled up and parked. Donna looked at me without saying a word.

"We pride ourselves on being a connectional church," I told Donna as I got out of the car. "I'm going to see just how connectional we really are. It's just a shot in the dark, but let's see if the pastor might be in. I will feel better if I have some additional points of contact up here."

As we made our way across the parking lot to the side office entrance, I noticed a man in his forties walking from his car to the same door.

"Are you the pastor?" I asked as I held out my hand.

"Yes, I am," he said as he shook my hand and introduced himself. I wondered for a moment if what people always said about pastors looking a certain way was indeed true. I also wondered if he could tell I was a pastor as well.

After explaining ourselves to him there in the parking lot, he gave us reassurance.

"You tell Tyler if he needs anything to come and see me," he said with a big smile. "And if you ever want me to check on him, just give me a call."

Feeling much better about the whole situation, we consoled ourselves with the hope that after a summer of touring, Tyler would either be convinced of his career choice or ready to pursue something else.

Now I stood on a boulder watching violent waves. Even though I knew Tyler would be safe on this well-prepared tour and that it could very well be the chance of a lifetime for him, I still felt unready for such a change.

As the wind whipped past me mercilessly, I began to appreciate the beauty of the rock upon which I stood. I knew it had been there for longer than I could imagine and even with the fierceness of this inland sea, the rock would last for centuries yet to come.

Donna and I both found the North Shore Drive to be more beautiful than we could have imagined. She looked startled when I suddenly turned the car around.

"I'm sorry," I said while laughing over Donna's objections. "I know we want to get to Canada and back before dark. But right back there on the edge of the lake, I saw a big granite monument. Why would anyone put a big monument on the shore of the lake way out here in the middle of nowhere? It's too much for my curiosity! I have to stop and read it."

Donna laughed and agreed even though we both knew she didn't have a choice. My curiosity always won.

As soon as we parked and opened the doors, Donna backed out of the little excursion.

"Last week we had temperatures in the 80's," one of the band member's parents said with a laugh. "This week, it's cold. I guess it's just so you can get a little feel for what our winters are like. The only time I mind the snow is when it gets to be 36 inches deep. At that point," he said with a grin, "it's just too hard to walk through."

Donna and I each packed light jackets but nothing sturdy enough for this kind of wind. When we stepped out of the car to walk down to the shore to read the monument, we realized our northern drive out to a desolate and beautiful place had brought us to a new kind of cold and wind.

"There's no way I can go out there," Donna said while getting back in the car. "But you go and look. I know you want to."

I made my way down to the shore and stood before the large monument. There, to my surprise, I discovered it had been placed by former residents of an abandoned community.

The engraving on the monument read in part:

"The place though little less than wilderness was the seat of the U. S. Land office for the northeastern district of Minnesota. After the removal of the land office the settlement disappeared."

"It marks the spot for a town that no longer exists. All that's left is this granite marker," I said aloud.

The wind captured my words as though trying to force them away. The rocky shore beckoned me. I looked back and waved at Donna who waved at me. I pointed to the shore and she nodded as though understanding my desire to explore.

"I'll only take a moment," I said to myself.

The boulders demanded my attention. One after another they beckoned me to keep on climbing and hiking. Each one gave a greater view of the lake and the powerful waves. Soon I stood on a black boulder, frozen in the wind and the waves but unwilling to leave.

I heard a scream. Turning, I saw Donna climbing up the edge of the boulder. The wind melted her scream as her hair, now wet from the spray of the crashing waves, was tossed to one side of her head.

Her face was distorted in fear.

I ran to her and hugged her tight. I turned her away from the wind and the water trying to shield her and warm her at the same time.

"I thought I had lost you," she sobbed into my shoulder. Her whole body shook from cold and fear.

Morning

"I'm sorry," I said quickly, "I'm so sorry. I thought you understood I wanted to climb these rocks. I shouldn't have come."

"I understood," she said while still shivering and crying. "But you were gone so long. I thought you had fallen into the waves, and I knew I could never get help up here in time to save you."

She pulled me even tighter to herself.

"I thought I would never see you again," she sobbed. "I thought I had lost you forever."

Chapter 27
The Beginning

"It's Tyler!" I shouted to Donna after hearing his voice on the phone. Donna immediately picked up the phone in the bedroom.

"Tyler B!" she said with a laugh. "Where are you? How are you doing? Have you arrived in New York yet?"

"Yes, ma'am!" he said enthusiastically. "You'll never guess what I'm doing right now. Just try to guess."

"Well, I hope you aren't driving," I said with a laugh. "You must be in the van. I hope none of you got sick from your swim in the pond in the middle of the cow pasture."

Tyler laughed and I could hear other laughter from the guys in the band.

"We were all so excited about finally getting to take a bath," he said quickly. "We didn't know a pond in a cow pasture by the side of the road would be filthy!"

"Where are you?" Donna repeated on the other extension.

"I wanted to call you to let you know I am now driving our van and pulling the band's trailer through Times Square!"

"Tyler!" Donna exclaimed. "That's amazing!"

"Maybe you should get off the phone and pay attention to what you are doing," I suggested as again I heard the other guys laughing.

"Where are you going?" Donna said to change the subject from my useless parental guidance.

"It's great," Tyler exclaimed. "You're not going to believe it. The show last night was unbelievable. Lots and lots of people. And afterwards they kept coming up to us and wanting autographs. It was amazing! I can't wait to tell you all about it. But right now we're headed to see the Eiffel Tower."

Silence and then shouts of laughter followed from the van.

"Oh!" Tyler said while laughing. "It's not the Eiffel Tower. We're on our way to see the Empire State Building."

"*At least both places start with an 'E'*", I thought to myself.

"We're headed to Kentucky next!"

"Kentucky?" I asked. Before I could say anything else, more laugher and shouts came from the van.

"Oh, Oh!" Tyler said while laughing. "Not Kentucky. Connecticut. I knew it was one of the "Ku" states, I just forgot which one. Love you. Gotta go."

Morning

Donna came down the steps laughing and coughing. We hugged as we laughed together in mutual relief for how this strange experiment seemed to be working so well. Our son was living his dream and experiencing a whole new way of life. Testing the waters and obviously growing through these events was working for him. This bold step appeared to be successful. We both knew any and all moments of parental bliss were to be fully relished.

"I do hope he can find his way home," Donna said with a look of exasperation. She sat on the couch exhausted.

"I guess all of this will turn out alright," she said with relief. "Those band members seem like great kids."

"I really think God provided this opportunity and then somehow let us know it would be alright to let him go," she said. "I still can't believe we did it, and I can't believe he worked it all out. This whole thing is just amazing."

"It's one of those things you do and then wonder why in the world you ever did," I said as I sat on the couch next to her and held her hand.

A bluebird landed on a tree branch in the small backyard. The windows of the sunroom allowed the bird to examine us as much as we examined him. Bright sunlight made its way through the dancing leaves of the sweet gum trees inviting us to come out and play.

The talking stopped as we watched the bird. The bluebird of happiness. I wondered if Donna was thinking about the same thing. I rarely worried about her happiness. She always ran into each new day with enthusiasm as though each morning brought its own means of joy.

I stared for a few moments more at the bluebird on the branch right outside the window. Without hesitation, the little bird returned my gaze. Since Donna never seemed to need a happiness bird, I began to think the bird must have been for me.

Sitting in our favorite room of the house while holding her hand and knowing Tyler seemed happy, excited, and motivated by his new adventure, I wondered why I needed the bluebird of happiness. My journey with God and family made me happier than I could have ever imagined.

"It is unbelievable," Donna said after a cough. "But faith is about doing the unbelievable."

"You sound like you might have some bronchitis going on," I said casually.

Donna and bronchitis were old friends. Normally she had about two bouts of it each year. We both became very familiar with the signs and with the fact that a doctor's visit normally took care of it.

"I'm going to the doctor tomorrow," she said with a shrug. "More antibiotics. Same old story."

I knew she could not possibly be feeling very well. I also knew she would not slow down nor stop from her normal pace of getting everything done. Her way of being sick was to medicate and ignore until better.

Summer came to an end. School began once more. I loved to watch Donna as she made preparations for the new school year. Even with her years of experience, she could not help but joyfully anticipate getting to know new students, becoming a part of their lives, and helping them learn.

Her enthusiasm grew as she worked for several weeks before her first day back. Bulletin board materials would be examined and readied. Boxes of supplies and displays would be removed from our attic as she carefully decided which ones would be used to make her room as inviting as possible for the return of the students.

Always frugal, she would only purchase a few new and carefully chosen items to change up the appearance of her room from the last school year. On her first day of the new school year, her car would be loaded with everything she could possibly need.

The school year started. Tyler returned home after his interesting summer with the band. He began to discuss options for furthering his education.

"Touring with the band was fun," Tyler said after telling us the details of his summer. "Playing in front of big crowds of people seemed sort of unreal, but I realized I don't want to be in a band for the rest of my life. Constantly performing and then traveling to the next location to do the same thing over again and again…it got old."

"But what a great learning experience," Donna said while we sat at the table finishing our dinner. "If you had never done that or never had the opportunity, you might have always wondered what it would be like. Now you know."

"And the main thing," I said while looking at Tyler with admiration, "is you made it happen. You saw the chance and you took it. I'm very proud of you for accomplishing it."

It felt so good to be able to look at my son and tell him of my pride in his accomplishments. I wanted him to know the importance of positive steps and choices. As I looked into his eyes, I wanted him to fully grasp my love and my respect for him.

Donna and I often doubted our abilities and skills in parenting, but I knew I could make this one precious child know that no matter what, no matter how often I did not pass the parenting test, I could and would make sure he knew how much I admired him for the person he was.

Morning

Our lives continued in the normal progression of ordinary events. Donna's school, the church, Tyler's plans, everything moved in harmony as though at this point in our lives, we finally moved into a deeply satisfying time of simply living.

One evening in October, Donna finally settled down on the couch in the sunroom to watch some television with me.

She began to cough and then laughed.

"The teachers at school have started laughing at my cough," she said while finishing her coughing. "They say they can hear me coming down the hall and always know it is me by my cough."

"It's been going on for a while," I frowned. "You've been on antibiotics. Are you still taking some?"

"No, I finished them," Donna said while watching the show on the television. "That was my second round. I don't feel very bad, but I can't get rid of the cough."

I knew it didn't make any difference if she said she didn't feel very bad. I wished for a moment I could really tell how bad she felt. I knew if I felt the way she undoubtedly did, I would probably be in bed.

"You always just keep going," I said with a smile, "but I think we need to see someone about this."

Before she had time to contradict me, I continued.

"I want you to see one of the new internists at the office up the street from the church. Several people have told me how wonderful those doctors are. I've never been to an internist, but I don't think you have to be referred from another doctor."

Much to my surprise, Donna agreed to call and make an appointment. The next day she told me when she would be going.

"I want to go with you," I said quietly.

To my surprise again, she agreed. After I hung up the phone, I paused.

Why do I want to go with her? I thought. *I never go with her to the doctor. She certainly doesn't need me to go. She's always taken very good care of herself and has no trouble communicating with any doctor.*

At the appointment, the doctor immediately gained our trust. His questions and the easy conversations were in no way rushed. He knew how to phrase his comments and inquiries so Donna could effectively describe her long-term coughing in great detail.

"I want to run a few tests," he said with a warm smile. "Let's get a chest x-ray first."

As Donna prepared for the x-ray, she looked at me with a slightly worried look.

"I know he must be thinking it's pneumonia," she said quietly. "I don't think it is. I really don't feel bad. I don't know what it is, but I've got to be back at school tomorrow. We have too much going on right now. I hope I don't have to miss school just so he can continue to try to figure this out."

"Let's just see what the x-ray shows," I said calmly. "I don't think you could have too much pneumonia or you would be running a fever, I think."

After she returned to the exam room from the x-ray, she looked better. I could tell her endless determination had set in and now she was ready to stop all this foolishness and get back to normal.

"I'm feeling better," she said firmly. "I think this is just a simple cough. Probably just allergies. They're always changing the cleaning supplies they use at school. I bet I'm just sensitive to some of them."

The doctor walked into the room. He wasn't holding the x-rays.

"There's something going on," he said. "If it's alright, I would like for you to go right up the street and get an MRI done. It won't take long."

I drove us up the street and would not allow myself to wonder what was happening. They immediately took her back to begin the process. I sat in the lobby and did not think.

About an hour later, she came out smiling. When we got into the car, she began to cough. I knew she had not allowed herself to cough while in the office. By sheer force, she had kept everything under control until she was safely with me.

Much to my surprise, we were told to go to the internist's office after the MRI since he would have the results immediately. I knew the normal delay involved in reporting the results of these sort of tests. All of this was happening with lightning speed.

We sat in the exam room and waited. With the determination I had learned from Donna, I kept my mind blank. She continued to very calmly speak about how unnecessary all of this was. I reassured her we needed to get to the bottom of what was causing her to cough this much.

"Maybe this doctor can stop you from having bronchitis so often," I said in a reassuring tone. "It's hard on you to have to go through this twice or more every year."

The doctor came back into the room and began to speak. I watched his expressions and his movements more closely than I listened to his words.

"There is definitely something going on," he said with a calm voice. His face was devoid of all emotion. His forehead did not furrow. No hint of perspiration. Nostrils did not flare. Even his lips seemed calm.

He prepared himself before he came back into this room, I thought. *Even at this young age, he's learned to become expressionless.*

He looked down. Searching for any clue of hope, I noticed how his arms drooped uselessly at his sides as he talked. Even his fingers appeared limp as though all strength and ability had vanished from them. This highly skilled doctor, the fighter, the healer, the one with all of the amazing abilities to conquer illness had been bested.

I stopped breathing for a second. The quietness. The unbearable stillness.

Waiting for the moment to end, I looked at Donna. Her arms folded gently in her lap, she looked completely at ease as though waiting for some good news.

I knew she saw what I saw. His downward glance did not seem to faze her. Her eyes looked kindly at him. I wondered if she felt pity for what he must have been going through to come into this room and speak with us.

She did not dare look at me.

"There is definitely something going on," he repeated. His face took on the look of determination.

"The MRI showed a spot on your lung," he said simply. "It also showed a spot on your liver."

Silence.

"We will not know exactly what is taking place until a biopsy is performed. I've arranged for you to leave from here and go to Carolina's Medical Center in Charlotte to be admitted today as a patient. Because of your kidney transplant, you are considered a very special case. A team of doctors including a nephrologist will be in charge of your care there. They will perform a biopsy very quickly so we can determine exactly what must take place."

Silence.

Chapter 28
Hospital

A DOCTOR FROM THE CHARLOTTE MEDICAL TEAM stood at the door of the hospital room. His arms, folded in front of his chest as though protecting his heart, held a flat notebook. His straightforward and professional manner did not allow for any visible emotion. In a confident and calm voice, he introduced himself and reported that a full diagnosis and prognosis had been achieved.

"Please tell me exactly what you have found," Donna stated with strength and without hesitation. "I want to know what you now know…the entire truth of the situation. You can speak in front of everyone in this room."

Her mom, Thelma, stood by one side of the hospital bed while I stood on the other side of the bed closest to the doctor. Our friend from church, Teresa, stood next to me.

The doctor did not smile; his expression did not change, but I could sense admiration in his voice when he spoke. Perhaps he could tell from our calm reaction to her words that we knew she could handle anything he could possibly say. Perhaps he also knew that through her strength we would find strength.

"You have carcinosarcoma of the lungs," he said with a confident voice. "It appears to have already metastasized in the liver. This is a rare and aggressive cancer."

"Rare and aggressive." The words hit me hard; I felt my muscles begin to tighten from head to toe. On several occasions, I had heard the same words from other doctors as they gave a diagnosis to my parishioners. I knew exactly what those words meant.

The doctor paused for a second as though making sure he had Donna's permission to continue. In his next words, I sensed more kindness in his voice as his eyes began to show pride in his new patient.

"This cancer is a combination of two cancers of the epithelial and connective tissues of the body," he said scientifically. "This type of cancer is difficult to effectively treat."

"Exactly how long do I have?" Donna stated calmly with a strong voice.

"If the treatments work very well," he stated without hesitation which acknowledged her strength, "you have six months to live. If the treatments do not work very well, you will have less."

Morning

"I need to get back to my students" she said firmly. "We are just getting started with the school year. This is a terrible time for me to be absent. When will you be releasing me so I can return to my classroom?"

The doctor hesitated. I wondered if his armor was beginning to crack. He almost took a step closer to the bed but then stopped himself. As he answered the question, I sensed remorse in his voice as though he regretted having to give this news.

"Your teaching days are over."

Chapter 29
First Night Home

"WELL, THAT'S THE WORD FROM THE DOCTOR," Teresa said defiantly as she shut the hospital door behind the doctor. "But he doesn't have the last word. God does!"

Teresa began to pray after we all joined hands around Donna's hospital bed. Each of us had tears running down our faces. I uselessly tried to contain mine afraid of a complete and unending breakdown.

Teresa began to pray as I felt Donna's hand in mine. Warm and soothing, her palm and fingers in my hands assured me not only of her presence but also of her love. Calming waters of relief flooded around my heart as I realized the force of life existing so strongly in her touch. I held her hand tightly as Teresa made our requests known to God for her complete healing.

As she finished her prayer, Teresa left the room. In private, the three of us did not go immediately to the endless grief of the news. Our tears continued as we tried to be brave.

"You've been through so much in your life," Thelma said while smiling down at her beloved daughter. "I just feel you will come through this as well. You always have with God's help and blessings."

They embraced and quiet tears continued.

I thought of Teresa's great statement of faith. No matter what the doctor's might have to say, God would have the last word. I knew the truth of her words. I wanted to believe that God wanted healing for his wonderful and obedient servant, but the absoluteness of the doctors words seemed to wring the faith right out of me.

Wishing I had the relentless trust of Teresa, I began to pray not only for Donna but for my faith during the times ahead. I beseeched God to heal and, through the healing, to strengthen and confirm my faith.

In every situation, Teresa maintained her faith and her desire to let everyone know about God. Now, without even realizing it, she lifted me from the confines of sorrow and gave me hope.

After returning home, Donna and I sat on the couch in the sunroom watching as the evening approached. The events of the day swirled in my head. Everything seemed to turn from anguish to a deep dark fear.

"I'm not afraid of dying," Donna said quietly as she squeezed me gently. Her head was on my chest, my arms around her. She had cried while I held her. I knew she felt relieved to be alone with me so she could let her guard down.

On some level we both knew that in all likelihood we would not die together. We saw many widows and widowers at the churches we had served. In getting to know them, we understood how life for one of them continued. The one left had come to understand the new way of living without the other.

Even though life continued for these individuals, it was never the same. Some of them remarried, some remained single, some adjusted to the new normal, and others seemed to never adjust.

Sitting there, holding Donna, I began to grieve. The first grief came as I realized that our life together from this moment on would never be the same. Now the uncertainties of the future no longer presented themselves as something to imagine. Now the future shaped every precious moment of the present. Now each day became the dreaded reminder of the constant ticking of the clock.

Time could not be stopped. This future would occur as the doctor predicted unless God intervened. Even with our faith, it felt as though the cards had already been played.

I feel like a child, I wanted to say softly to Donna. *I feel like everything is now new, except it isn't new and wonderful. I used to dream about everything life could be. I used to think nothing was impossible. Now I look at the future, and I'm not only terrified of what it will bring, I also don't know how to cope with it. There are no roadmaps. I'm feeling lost and alone already.*

As I sat in silence holding Donna, I knew I would never try to explain this disaster to her. I accepted the utter failure of my pastoral words to make any sort of sense out of this situation. I also knew she already understood exactly what I felt without the words. Tears ran down my face, and I hugged her more tightly.

"I'm so sorry," I said in a broken whisper. "You know I'll be strong for you. Everything will be alright."

"It's okay," she said softly as though being awakened from a long slumber. "We always think alike. I'm having the same fears. But for now, we have each other."

The stillness of the room calmed us. Our hearts began beating in rhythm. We awaited the storm as it approached, knowing of God's love for us and our love for each other.

"I'm not afraid of being sick," she said gently. I knew her words were true.

"I'm not even afraid of what the treatments might do to me," she paused as if needing to check the validity of her thoughts.

"I'm not afraid of the pain or the unknown," she said simply.

While she paused, I began to wonder how I would feel under the same circumstances. How would I face the reality of a fatal illness? I began to question my bravery as I wondered about the moment of death. I had watched many people die. I had witnessed their last breath and the moment they had gone to be with the Lord. I had watched as they gasped for the last bit of air and their heart slowly quit its lifetime of beating.

How will I face the moment of my death? I thought.

Donna stirred in my arms. I did not question her ability to face what might be while I fully doubted my capacity to endure the days ahead.

"Fear is not the problem," she said as she held me tighter.

"I just can't stand the thought of leaving you," she whispered. "I just can't stand the thought of leaving Tyler and you."

"I can't believe I will have to."

Chapter 30
Treatments

"I'M WILLING TO TAKE HER ANYWHERE, ANYWHERE in the world to get the very best treatment possible."

I wanted to make sure my friend and church member, Dr. Sunil Lalla, understood the importance of the task I had asked him to accomplish.

"Please contact all the people you know," I said to this very skilled surgeon who had stopped by the parsonage to speak with me. We sat in the living room beneath the loft near the master bedroom. We spoke quietly even though I knew Donna was fast asleep.

"I'll contact everyone and find out exactly what the situation is," Sunil said. His countenance changed from being just a supportive friend to a highly trained and dedicated health care provider.

"They have everything arranged for Charlotte," I said with a shaky voice. "I know they will do a great job, but I also have to know there are no other options available. I have to know…I have to be certain…I don't want to leave any stone unturned."

I knew Sunil could have questioned my faith right then. He could have told me about God's healing abilities for everyone. He could have even spoken about the will of God. I knew he possessed a great understanding of our Lord. I wondered if he thought less of me for not expressing my full reliance on God right then and there.

"I do want you to realize something," Sunil continued slowly. "This cancer is rarer than you probably understand. Right at the moment, the people in the United States who have this cancer could easily fit into this living room."

"Oh," I said, "and the doctors said it is aggressive as well."

"The thing you need to understand is since it is so rare," he paused as if making sure he should tell me the rest, "there is not much medical research being done on it."

I let those words soak in.

"The scarcity of resources," I surprised myself with the amount of disgust in my voice. "It's always the problem."

"You have to understand," Sunil said gently, "there are many more people with the common types of cancer who also need a cure."

"Since there is so little research being done on this cancer," he continued, "the treatment options are very limited. I'll make contact with the major hospitals in the country and see what I can find out."

"I know. I'm not trying to blame anyone; I believe everyone has done everything they possibly can do," I looked down at the sofa instead of at him.

"But," I hesitated, "she had a cough for a long time…months." I paused as I realized the intensity of my anger and frustration. "She kept going to the doctors and they kept giving her antibiotics."

"I have to know," my voice got louder, "I have to know," I repeated as I looked up from the sofa and directly in his eyes, "could we have saved her life if we had found the cancer sooner?"

Sunil looked straight at me. His eyes did not waver. I knew he understood that only the truth would suffice at this moment and his answer, one way or another, would make a huge difference to me right then and in the future.

With ease coming from great sincerity, Sunil returned my searching and desperate stare with perfect assurance.

"Dan," he said calmly, "if she had been diagnosed earlier, then you would have known for much longer she was going to die."

Within a few days, Sunil called to say that the heads of the sarcoma units at the major cancer treatment centers around the country had assured him the treatment protocol being offered at Charlotte would be the same as any other hospital.

"All that can be done, is being done," he said with gentle compassion.

I found myself somewhat relieved that the best treatment could be found nearby. I knew if another more costly option had been available, Donna would have refused. Even though I would have gladly spent every last dime we had and put us in overwhelming debt to have her cured, Donna would have never agreed.

"God can heal me in Charlotte as well as any other place," she would have said to end the conversation once and for all.

A few days later, Donna and I sat in one of the most modern medical facilities I had ever seen. Walls of glass overlooked gardens several stories beneath us. In the distance, the impressive skyline of Charlotte shimmered in the sun of a bright and cloudless day.

Nurses, who cared beyond belief, surrounded us. They mixed the chemotherapy drugs in the same room where the infusions would be given. In an odd sort of way, the large room reminded me of an upscale chic restaurant. Working under the fume hoods, the nurses in their white

Morning

uniforms reminded me of chefs concocting gourmet dishes to be served to all who waited.

"You will receive chemotherapy three days a week for six weeks. We will then see how you are progressing," the doctor said in a pleasant and cheerful manner. I could see his training in being always positive and hopeful in every word and expression. At this point, there was simply no need to go into the dim prospects of the situation.

"We will give you plenty of information about the side effects of the chemotherapy," he continued. "I don't think you will have any problems, but if you do, we will handle it quickly."

"This cancer is a combination of two types of cancer," he said becoming less cheerful. "A lot of times it will work on the one type of cancer and have little or no effect on the other type of cancer present."

"What will you do if the other type of cancer will not respond to this treatment?" I interrupted.

Donna looked at me with compassion even though I knew she would have preferred to have asked the questions.

"Then we will look at what other options are available," the doctor stated easily maintaining his friendly and hopeful countenance.

"But let's take one thing at a time…one step at a time," he said.

"I have this one lump on my thigh," Donna said pointing to her leg. "Do you think it is cancer or something else?"

"Let's take a look," the doctor said cheerfully.

After an examination, he looked through her records before turning back to us.

"Everything would seem to suggest this lump is cancer," he said cautiously. "As you know, our tests show the cancer is spreading."

Donna and I nodded in agreement.

"This is one place where the cancer can be seen as a lump under your skin. Has it grown recently?"

"Some," Donna said as though discussing a rash on her skin. "But not too bad. It's much bigger than when I first noticed it."

"We'll keep an eye on it to make sure it doesn't bother you," the doctor said with confidence. "I don't think it will be a problem."

"Now," the doctor continued, "I'll have someone take you on a tour of our facility and let you know what to expect during your treatments."

Always upbeat and cheerful, Donna laughed and talked with the nurses and made friends with them along the way.

The forty-five-minute drive from Lancaster to Charlotte became in some ways a return to normal. I would drive with one hand on the wheel and my other hand holding hers in her lap just as we always did. It felt as though everything was just as it had always been. For those moments in the car, we did not discuss the cancer nor the treatment. We simply chatted about the ordinary and mundane details of the day as though nothing was unusual. It became our escape from the reality of the situation as though by going on this journey together, all would be well. For those minutes in the car, we were just Donna and Dan enjoying each other's company.

Even though a private television screen was cleverly attached to each infusion chair, Donna normally read a book while I sat next to her doing the same. When lunch time arrived, I would bring in something and we would eat and talk and laugh. Sometimes we would play card games to pass the time. For some reason, the hours of the treatments seemed to pass very quickly.

"I think something's wrong," Donna said one time after the infusion started. "Something's leaking."

I looked down and saw chemo fluid puddling on the floor. In panic, I ran to the nurse who had begun to help someone else.

"She's not getting the chemo!" I said in a startled tone. "It's all pouring out on the floor!"

The nurse came directly over and stopped the flow and adjusted the tubing and then restarted everything. She used sterile looking cloths to clean the floor. Donna calmly thanked her as the nurse apologized for the leak. She left to go to other patients who sat in their overly comfortable seats looking out glass walls to the beauty of a gleaming city full of hope.

She didn't care that Donna would not receive all the chemo, I thought. I smiled at Donna hoping she could not sense the great dismay in my heart. *It didn't make any difference to the nurse*, I shouted to myself. *Donna will not receive a cup or two of the chemo! How can it be alright?*

I wanted to scream and make a huge scene. I wanted to proclaim that this was our last best hope and they had messed it up. I wanted them to make it all better, to give her a new full bag of the chemo and to make sure something like this never happened again.

But the real message of the nonchalant attitude of the nurse dispelled my anger. The message of her actions spoke more loudly than all the wonderful care Donna had been receiving.

The nurse knows full well that a cup or two of this fluid will make no difference, I suddenly realized. *This isn't life-giving medicine. It's a long shot at best. It's more than a long shot, it's just something to try so we can be satisfied that something is being done. They all know it's completely and utterly useless!*

Morning

I went into the bathroom and stared at the mirror without seeing myself. I needed to be alone so I could readjust my mask of hopefulness in order to continue the charade.

Chapter 31
Christmas Gifts

AFTER LEAVING THE TREATMENT CENTER ONE DAY, Donna suggested we buy some Christmas gifts. A very large outlet mall was not too far away, so she thought it would be a good place to get most of the presents we needed.

"Are you sure you feel up to it?" I asked even though I didn't want to discourage her. I knew my anxieties would always show.

"I'm fine," she smiled. "I feel pretty good today. We need to get the shopping completed, and this is a great chance."

I parked as close to the entrance as possible, and when we entered, I looked around to see if a wheelchair might be available. I knew better than to mention the need of any sort of assistance to her, but at the same time, I needed to know what was available, just in case.

We walked from store to store. Donna's carefully prepared list only included items easily found in this large mall. With great efficiency, she led the way as we quickly made purchases of exactly what she wanted for everyone.

My arms filled with bags, Donna spotted a cute little store and decided it would be her last stop.

"I need one thing for Teresa," she said cheerfully. "I'm her Secret Santa with the United Methodist Women, and a small gift will finish it out."

The store looked like something from a Dicken's village. Its large windows with many rectangular panes had been decorated with holly and piles of fluffy small snowflakes. Christmas lights and candles glowed through the windows.

I spied an empty bench in front of the store entrance in the middle of the busy corridor. Decorated with Christmas lampposts and trimmed with holly and poinsettias, this wooden bench almost looked too pretty to be used.

"I'll stay right here with all these packages," I told Donna. "I don't think there's room in that little shop for me to walk around carrying all these things. I'm afraid I'll be a bull in a china shop."

Donna agreed and went into the store as I situated the packages on the small bench and then sat down. It felt surprisingly good to free my arms and rest for a moment or two. Constant streams of people passed me on either side of the bench, and I began to feel as though I were sitting on an island in the midst of rapidly moving currents.

Morning

I looked up and saw Donna standing in the Christmas window looking at a display. She smiled, not at me, but at the selections of gifts she had discovered. She looked completely happy, contented and a little excited to be getting the perfect gift for our friend. I watched as she picked up one item and then another while examining them. Her peace seemed complete. No doubt or fear existed as her unabated joy continued.

Tears began to run down my face, and I quietly sobbed. I didn't want to worry the many people passing around me, but I couldn't stop crying.

How could someone who finds such joy in doing for others be dying? I thought. *How could her kindness and love for every person be coming to an end?*

Once more I imagined what she must have looked like as a child running down the hospital hallway to escape the doctor. In my mind's eye, I could see Donna's mahogany brown ponytail waving to anyone who cared to see. I imagined her innocent smile and could hear her defiant laughter as the young doctor ran to catch her.

How could someone with so much spirit be taken away?

I could no longer look at her as she stood at the window making the selection of the last Christmas gift. She still did not see me, but I had seen more than I could stand.

Her last Christmas, I kept thinking. *How can this be her last Christmas?*

My tears fell onto our packages as grief overtook me. No one seemed to notice as the shoppers continued to walk quickly around me. The cheerful decorations did not fade, the lights did not stop twinkling, and the Christmas music filling the mall wished us all a Merry Christmas.

Chapter 32
Beauty

DONNA AND I WALKED UP THE FLIGHT OF STEPS to the top level of this small shopping center in Charlotte. We had followed the precise directions given to us by one of the very efficient and helpful nurses at the cancer treatment center.

"I think I am at the point of needing something done about my hair," I heard Donna tell one of the infusionist.

I tried not to look surprised nor alarmed even though both emotions welled up swiftly and simultaneously within me. I wanted to step over and hug her tightly and assure her everything would be alright.

In calm and matter-of-fact tones, Donna told the nurse what had been happening. "Every morning, I notice more and more hair on my pillow. I think it is time for me to get a wig. Do you know of a wig store specializing in care of cancer patients?"

The nurse told us of several shops. She then recommended one of them above the rest.

"I really like the lady who runs this shop," the nurse said with a reassuring smile. "All the patients who go there speak very highly of her. I would try there first."

On the way, I mentioned how sorry I was for her hair loss and how unobservant I must have been not to have noticed the hair on her pillow.

"I cleaned it off every morning so you wouldn't notice," she said with a sweet smile. "I didn't want you to worry about me."

"Please don't worry about me," I said with a slight laugh. "We're in this together. But I'm glad you asked the nurse about it. It's good to take care of things as they arise."

The fantasy of normality continued. We both understood the simple reality of the enormous quantity of the unknown surrounding us. No level of striving to plan every reaction to this situation would make it any less surreal. We could only move from one moment to the next.

"We can handle anything together," I said as I reached for her hand and squeezed it tightly in mine.

As we entered the shop, I was surprised to find it rather dimly lit. Instead of bright and cheerful, it seemed very subdued. A few wigs tastefully displayed on shelves seemed to be the only reminder that this place was anything more than just someone's cozy parlor. Comfortable chairs and a couch done in light pastel floral fabrics made the interior inviting.

As soon as we entered, a tall lady in her fifties came from the back room and greeted us. Donna quickly explained why we were there and who had sent us.

"It's so good you are handling this before it gets to be a big problem for you," the lady stated with great kindness and concern. "It helps everything be less traumatic if you get a wig you love and feel good about wearing right now. What sort of wig are you interested in?"

"I've always kept my hair rather short," Donna said. "Of course, it's been gray for so long I'm not actually sure what the natural color would be."

Donna and the lady laughed.

"Mahogany," I stated with a smile. "It's always been mahogany."

The lady looked at me and winked a cheerful wink.

"Leave it to the man to know exactly what her hair looks like," she said in appreciative tones. "Short and mahogany," she continued. "I think I have exactly what you're looking for."

"Let's go to the next room to get started."

She led us through a curtain from the main room to another room. The coziness of the first room changed to the efficiency of the fitting room. A single white salon chair sat in the middle of the room facing a wall of well-lit mirrors.

The lady examined Donna's hair and ran her fingers through it as though getting ready to style it.

"The best thing to do at this point is to cut it all off," she said while examining it. "I know it's a little bit early, but it really is the best thing. It's falling out now, and every morning you are going to be reminded of how much more you are losing as the days go by. I suggest you just go ahead and make a clean sweep of it."

I realized how completely unprepared I was for this new development. I wanted to emphatically state that it was too early for something this drastic. I started to say Donna would have to think this over and we would come back next week or so with a decision. I opened my mouth to protest that she should have been forewarned that by coming here she would have to make this decision right at this moment.

I was simply not ready.

I knew Donna could handle it. Her strength and determination through all of this could be clearly seen. She continued with the great fortitude that God had always given her. It never failed her. I knew she would agree with the lady because it was the reasonable thing to do.

But I wasn't ready to be reasonable. Nor strong. I wasn't ready for this change. I would never be ready for what would inevitably come next.

Donna agreed without consulting me. I knew she could see me in the mirrors and even though she did not acknowledge my fragility at this moment, she understood.

She would always be strong for both of us.

"This won't take but a moment," the lady said as though getting ready to put cookies in the oven. "Then I'll get the wig that is just right for you. I think you'll be very pleased."

With great efficiency, the lady quickly shaved Donna's head. I watched and smiled at Donna from behind her in the mirror. I found myself looking at my smile to make sure the reflection of myself looked genuine enough.

Donna sat with great poise and held her head high and straight as she watched her natural hair disappear. I knew we both understood her hair would never reappear. This step was done. We would need to be prepared for the next step.

"There," the lady said with unbelievable cheerfulness. "It's done. Now hold on while I get your new hair."

I tried to look into the eyes of the lady as she glanced at me, but she quickly looked away. She probably had no indication of Donna's prognosis nor did she seem to want to know. Her job was to make this procedure as painless as possible. She did not need to see my face or look into my eyes to see that harsh reality was cruelly assaulting my wife. Her task was to make this transition as easy as possible. I knew she cared deeply and understood our pain. She was doing everything she could to help us with the inevitable. It was her gift to us.

Donna would not look at my reflection in the mirror as I stood behind her. She simply lowered her head. I could not tell if she was embarrassed or hurting. I knew she would have gladly looked at her shaved head in the mirror for an hour but she could not look at me for a moment.

"You have a remarkably beautiful head," I said softly.

She laughed quietly.

The lady came back holding the wig with both hands. She deftly pulled the wig over Donna's head and then stepped back.

In that moment of transformation, everything returned to normal. Her mahogany hair had been restored, but even more than that, in that second, something miraculous happened. For a moment, her beauty brought the past back in completeness. Everything was the same as it had been. Nothing had changed. No time had passed since the first time we had kissed. No events had taken place. No sickness. No cancer. No treatments. No prognosis. All was restored to blessedness.

Donna smiled.

"My goodness," the lady said looking at her creation, "I don't think I've ever had one look this good right from the start. It looks like it was made just for you. You've even brought out more of the mahogany tones I didn't see in that piece before. It's just right."

Donna looked at my reflection in the mirror and smiled.

"You're beautiful," I said.

I kept staring at her as she continued to smile at me. Her face glowed with the peace of accomplishment. She looked just as radiant as the first day I met her. She looked as ravishing as the moment I fell in love with her. No longer sick, no longer preparing for the next step in the process. All was as it had been. All was well. Her gift of beauty made everything seem alright.

That evening I sat in the loft as Donna bathed in the next room, I kept thinking about her beauty and wondered how she could keep her strength after all she had been through. I heard her get out of the shower and then begin to put on her gown. I nestled into the big wingback chair and propped my feet up on the ottoman waiting to see her once again.

She emerged from the bathroom and then came out onto the loft and smiled as she walked to me. She looked perfect as she moved gracefully across the room. Her long gown flowed around her legs and brushed across her bare feet. I held out my hands to her and she came and stood next to me.

I looked up to her face. Her beauty, intensified by her serenity, overwhelmed me. I put my arm around her waist and pulled her closer to me. She sat in the chair next to me and caressed the back of my neck in slow soothing motions.

"Look," she said softly.

She gently pulled up her gown and exposed her right thigh.

"The lump has gone away."

Chapter 33
Merry Christmas

"THE TREATMENTS APPEAR TO BE WORKING," the oncologist stated quietly. "We will continue to monitor, scan and study this situation, but for now you have finished this round of chemotherapy. We will see you again at the first of the year. Merry Christmas."

He stood and left the room without further explanation. Of course, no further explanation was necessary. I jumped to my feet and hugged Donna as we both began to cry.

"I can't believe this, I can't believe it," I said while trying not to shout with joy. "It's greater than anything I could have ever imagined! God gave you that lump so we would know about the healing. It's amazing!"

"Merry Christmas!" Donna said through her tears.

The unexpected Christmas miracle news spread quickly. All our prayer partners around the world were notified about the current need for prayers of gratitude and thanksgiving as well as those for continuing recovery.

I returned to work since the many events of the Advent season at the church needed my attention and since we knew we needed to celebrate with the church family. My sermons during this season always centered on the anticipation of hope, peace, joy, and love, but this year they emphasized the coming joy in a new and more intensely passionate way.

Every worship service during the season became an opportunity for all to see the goodness of the Lord.

As she continued to recover from the treatments, Donna could not attend all the festive parties and gatherings of the church and community. I participated in worship and the work of the church but then spent time with Donna enjoying a quiet Advent with her.

After our very first Christmas when it came time to pack away the ornaments, we realized how many decorative cookie tins had been given to us by friends. Donna made the suggestion that we should not discard the sturdy colorful tins but should use them to store our ornaments. Over the years, we collected an amazing assortment of ornament filled tins.

This year, Tyler unpacked the tins from the cardboard boxes in the attic and put them around the Christmas tree. While listening to our favorite Christmas album, we carefully opened one tin at a time and unwrapped each ornament from the white tissue paper protecting it. As each ornament was hung on the tree, we told its unique story. Every one brought to our minds

Morning

some particular thoughtful person or a place where we had visited or lived. We knew Tyler had heard of these people and places many times, but he accommodated our slow method of hanging the ornaments.

A very special blue tin held the last of the ornaments to be hung in the front center of the tree. Each year we would marvel as we opened that tin and very carefully removed the egg shell ornaments from our first Christmas together.

Even though they looked terribly fragile, they survived many moves and many extremely hot attics. Each year they looked as though we had just made them in the tiny kitchen of our prefab home in the dairy fields of Pendleton.

During our Christmas Eve candlelight communion service, before a full sanctuary of the worshipping faithful, I thanked God for the gift of salvation and redemption through the birth of Emmanuel. I paused and thanked God once again for the eternal hope given to us through faith.

As the congregation completed the liturgy and said amen in unison, I could unmistakably hear their voice of faith. I knew they understood our God always shepherds.

After the services were finished, I served Donna hot spiced tea in the loft using my grandmother's old and overly ornate silver service. It had become a holiday tradition for us to have this quiet time together to prepare for the rushed Christmas morning.

As I poured her tea, we did not discuss the past nor the future. Instead we delighted in being with one another. The joy of sitting with her as we anticipated Christmas morning, made the movement of life seem complete.

I held her hand and kissed it. I thanked her for all the ways she continually blessed me.

Smokey and Thelma joined us for our quiet Christmas day celebration the next morning. The day after Christmas, Thelma called me to come to the master bedroom.

"I'm having a hard time breathing," Donna said with a gasp as soon as I arrived. "I think you should call someone."

Without pausing to ask questions, I called our Hospice nurse.

"It will probably be a day or two before the needed equipment can be supplied," she said over the phone. "I'll keep you posted with whatever I can do in the meanwhile."

I then called one of our faithful church members who ran a medical supply business and made my urgent request.

Within minutes of my phone call, an oxygen tank was in place and Donna was breathing with ease. As she went to sleep, I began to try to make sense of what was happening.

"I wonder if this is just some sort of delayed reaction to the treatments she received," I whispered to Thelma as we watched Donna sleep. Neither one of us wanted to leave her bedroom.

As we developed theories from blood clots to allergies, no explanation seemed adequate for such a rapid change of events.

A few days after Christmas, at our scheduled appointment with the oncologist, scans were done. Once again we sat in the examining room waiting in great anticipation for the results.

"The treatments have failed," the doctor stated. He spoke with the same calmness as when he told us the treatments appeared to be working.

"I don't understand," I said interrupting what I was beginning to think was nonsense. I didn't want to hear about failure. We had secured hope in the face of all odds. She was being healed. All things were succeeding in joyous answer to many, many prayers.

The doctor looked at me and then slowly began to speak with great care.

"The treatments worked very well on the cancer of the epithelial cells," he said without sounding condescending. "But this cancer is a combination of two cancers. We now can tell the cancer in the lungs is not responding to the chemotherapy. It has grown and continues to spread."

For a moment, I was examining this place from a distance. I could hear each word as it was spoken and see each movement, but only as an objective observer. None of it made sense. It was as if I had entered the theater too late and now the final act had started. With all my points of reference gone, an extremely important event was taking place right in front of me, and I was powerless to comprehend. I looked at Donna as she wiped away a tear from her eyes.

"Thank you, doctor," she said in a normal fashion. "What do we do now?"

The doctor looked at me as if observing if I would be able to continue with this conversation.

"Well," he continued while looking at Donna, "the treatments are finished. There is no reason for you to take another round. Your only other option will be to receive radiation. I have arranged for you to see a radiologist in Rock Hill."

Once again, Donna thanked the doctor as I sat there motionless.

"I don't understand what just happened," I said in a weak voice as soon as the doctor left and shut the door.

All of a sudden, the play came to an end. All of a sudden, the curtain dropped and all was finished. All of a sudden, I figured out the final scene.

Morning

"How could everything change overnight?" I said in rage and disbelief. "He said the treatments appeared to be working! It was just a week or so ago. How could this be happening so quickly? I don't understand anything anymore!"

Realizing my voice was getting too loud, I stood up and hugged Donna. I wanted to be able to explain everything to her, to somehow make it all better. I didn't want her to give up hope just because the doctor had changed his mind about how things were working.

"I'm so sorry," I said through my tears. "After having your hopes built up so high, the unbelievable is happening. I don't understand, but we can get through this. I think it's all just some sort of terrible mistake."

Donna gently pushed me away. She looked up at my face and then looked deeply into my tearful eyes. Her clear green eyes examined my pain in careful detail.

"I knew," Donna said carefully while still holding her eyes in a steady unblinking lock with mine, "the cancer was not going away even when the doctor said the treatments appeared to be working. The lump had gone away, but," she paused as though to give me time to prepare for her next words, "I knew how I felt. My breathing was getting worse every day. I knew the cancer was growing and spreading in my lungs."

"Why didn't you tell the doctor, why didn't you tell me?" I said while choking down sobs.

"Because, Darling," she said as her eyes began to smile into mine, "I wanted you to have one last Merry Christmas…with me."

Chapter 34
Radiation

"THEY BROUGHT HER HERE IN AN AMBULANCE," Donna stated calmly.

We had just arrived at the radiologist's office in Rock Hill. The modern facility stood right next to the large county hospital. I did not realize we had parked near the ambulance entrance.

"Why would they need an ambulance entrance at a radiologist's office?" Donna stated as though out of normal curiosity.

We sat in our car and watched as the ambulance personnel continued to slowly and carefully wheel the stretcher up the ramp. Even from a distance, the frailty of the lady on the stretcher was evident.

"I can't believe she is still taking radiation when she is in such terrible shape," Donna said emphatically. "Why would anyone put her through that? It doesn't seem right."

Our wait for the doctor did not take long. Obviously very familiar with Donna's case, he came in and began to explain exactly what would take place. As soon as he was finished giving the general overview of the procedures, Donna began asking questions.

"Will the radiation be severe enough to cause burns on my skin?" she asked in a tone implying she already knew the answer.

I waited for him to assure her that modern radiation never produced such burns.

"In order for this radiation to be effective," he said, "the radiation will cause some burns on your skin."

"Where and how much burning?" she asked as though trying to negotiate a deal.

The doctor looked mildly uncomfortable. "The burning on your skin will cover most of one side of your body. Since we have to make sure the lung and liver are treated, it will involve burning of the skin on one side from your shoulder to at least your waist."

"What other side effects can I expect from the radiation?" Donna continued without hesitation.

"You will notice a decrease in your energy level. You will have difficulty walking around and will probably have to remain in bed most of the time."

"I already have decreased energy now," Donna said negotiating to remove this point from the bargaining table.

Morning

"It will be worse," the doctor said as though refusing to bargain on this point.

"In your estimation," Donna continued without showing any reluctance or fear, "how much will this add to my life expectancy by undergoing radiation therapy?"

"We will probably be able to add one month to your life," the doctor stated with finality.

End of bargaining.

"What do we do next to get all of this started?" I said in a somewhat cheerful tone. "When can we expect to begin the treatments?"

The doctor turned to me obviously pleased the bargaining had led to my decision to proceed under his terms.

"Thank you, Doctor," Donna said as she held out her hand to shake his hand. "I'll have to pray about this decision and get back to you."

Now the bargaining was really finished.

Donna bowed her head when we got back in the car. I knew she was praying for guidance and, perhaps, for the right way to break the bad news to me.

Once her prayer was finished, she looked at me.

"I'm not going to spend the few weeks I have left completely burnt on one side of my body and confined to bed," she said without emotion. "It's not worth it."

My friend, Sunil, came to the house later that evening. Donna had already gone to bed. We sat in the living room so I could hear from the loft door above if she called for me.

"She made the right decision, Dan," Sunil said with confidence. "There is no good reason for her to go through radiation. It's simply not worth it."

"I know you are right, and I know she is right," I stated through my tears. "But I'm not ready to accept the idea…I'm not ready to say we have done everything possible. It can't be over yet."

Chapter 35
Hospice

I STARED INTO THE OPEN KITCHEN CABINET next to the refrigerator. Following the instructions of Debbie, our very capable and kind Hospice nurse from Mint Hill, I had emptied this one cabinet and then stocked it with every medicine and supply necessary for Donna's palliative care.

"Do you see it?"

It was two o'clock in the morning. Donna had awakened feeling some discomfort. We both had been instructed about the medicines to be given in this situation. All I had to do was go downstairs and retrieve the medicine and give it to her.

I had offered to keep the medicines in our bathroom cabinets upstairs.

"The Red Box needs to be in your refrigerator," Debbie stated with her usual care. "If we need the medicines in the Red Box, everyone must know exactly where it is."

I knew the Red Box contained stronger medicines to be used only under the specific instructions of the Hospice nurse. I also knew the time had not yet come for them to be used.

"Since the Red Box is in your refrigerator," Debbie had continued, "I find it is best to have all of the medicine near the refrigerator. It saves on confusion."

Debbie came on Monday, Wednesday, and Friday of each week. She spent at least an hour with Donna and me checking on everything. I knew she would stay as long as necessary and wanted not only to make sure Donna did not suffer but also to see how I was coping.

On Tuesday and Thursday, a delivery truck would arrive with the new prescriptions for that week. The system worked like clockwork. Debbie would make sure the old prescriptions were discarded and the new ones were ready. She always checked the cabinet next to the refrigerator.

"I know the medicine should be in here," I tried to remain calm, "but it isn't. I remember seeing it. I remember Debbie checking it. But it isn't here."

The Hospice nurse on the phone spoke to me as if discussing the beauty of roses. In a peaceful voice she reassured me.

"It's perfectly OK," she said. "We can handle this situation. Everything will be OK."

I tried to steady myself as I realized I had to make sure Donna didn't suffer.

Morning

"I will dispatch someone to come to your home immediately," she said as though it was already accomplished. "There will be a delay in the courier arriving at your home since we are about forty-five minutes away, but I'm going to contact our doctor to see if one of the other medicines you have can be used as a substitute in this case."

I wonder if she will have me open the Red Box? I thought. *I'm not ready to do that, but it doesn't matter. Donna is suffering.*

I had already questioned Debbie about the heavy use of medications.

"I worry about her taking so much medicine," I told her after I walked her out onto the front stoop. "In the past, medicines have had strong effects on her. I don't know if she can handle all these drugs."

Debbie smiled at me and then looked me squarely in the eyes. Using a pastoral tone of voice, she eliminated this concern.

"Remember Dan," she said with a kind but saddened smile, "the medicines are not killing her. The cancer is."

Suddenly I saw the bottle of pills in the cabinet on the shelf eye level with me. In my panic, I literally failed to see what was right before my eyes.

"I'm terribly sorry to have bothered you in the middle of the night," I said quickly to the Hospice nurse on the phone, "but I just found the medicine. It is right here. I've been staring at it the whole time. I don't know how I didn't see it."

"Oh marvelous," the nurse almost shouted over the phone. "That's wonderful!"

Even though she had done a very good job of remaining calm and giving me reassurance, she was actually very alarmed.

"I must have been more panicked than I thought," I said with embarrassment. "I'm sorry to have bothered you."

"No bother at all," she said with sincerity, "that's what we're here for."

Hospice exceeded my expectations in everything. The doctors, nurses, social workers, and chaplains who came to visit all appeared to have been called into this profession. Since Donna could take care of herself, many of their services were not necessary in our case. But everything was offered.

"I do have one question," Donna asked as we were trying to get everything organized on the day of Debbie's first visit with us. "Our bedroom is large and has the wonderful loft attached, but it's upstairs. I know it would be much more convenient for everyone if I moved to one of the bedrooms downstairs. What do you think?"

Donna always worried about being any sort of inconvenience to others so her concern did not come as a shock to me. While I waited for Debbie's response, I immediately began to plan the move.

"If you really like this bedroom," Debbie said with her combination of extreme kindness and professionalism, "then you should stay here. But whatever you decide to do, just pick a place you like very much because you will be spending a lot of time there."

Reminders of the stark reality of the situation always took me off guard. I wondered if I continued to refuse to face the truth. I also wondered how Donna took the wise statement. Did it catch her off guard?

"Well," Donna said cheerfully, "that only makes sense, and it makes the decision easy. I love this room with the large windows overlooking the front of the house and the fireplace and the loft. I'll just stay here."

She smiled and looked at me.

"I hope everyone doesn't mind running up and down the stairs!" she said with a laugh.

"I do have one other thing to go over with you," Debbie said.

The initial visit had gone very well, and I had been able, somehow, to not feel overwhelmed. Something in the tone of Debbie's voice made me think her next task might not be so painless.

"As a part of Hospice care," she said, "we need both of you to understand that a DNR is not just a good idea, it is necessary."

DNR. Do Not Resuscitate. Plain and simple. Rubber hitting the road. Cancer wins. Death is the only outcome. No other options are available. All other choices are unwise. All other paths lead to continued and unnecessary suffering. Pain is to be avoided.

I stopped the screaming in my head. I shut down the flood of emotions.

This is necessary, I told myself.

"Of course," Donna said with a weak smile. "I completely understand. That's a good idea."

Debbie turned to me as if seeking my approval, my permission. I knew she did not need my consent, but at the same time I realized that without my cooperation, things could get complicated.

I nodded in agreement without saying anything. Words could bring tears. Tears would not help. Emotions are not wanted at this time.

"We need to post the DNR right above the bed," Debbie said.

Her tone had changed. She now sounded sad. She now sounded real. She understood what the posting meant.

Constant reminder. Marked person. Marked and posted as one who is near death.

Morning

"Just in case someone else other than Dan is present," Debbie said softly, "we need to make sure if emergency personnel are called, they will understand. A DNR is for your protection."

"Of course," Donna said. "That's also a good idea. Very practical, just in case."

I watched in horror as Debbie took the completed form and posted it on the wall right above Donna's head. The yellow form looked officially unkind. I wanted to walk over to the wall and punch a hole through the sheetrock and send the form to perdition.

I sat and smiled as though wondering if the tape would leave a mark on the paint.

Chapter 36

Prayers

OLIVIA KNELT TO PRAY.

"Get ready, Heaven. She's on her way!"

When I found out about Olivia's prayer, I wanted to discuss it with her. I wanted to discover her reasoning and her understanding of what was happening. I wanted to know why heaven should prepare itself for Donna. I needed to know why the prayer was for the readiness of heaven instead of for healing. I needed to comprehend her thoughts.

I wanted to sit at Olivia's feet and be nourished by her strength of faith and her incredible grasp of the divine.

She impressed me the very first time I met her. Listening to her comments on my sermons and how she took my ideas and caused them to blossom much further than I had seen amazed me. She saw things more completely than I did, almost as though she understood the eternal through experience.

When I heard of her prayer, I knew it had been an assurance of the goodness of God, of Donna gaining everlasting life through Christ, and a statement of peace for me. I wanted to cry with her and confess my doubts and my fears and hear the message of the ages from her wise lips. I knew she understood more than I could ever imagine.

But I knew I would have to speak with Olivia's parents first since she was only nine years old.

Donna sat on a small chair in front of the large double windows of our bedroom. I raised the windows and the storm windows so she could be clearly seen. I knew she would have preferred to have gone downstairs and stand at the front door, but she was no longer able.

I had helped her dress in a navy-blue robe with her beautiful wig. She always looked best in dark colors. She sat there and smiled; I stood beside her and silently cried.

Below us on the stoop and the walkway, church members had gathered this evening. Each one held a lit candle. In unison they prayed a litany requesting God's healing. Together they prayed for the blessed presence of our Lord to be seen and felt. As they lifted their candles high, they praised God for being the Shepherd of us all.

Morning

Donna waved to them as they called out how much they loved her and how she would be continually in their prayers. They did not tarry. I knew they could tell how tired Donna appeared. I helped her out of the robe and back into the bed. She immediately fell asleep before I could even close the windows.

"Get ready, Heaven. She's on her way!"

Anointing oil had been placed upon Donna by the faithful with many prayers. Prayer services and vigils had been held. Prayer requests had been sent to every continent. Missionaries we would never meet were keeping Donna's need for healing before the Lord.

At night, I would sleep in the bed next to her as I had always done. I would not sleep until I knew she was fast asleep. Then I would begin my nightly routine. With as little movement as possible so as not to disturb her, I would lay my hands upon her in prayer. Starting at her shoulder and then moving over her body, I would touch her as I prayed for healing. I prayed God would send healing to her through the laying on of my hands. I would pray in faith for my earnest request to be heard and for complete healing to take place. I would pray that through the power of the Holy Spirit a miracle would occur so glory could be given to God.

I would also pray that God's will was accomplished. Not mine.

"Get ready, Heaven. She's on her way!"

A church member stopped for a visit and insisted I should go on a drive.

"You need to get out of this house," she said in a mock scolding tone. "All you do is just sit by her bed all day long. You know that's not good for you. Now go out and enjoy a nice ride or go get a cup of coffee or something. I'll make sure everything is alright. Stay out there as long as you like. Go!"

I knew her advice was sound, so I got in my car and drove in the direction of the country. I thought I wanted to get out of town to the pastures which would remind me of our farm. As I pulled out of the driveway, I immediately regretted leaving.

Just keep driving, I told myself. *You need a break. This will be good for you.*

I drove up the street and made a right turn away from town. My heart began to break.

I must be by her side, I thought. *It's not an obligation. It's not a job. It's not tiring. I'm not exhausted. I need to be with her, while she is still here!*

I continued to drive hoping the pleasant March day would make me feel refreshed. As I made a turn, I instinctively reached my hand across the seat for her hand. As soon as I did, I began to cry.

This is what it is going to be like very soon, I thought. *I'm going to be alone. She is not going to be with me. How can I face this? I don't want to live without her. I want my life back, and I want my life to be with her!*

I turned the car around and sped back up the country road trying to get to her side as quickly as possible. Wiping away more tears, I tried to calm myself so I could continue to drive. As I entered into town and turned onto a four-lane road. I was driving on the wrong side of the road.

Car horns began to blow at me in frustration and tires could be heard screeching. I drove over a concrete median and almost hit another car coming up the road on the other side. Embarrassed and angry with myself, I arrived home. When I finally got back into the garage, I said a prayer of thanks that in my sorrow, I did not harm anyone else.

"Lord, I can't live without her," I cried in conclusion to my prayer. "Please don't take her away from me."

"Get ready, Heaven. She's on her way!"

I walked Debbie back down the steps and out onto the front stoop.
"She's not quite our Donna anymore," Debbie said with a sad smile.
"I don't understand," I said in complete honesty.
Normally our little meeting on the front stoop consisted of helping me to feel confidence in what I was doing. Rarely did anything need to be drastically changed or done differently, but Debbie knew I needed a thrice-a-week encouragement from a professional. Now she was bringing up something different. Something I didn't understand.
"You haven't noticed?"
"Noticed what?"
I thought back to Donna's appearance. She continued to remain the same weight. She did not look pale. She showed her strength in her smile.
"Maybe it's because you are with her all the time," Debbie said in a gentle tone, "but I can see she's changing."
"What do you mean?" I asked. I actually wanted to shout, "Please don't tell me anything more. I don't know how to respond to anything else. I'm going to completely stop living when she dies."
Before Debbie said another word, I realized the fear lurking in the background and now springing forth.

Morning

I'm not going to be able to handle her death. I will simply cease to function, I thought. *I will not just grieve, I'll lose every ability I ever had. I will become so filled with grief my mind will refuse to accept the reality. I will not be able to cope.*

"Well," Debbie said cautiously, "I hate to tell you, but in my opinion, the cancer has now spread to her brain."

"I hope it does not spread to my brain," I heard Donna say not too long ago. "I've heard of that before, and I think it would be the saddest thing in the world. I can take anything except losing my ability to think."

"Are you sure?" I asked as tears began to flow. "How do you know?"

"We won't know for sure," Debbie continued. "The only way to know for sure would be to do a scan, and we're not going to do that. But, all the same, I've seen this many times. I would say it has spread to her brain from my interaction with her today. It's definitely a marked change from the last time I saw her. You're probably too close and too involved to notice those changes. But it's okay. This is normal. Please don't be too upset."

Debbie left. I closed the front door and started up the steps to once again be at Donna's side. I stopped climbing and held on to the railing.

She's already leaving me, I thought as I began to sob. *I'm walking up the steps to a Donna who is not completely still there. She has changed and will never be the same. It's all happening too fast. Please, God, please help her. Please, God, please help me.*

"Get ready, Heaven. She's on her way!"

Chapter 37
Ides of March

MORNING CAME LIKE ANY OTHER MORNING. I opened my eyes and looked out the windows at the beautiful March day that beckoned me to enjoy.

Beware the Ides of March.

I knew exactly why I thought those words.

I turned to look at Donna and gently placed my hand on her chest to make sure she was still breathing. Her heartbeat felt regular through the palm of my hand and her breathing continued.

In a few hours, Debbie arrived.

"I'm here for the duration," she said, "I don't think it will be long."

We gathered a few extra chairs for the bedroom and held a daylight vigil. Debbie now felt like family. She even told Donna that she thought of her as a sister.

"A blessed sister," I told her in response. "I don't know what we would do without you."

Her presence on this beautiful spring day meant everything to us.

I sat on the bed next to Donna and kept my hand in hers. Tyler sat on the bed next to me. Smokey, Thelma and Vernon sat in chairs around the room. Debbie sat in the window seat next to the bed.

Donna's condition did not change for most of the day. She simply slept as though at any moment she would awaken and start asking why we were all in the bedroom with her. Just the day before, she took a shower without assistance. I continued to marvel at how easy she seemed to be making this process work. I knew she would have it no other way.

At six o'clock, Debbie reluctantly stated she had to leave.

I walked her to the door.

"I don't know if you normally attend funerals," I said to her as she was starting down the steps, "but I would like for you to attend. I would even like it if you would sit with the family. You have helped us so much during this ordeal. I know Donna would want me to let you know how much she and I appreciate all you have done."

I returned to my place by her side. Ladies from the church had been bringing meals to us for many weeks. The food arrived this evening as usual. Life seemed to be continuing as usual as I waited for the impossible to happen.

Morning

"The day after Jack died," my Aunt Pat had told me years ago referring to her late husband, "I went up to his store to get some things. I stood outside the store as cars continued to drive by on the road. I wanted to scream at them and tell them they must stop. Everything had to stop…because Jack died. But nothing stopped. Everything kept going as if nothing had happened."

I knew people were continuing in their regular routine even if I couldn't understand.

As eight o'clock neared, I sensed a change in Donna's breathing. It was subtle. Perhaps a little less often. Definitely a little more shallow. She did not change her expression. She did not struggle.

"I love you," I said leaning down close to her. "I will always love you. It's OK to leave. I'll take care of Tyler. You have nothing to fear."

As I leaned up, I looked at her face. The beauty I beheld amazed me.

The azure moon was shining on her once again. I could hear the gondolier from many years past telling her to look into the reflection of the lantern on the waters of the river to see her future.

"Your face is full of wonder once again," I whispered to her. "Now I know what it means. I know Who you see."

At a little past eight o'clock she breathed her last.

Chapter 38
Underwater

AS CHILDREN, WE EAGERLY ANTICIPATED OUR twelfth birthdays when we would be considered young adults. During those years, we often swam in the cold mountain waters of Table Rock Lake to escape the summer heat. After an afternoon of splashing and swimming, we would begin to play more risky games.

One of our favorite ones involved seeing how long each one of us could stay on the bottom of the lake in the deeper waters near a wooden platform positioned out from the swimming area. I quickly learned from the mutual experiences of my brothers and cousins that the best way to sink to the bottom included not only diving and swimming to the lake bed but also to expel all the air from our lungs.

Even though we thought of this game as harmless fun, a big part of the attraction of this activity involved the thrill of realizing the rather great difficulty involved in getting back to the surface.

Sometimes I would do practice runs while the others were playing.

I would start by getting as much air in my lungs as possible and then quickly jumping from the platform feet first. Once the initial decent took place, I would try to make my body as sleek as possible with legs tight together and arms held close at my sides. Just when my descent seemed to be slowing to nothing, the exhaling would begin.

With every muscle in my chest, I would force the breath out of my lungs. Surprisingly, the air would make wonderful bursts of bubbles which frantically rushed to the surface as if in a great hurry to join the air of the skies above.

With the release of the life-giving air from my lungs, I would again be descending. Eventually, I would push the palms of my hands in upward motions to complete the final few feet until my feet hit the bottom.

At those times, in the cold murky darkness, I would realize that no one actually knew where I was. As my feet would slowly sink into the soft brown mud, I would wonder if they might become so mired in the lake bottom as to be trapped. I would open my eyes trying to see through the dark waters only to find very little visibility. Looking up to the surface, I could see some shimmering of light and hear distorted sounds resembling voices.

I knew the object of the game was to simply stay down there with my feet in the mud in the darkness until I felt I could not hold my breath any longer.

Morning

The great risk involved the fact that I never knew exactly how long to stay down there. I also did not know how long it would take me to swim to the surface.

We were never scientific in playing the game. We would jump from any side of the platform without considering that the depths of the lake changed with every few feet. We also never thought of counting off the seconds so as to have any indication of the passage of time.

Instead of taking any safeguards, we would foolishly play the game thinking we could always make it to the surface before it was too late.

The exertion and the anticipation of the first glorious gulp of air when my head burst through the waters to the bright summer day would make my lungs scream more and more.

Once my lungs were screaming for air and my head was starting to feel dizzy, I would kick off the muddy bottom and start my frantic race to the surface.

Just then, a quiet panic would begin.

What if I can't make it to the top? I would ask myself. *What if my arms and legs stop working due to lack of oxygen? What if I have misjudged the depth of the dive and there's no way to reach the surface?*

To intensify the panic, I would then realize the great stupidity of undertaking this dangerous act without letting someone know what was happening.

At the very second when I thought I could not endure the pain, fear, and panic of never reaching the air again, I would break through the grasp of the water and see the sunshine and breathe.

Watching as Donna took her last breath, I finally understood what it meant to be forever trapped in the dark waters. Even though in my childhood I had always reached the surface, this time the reality was different.

Just like my beloved Donna, I would never truly breathe again.

Chapter 39
Watching

THE MORNING AFTER THE FUNERAL I STOOD at the large window in the dining room of the Homeplace. I remembered seeing my grandfather's casket against the dining room wall and the room filled with people. I remember standing here and watching the sunrise over the tall trees on the other side of the road the morning after Dad died and the morning after Mom died. I remembered the golden light of dawn flooding through this window and into the entire house giving me hope.

Now I stood alone at the same window watching for the dawn.

My family had gathered at the Homeplace after the funeral and the interment. My cousin, Leanna, prepared a meal and we shared it in the same house where as children we celebrated every holiday. Slowly the friends and family left as the night grew darker. My brothers offered to stay with me, but I insisted they leave. After everyone left, Tyler said he would be going back to Lancaster.

I knew the Homeplace held too many memories of Donna for him. It held too many memories for me as well, but it was the place I needed to be right then.

It saddened me to think the Homeplace was now a point of pain for Tyler. His room at this house still held some of his childhood toys. I had planned for this home to be his anchor in the midst of pastoral itinerancy, but now he had to abandon it.

I was alone. I went to bed but did not sleep. After hours of trying to rest, I awoke and stood at the window waiting for the morning.

Joy comes with the morning, I thought to myself.

I had requested Psalm 30 to be read at her funeral and used the text in the material I wrote about her for the service.

"Donna always felt the morning was the best time of the day," I wrote. "She told me one reason she enjoyed teaching so much was because she had to leave so early in the morning, she got to see the sunrise on her way to work."

"There's nothing like a sunrise," she told me. "It tells of the wonder of God and reminds us God is there each and every day."

An artist from Lancaster, Betty Hodges, called me one day and offered to paint a picture for Donna.

Morning

"Ask her what sort of picture she would like," Betty requested. "What should the subject matter be?"

I went to Donna and asked, and she immediately answered, "Ask her to paint a sunrise."

Now I waited alone for the sunrise. I wanted to see it. I knew I would never again fully experience the promise of a day filled with joy. I simply wanted to see the golden light and know this dark night had passed.

"More than those who watch for the morning," the Psalmist wrote.

I wondered what it must have felt like to be watching from the gate towers of a city in Biblical times. What must it have been like to have known the enemy could be approaching at any second during the night to kill and destroy? The only hope would be for morning to arrive.

"More than those who watch for the morning."

I now stood watch. The funeral, the mass of people, the faithful friends, the shared hugs and tears, everything seemed to be like a murky haze. I could barely sort out the details.

Even as I tried to remember, I knew we had worshipped God and celebrated Donna's life and her passion for helping others

As I stood at the window, I thought back to the many days in my childhood when I would go with my mother and grandmother to the cemetery at Ebenezer Church. We would check on the family plots and make sure any stray grass growing on the inside of the marble coping was removed.

On the day of the funeral, I drove myself from Lancaster to Ebenezer Cemetery. As I drove into the graveyard and then to the grave, I was touched at how many people had gathered for the burial. In the family plot alongside my parents, grandparents, great-grandparents, and my sister-in-law, Donna was buried. I also knew my place waited next to hers.

"This hillside has an amazing view of the mountains," a fellow pastor noted after the burial. "Table Rock is so visible from here."

I turned away from the plots of my loved ones and looked to the East. There in the distance, the Blue Ridge Mountains shone in all their glory.

"I never realized that before," I told him. "I guess every time I've been here, I was only looking down."

The women and men of Ebenezer claimed parts of my life. With every burial, I felt like a fragment of me was lost into the grave.

Now the shattering was complete. I would never again hear that sound as I did in the lighthouse on Amelia Island. I did not have to hear the clay pot breaking into pieces because the shattering had become real. I didn't just hear the sound, I was hopelessly broken. Donna unwillingly took all my shattered pieces with her to the grave.

I could never be whole again.

The dawn would not come. My watch for the morning would now have to cease since I felt a strong desire to leave and be in Lancaster with Tyler.

I walked away from the window where I had seen the golden light of dawn in past days of mourning.

As I ended my watch, I could see only darkness.

Chapter 40

Labyrinth

SHE STOOD BESIDE THE LARGEST TREES at the edge of the fields. Dressed in a simple white shirt and pants, she appeared pure against the varieties of colors of the pastures, the small lake and the woods.

This friend, this companion in Christ, had prepared a prayer labyrinth in the forest. Painstakingly she had removed white rocks from the pastures and used them to outline the classic patterns of the maze. Bleached by years in the sun and washed by country rains, the white rocks formed a perfect border for the paths leading one to a closer understanding of our relationship with God.

Each rock was roughly the size of a large round loaf of bread. Resting in the smooth brown soil, each one looked ready to be baked, broken, and given for the good of others.

Nancy had invited me to come and walk the labyrinth.

"I would really like to do that," I said hesitantly. "But I think I need to do it alone."

She nodded in agreement. A strong woman and faithful disciple of Christ, she did not need to seek a lot of explanation from others. She tended to accept and understand each person's limitations.

I knew she understood the experience of the labyrinth would be very difficult for me. Even though I knew it had the potential of healing, I expected pain as a part of the journey.

A spiritual walk through an ancient pattern of white quartz field stones in an old forest seemed like the perfect place to bolster my abilities to cope.

"You go at your own pace," she said in a quiet but firm voice. "As you go through the paths of the maze toward the center, you focus on all of the things you need to let go. At the center, you focus on where you have been. You also focus everything on God. As you begin your journey from the center back out of the maze, you focus on what God is giving you."

Without further elaboration, she left my side and walked to the edge of the forest. I saw her slowly bow her head in prayer. My sentinel stood ready to defend me from the distractions and the turmoil of the present. She stood in quietness as though prepared to do whatever was necessary to make sure I would have the opportunity to be on my journey of spiritual exploration and awakening.

My sentinel stood and guarded my time of solitary healing.

As I began the journey, I noticed the beauty of the forest and the quietness of the surrounding countryside. All I could hear was the soft movement of my feet.

What do I need to relinquish? I asked myself. *What is holding me back from the potential of healing?*

I thought about the demands of my day, my work, and the normal activities distracting us from growing closer to God. One by one, I prayerfully gave them to God. Finding relief in the removal of those things occupying so much of my daily energy, I felt the journey becoming more fulfilling.

Then as I turned the first curve of the pattern and started on the second path which drew me near the center, I began to think of the ways I distanced myself from God. Asking for forgiveness and pardon for my acts of selfishness and sin, I began to realize the lightness of mercy and grace upon me.

What a wonderful way to seek forgiveness and focus on repentance, I thought. *By walking the path, I physically distance myself from my prison. I can sense through my movement the joy of moving beyond my mistakes and becoming closer to God.*

As I took the third corner and began this new path, I thought I would continue to seek and find aspects of my life desperately needing to be placed in proper perspective. I eagerly took the next steps and turned the corner and faced a new and untraveled path deeper into the circling maze.

I took one step on this new path and then stopped. My spiritual renewal and the potential of awakening a closer walk with God came abruptly to an end. I saw clearly the road and avenues awaiting me not just through the labyrinth but also through all of the days of my remaining time on earth.

Every step brought me closer to my grief. My relationship with God and my journey as a pilgrim would never take place without the constant presence of pain. I began to cry. Sorrow surrounded me. I cried in the knowledge this suffering would never come to an end. The anguish of missing Donna and the fact I would never again walk this path of discipleship with her crushed me.

I found myself in the center of the enclosing circles. Looking around, I began to wonder how I could find my way back out to the comfort of the forest. I sought my gentle sentinel and saw her looking at me in shared sorrow for my plight.

I stepped over the beautiful white stones and violated the direction of the paths to seek release from this bitterly cold reminder of my misery.

The sentinel sat on the edge of the forest overlooking the small lake. Evening approached as I sat next to her. I knew she would not seek any

Morning

explanation for my actions. She smiled at me as though to say she understood.

I returned to my empty home and slept for a few dark hours in my empty bed.

Chapter 41
Hardest Things

"START WITH THE HARDEST THINGS FIRST. Then every day will get easier."

The lady smiled at me as if she knew I needed to hear a bit of advice. She took another bite of birthday cake. This small gathering of people from around the state took place in the fellowship hall of the church. Somehow, I had started speaking to this well-dressed and very friendly older lady from Fripp Island. I thought we had nothing in common except our mutual friendship and admiration for the person being honored at the party. As it turned out, we shared some of the same life experiences.

The lady had become a widow just a year prior. She brought it up casually at first and then in a much more compassionate manner when I mentioned my wife's recent death. I knew where the conversation would lead and became momentarily uneasy fearing this encounter might bring out my tears which were always near. I decided to guide the conversation quickly away from me.

"That's great advice," I said with a genuine smile. "I wish someone had mentioned it to me a few months ago. It really makes sense."

"I followed it to the best of my abilities," the lady continued, "because I knew the man who was telling me understood exactly what he was saying. He lost his wife several years before and wanted to help me with the process."

"I have things I have been avoiding because I felt they would be too painful." I stopped talking realizing almost too late the conversation centered on my grief. I felt my eyes beginning to water and tried to think of something else.

"I understand," the lady said in a calm and soothing tone.

She looked across the room as though she realized our conversation needed to take another turn. Even though she was not the hostess of the party, I could tell she knew through many years of experience how to keep everyone at ease and happy in a social setting.

Turning back to me, she smiled. "You'll have to try it with some of the things still unfinished. I think you will find it to be very satisfying."

With a pat on my arm, she turned to talk to someone else as though genuinely remorseful she had brought up a painful matter.

That night as I readied myself for bed I thought about the different points of advice others had given me. Aunt Pat told me a story of a widow who decided to sleep on her husband's side of the bed.

Morning

"She said it worked for her," Aunt Pat stated as she tried to give me advice, "because if she woke up in the middle of the night she wouldn't be looking at his empty place in the bed. It made it easier for her to see her place empty rather than his."

I followed Aunt Pat's advice. In the process of changing to Donna's side of the bed, I slept in the exact spot where she died.

I could have moved to one of the other bedrooms, but somehow I felt closer to Donna by remaining in our bedroom. Since her death, my sleep consisted of around three hours per night. After the first few weeks, I thought I might go insane with such little sleep, but over time I got used to long nights filled with sleeplessness. I knew I could have gone to my doctor for some safe medicine to help, but somehow the long nights filled with nothing fit the condition of my life.

I also made an odd decision. Donna had selected a white cotton duvet for our bed when we moved to this parsonage. We didn't use regular sheets since the duvet cover could be easily removed and laundered.

After her death, I couldn't bring myself to launder the duvet cover. It was not in need of laundering, but I knew most people would have either changed it or at least washed it. I found great comfort in sleeping in the very spot where she had breathed her last underneath the same duvet. Death had touched her there as the hand of God gently took her home.

I couldn't imagine the day when I would stop this sleeping arrangement. For now, it brought me a strange sort of comfort.

The next morning, after my customary three hours of sleep, I awoke with a purpose. After borrowing my son's pickup truck, I stopped by the store and purchased several boxes of large black garbage bags. Returning home, I went to the dressing room in the master bedroom and opened all the closets.

The room had four large closets. When we moved into the house, I told Donna she could have three since I would only need one. Even though Donna never obsessed about her clothes, she accumulated many outfits. I knew she had more than she needed. I also knew this accumulation was completely my fault.

Early in our marriage, Donna told me she hated to buy clothes for herself. With time I learned she preferred to spend money on other people.

Since she would not buy clothes for herself until it became a complete necessity, I began to buy her a few items of clothing from time to time. I quickly acquired the knack of selecting clothes for her. The more I mastered it, the more I enjoyed watching her receive my gifts of clothing. Donna looked best in bold colors. She did not like low necklines nor elastic waists. She needed something slightly fitted to show off her figure, but nothing tight.

She preferred skirts and blouses to dresses. A jacketed suit pleased her since she tended to be cold even in the summer.

Whenever I went through a department store, I would wander over to the women's section. At first I found this uncomfortable until I realized my kind of shopping could be done quickly. I would walk through the aisles looking at the clothes on the mannequins and immediately spot an outfit for her. Most of the time I would buy it on the spot to surprise her. She rarely had to return it.

I tended to buy her too many clothes. She protested but never complained.

The three full closets represented years of accumulation. Donna tended to keep all of her clothes since she never changed size.

In opening the closets, I realized each outfit brought back memories of a different time in her life. I looked through one section and then another and became amazed at how she had even kept some classic outfits from her college days.

I closed the doors.

A tear ran down my face, and I began to calculate a plan to have Tyler come over to the house and empty all the closets. I knew he would not be comfortable with such an undertaking, but feared I could never handle this task.

I think I will just leave all of it right where it is, I thought. *It's not bothering a thing. I don't need the extra closet space, and those items have too many memories associated with them. I'll just leave them right where they are.*

I started to close the doors.

"Those clothes can be used by other people who need them. There's no reason for them to hang in closets until they are useless. Help other people."

I could almost hear Donna admonishing me for waiting this long to use her clothes to benefit those in need. I knew she would not want me to keep the clothes. I opened the closet doors and began to carefully fold each outfit and place it gently in a bag. As if he knew I would need emotional support with this process, Tyler showed up and offered to help.

We continued until all of Donna's clothes were carefully bagged. After several trips to the donation center, the attendant asked me to stop bringing any more clothes until the next day.

"I can't stop now," I told Tyler as we drove back home. "This whole ordeal has to be completed today. Surely they won't mind one more load. Tomorrow will be easier because today we have completed a very hard task. It has to be finished now."

Morning

Without asking permission, I returned with the pickup truck filled with black bags of clothing. The attendant looked at me and smiled; she understood. She thanked us for the donations, and I assured her we were now finished.

We returned home and I looked through the attic and all the closets to make sure the job was indeed finished. I then went to a cabinet in the dressing room and removed an unused wig we had purchased. Sealing it carefully in a small box, I addressed it to the Red Cross.

I went to the loft and sat in one of the most comfortable chairs while Tyler sat on the small couch. Before he could begin to speak, I burst into tears. Much to his astonishment, my tears became sobs and then shouts of anguish.

"It's OK, Dad," Tyler kept saying as I continued to cry. "It's OK. Everything is going to be alright."

Slowly I stopped the crying and brought myself back together. I knew my grieving would have to be delayed for this evening since I had a wedding rehearsal to attend in a few hours followed by a wedding the next day.

"The wedding is in Columbia," I told Tyler after composing myself. "I think it will be beautiful."

Chapter 42
White Rose Petals

CANDLELIGHT UNVEILED HER FACE AS THE BRIDE stepped through the large, rounded mahogany doors of the sanctuary. As she moved through the soft glow, admiring gazes greeted her. At this one moment, everyone in attendance welcomed blessed certainty. The anticipation of years of planning and painstaking preparation crystallized in joyful clarity and reflected in harmony with the warmth of the groom's expression. With eyes locked on hers, he radiated the assurance that her steps down this aisle were taken not only in hope but also in complete acceptance found in the perfection of total love. Enshrined forever in this holy place, love everlasting created a new beginning.

The massive pipe organ echoed heaven's orchestration as though the unseen infinite became heard in this celebration of the very essence of the divine. Each slow and deliberate step of the bride reminded us we must approach and claim life and happiness. Her movements became not just the wedding dance but the dance of life. Her gentle smile glowed more strongly than the intense beauty of the candlelight filtering through the perfect artistry of floral creations within the room. Each petal of each carefully selected flower served to somehow enhance her radiance.

Anticipation of love fulfilled through the vows of a wedding completed the glory of this evening. After many years of shepherding flocks around the state, I joined with another old clergy friend as we prepared to officiate this passage to forever change the lives of this man and this woman. Together we would mark this time and place in the continuum of life. We would build a column of stones in the fast-flowing waters and say, even though things change more rapidly than imaginable, this point would indeed be noted and remembered. In the name of church and state, we would speak words of ancient liturgy in this sacred space which barely escaped destruction during the Civil War.

On our prearranged musical cue, my clergy friend and I entered the sanctuary from a side door to the chancel and slowly made our way to the altar area. Years of experience taught me the importance of walking slowly in order to emphasize peace, calm, and reverence. Even though many years and many weddings had made me accustomed to stepping from behind a closed door as the first of the wedding party, I still couldn't help but feel a bit of vaudeville existed as all eyes turned to us.

Morning

The presence of family and friends who filled every possible seat of this large hall of God and whose rapt attention was collectively focused on the details of the spectacle seemed to draw the very air out of the beautifully vaulted old chamber. Even with the unmovable traditions rigorously followed, elegant grace triumphed. The airless oppressiveness dissipated before the collective refreshing of the breath of life of the many who were present to celebrate this love as a reminder of all love. Each congregant participated to create the presence of the Spirit as love formed itself anew, not only in the couple to be married, but also in the lives and memories of everyone in attendance. Just for a moment, we would witness the creation of a different form of love through the act of creating a marriage.

Bride and groom would stand before us in the beauty of togetherness which was largely untried and untested. They would look at us with expectation, happiness, and the true conviction that life would always be this way. Their love made them immune to reason and experience. Their joy assured them nothing would ever change.

The groomsmen entered in formal attire. No more baggy shorts, tee shirts, baseball caps, or strapped sunglasses expressing the exuberance of youth. Now tightly contained in black tuxedos, the groomsmen looked as though they would be right at home at a Victorian dinner party.

Continuing the same music by which the groomsmen took their places, the bridesmaids entered from the narthex of the church, and with slow, carefully orchestrated steps moved to their places in front of the altar. They nervously smiled at the groom as though relieved to have made it without tripping. The colors and styles of their gowns became the last of the laboriously chosen and vitally important accents of beauty and style in the ceremony. Each young lady brought a new expression of early beauty. All of their many preparations served to enhance their natural radiance, but the final expression of joy was best seen in their smiles.

Unmistakably each attendant carried into the ceremony childhood and adulthood, awkwardness and freshness of youth, discoveries and mistakes, fights and tears, friendships and hatreds, school and sports, accomplishments and heartbreaks. They were close friends or relatives to either the groom or the bride. As they flanked the altar and the groom, their presence demonstrated more than mere approval. Their smiles at the groom as they went to their places stated their collective experiences. They formed not only a living wall of memories but also a necessary presence that would go with this couple, whether welcomed or not.

Beauty of youth and the frailty of innocence combined to illuminate the intensity of emotions in the sanctuary. After the entrance of the bride, the couple faced the altar. Their presence demanded notice of their lives undimmed and untouched by the jading of time and experience. Their glow brought new life to this place and reminded each one present of the glory of youth.

All was in place. Everything was ready. Now came the solemn vows and reminders of joy completing itself in the sacred. As the music reached its final crescendo, marking the point where our words would feebly begin to codify what was taking place, my mind returned to the rehearsal dinner.

As I remembered the laughter of last evening, I began to realize just how troubled I remained from that event. I was completely miserable as I stood before this couple and the gathered assembly and attempted to smile.

After the wedding rehearsal the day before, we took a quick trip into the heart of the city and stopped at a tall, modern building. As we entered through large glass doors, the receptionist smiled, stood and waved her hand toward the elevator as if welcoming honored guests. We took the elevator to the private dinner club on the top floor. Situated to overlook not just the city but also the state capitol building, this club stated for all in attendance that membership here demonstrated financial success.

Surrounded by the lights of the city, we enjoyed a wonderful meal. Traditional toasts were made and laughter filled the room as friends of the couple told funny stories and embarrassing secrets about the bride and groom. Just as the first guests had thanked the hosts and were preparing to depart, the wedding witch appeared in the banquet hall.

Dressed in old-style Bavarian clothing and using a thick accent, the witch had a difficult time getting us to understand her purpose. Finally we understood. With great flair and style, she performed her humorous role in the festivities. Laughter once again filled the large room, and the golden vested servers slid quietly against the walls to await the witch's departure.

One by one, the wedding witch took strange little items from her basket. With theatrical ability, this relative of the groom demonstrated how her talismans contained old magic making them capable of warding off all troubles of married life.

Each item possessed something of the ancient forests of Europe. A sprig of uncommon leaves placed in their hair was meant to keep them well. An earthy colored small feather was placed on their shoulders to help them bear the loads they would carry. A small dried fragrant flower was placed behind

Morning

each ear to help them hear the words of kindness spoken by the other. A stone from a mountain stream was placed in the pocket of the groom to help his pockets remain always full of riches.

More and more items appeared from her basket as the lady moved and spoke. As though invoking an old trance, the witch summoned a great and uncanny presence, and time appeared to focus its movement to this point. The clock stopped its incessant ticking; the evening ceased to move forward. Without knowing it, everyone in the room welcomed the chance to pleasantly travel into her spell.

The basket appeared to have more items than should have been able to fit inside its confines. The witch gave great pleasure in granting each talisman to the couple. Her speech, her manners, her clothing, and her unique items, carefully described and artfully placed, maintained the unmistakable and surprising magic of the moment.

The young couple did not seem to have known the witch would arrive, and of all the people in the room, they appeared to be immune to the powerful spell she wove. The bride and groom received the witch's items with graceful smiles. Their good humor spoke more of their winning personalities than the acceptance of the significance of the moment. In sadness, I realized each talisman, with its invocation of protective magic, only carried true power if the recipients realized the absolute necessity of many blessings. They did not yet understand what would be required to see their love through the many dangerous and grief laden paths of life.

I wanted to stand and join the witch in her maddening and startling dance of the reality of all things. I desired to embrace her and help her cast her spell of power so this—and every—young couple might never have to face the devastation. I wanted to cast aside everything holding me back and force them to see the pain and anguish of life that would inevitably be experienced. I wanted them to stop the clocks forever and live in this moment because I knew the future presented more than hopes and boundless joys.

As the young couple now stood ready to be pronounced husband and wife, I knew the witch was right. Her mighty spells had proven one point at least. It would take many talismans to keep them free from life crushing pain.

This couple had been prepared as well as any couple who comes to the church seeking matrimony. They had been prayed over and given all of the instructions from every possible wedding expert in what to expect and how to avoid the obvious blunders of an ongoing and deepening relationship. Even with all of these months of preparation and prayer, I knew they could never be ready for what the years would bring.

From beginning love intermingled with passions to the growing, maturing, stabilizing love that becomes the immense monument of lives shared, this young couple stood before us to begin their journey.

The old church, so filled with the history of this city, embraced the beauty of this occasion as though thirsty and yearning for all to experience the unseen radiance of the ages. Music lifted us from the material world and the amazement of the beauty of the present and took us to the spiritual realm from whence love is birthed. This woman and man asked us to somehow bring the collective sacred moment into the reality of the living out of their days.

In spite of the majesty of love expressed in art and worship, crushing brutal honesty forced its way into my unwilling consciousness. As I spoke the words and brought order into art making these two people one, I fought back dread and fear. Right then, the sheer innocence and ignorance of the young couple became bleedingly aware to me.

I had seen love. I had captured love. It had given birth to my true self and nurtured all of my previous wounds of living. While still giving me unbelievable strength, it had also torn me asunder.

I had been to the chasm of finality and knew, for this season, life itself no longer seemed worthy of pursuing.

How can you be ready to face the pain of life? I wanted to shout instead of the carefully scripted words of liturgy before me.

I wanted to tell them to run away and hide in their perfect love so it would never end.

A pause. Music began again. The beauty of an ancient song captured the image of a holy mother loving her holy Child. Familiar music, ancient music. Music which spoke of the mystical union of human love with the eternal truth of divine love.

The bride and groom stood perfectly still in their beauty. The candle flames did not flicker and the guests seemed to barely breathe.

Movement. I dared not change the position of my head. The flower girl, dressed in white linen with delicate tiny flowers ringing her dark hair, began to move from her carefully rehearsed position in front of the altar rail. She approached the bride and impishly walked over the flowing train of the dress. The bride looked to this radiant child and smiled as her train and veil were slightly pulled. The flower girl reached into her basket and, while still looking into the smiling face of the bride, extracted one perfect white rose petal.

The whiteness of its natural beauty glowed in the candlelight. Somehow the petal, in those not yet fully formed fingers of this young child, captured the light and the beauty. Somehow the petal began to speak in music as soothing as the song being sung in this holy place. Somehow another dance took place.

While everyone was still, the young child began her own magical movements. Her spell of grace clarified the completion of the dance of life. Her motions contained the meaning of life lived in love and faith. The petal spoke in exuberant tones that life and love were to be always exulted. The fingers holding the perfect petal demonstrated the necessity of everyone grasping what was offered and continuing to embrace hope and joy. Holding the petal gently in her tiny fingers, she appeared to move in this unrehearsed moment not out of uncertainty, but out of a desire for the bride to understand the enormity of all eternal things. In her innocence, she completed the wedding witch's spell and made it at one with life and pain, loss and victory.

As I struggled to breathe, the flower girl placed the pure white petal in the palm of the bride's hand and then gently closed the bride's fingers upon it.

Without a sound, and as the music of the skies continued, the scene was repeated with the groom who received this talisman with a smile.

The flower girl retreated back to her position as though nothing had happened.

Even though the music continued without interruption and even though the smiles of the congregation were seen and felt through the flowing waves of candlelight, and even though the bride and groom continued to look at one another with the same love and thrill and anticipation of all promises finally fulfilled, I knew everything had changed forever

Chapter 43
Night

I DID NOT STAY FOR THE RECEPTION.

The image of what the flower girl did at the wedding possessed me. I saw amazing beauty transpiring right in front of me and understood clearly the intensity of the other-than-natural occurring. The blessed sacredness changed me. Through the innocent child, the fears and devastations of life were boldly confronted by the unmistakable, eclipsing power of love. It changed my perception of God's presence in our lives. It changed my understanding of how God responds to our hopes.

It also changed my faith.

I could not stay for the reception.

I knew the bride's family expected me to be in attendance. I understood they had gone to great expense and trouble to make the reception spectacular and beautiful. But beauty and love and wholeness and promise wounded me more than I could endure.

Despite my joy of a new life built from two individual lives, I could not stop myself from wondering.

Why did they deserve such a blessing? Why couldn't the blessing be given to Donna and me? Why did Donna have to die when there are those who continue to experience blissful happiness?

I desperately wanted to echo the savagely bitter cry of Esau.: "Have you only one blessing, father? Bless me, me also, father!"

Why did our lives have to change?

I fully understood the selfishness of those thoughts. Fighting them with every spiritual discipline I could muster, I tried to force them out of my mind. As I drove out of the capital city, I prayed with eyes wide open.

"Please, dear Lord," I prayed aloud, "please help me move beyond this moment. Please help me relish the joy and beauty of what I just witnessed. Thank you for your love and dedication to others. Help me never be envious of the happiness they feel right now."

"Thank you for the many years of happiness you gave Donna and me," I continued while fighting back tears so I could drive. "I know we were blessed by your gift of love. You blessed us in more ways than we ever realized. Thank you for her life continuing in you…"

Morning

I pressed the accelerator harder as my last words echoed in the darkness. I did not want to be on this road all by myself. I wanted to be at home where I would be surrounded by the place filled with her lingering presence.

I wanted to wrap myself in the duvet that witnessed her last breath.

Then I saw the full moon.

It obviously had been shining on me the whole time since I left the church after the wedding. It had been piercing through the darkness of the cloudless sky, not glaring in brightness, but shimmering in radiance. Its gentle glow made all things beautiful.

I pulled the car over to the side of the road and stopped so I could continue to stare at something which was not a part of our world. Each crater seemed to be carefully outlined in shadows and brightness. I sensed the desolation of that faraway surface. I imagined how it must feel to walk through the dusty soil and create lasting pathways.

It felt good to be pulled away from this time and place. Escape from my heavy thoughts brought amazing relief. My mind eased into memories of sharing the full moon's transcendence with Donna.

I remembered standing with Donna on the beach at night amazed by the spectacle of the full moon shining on the gentle waves of the Atlantic. I could almost hear her laughter as we stood outside a mountain cabin and spoke of how the full moon made the surrounding valley and hills as bright as midday.

I remembered making her get out of the car on Hickory Lane Extension to look at the amazing rainbow surrounding the full moon. I remembered thinking how it meant only good things awaited.

Now I gazed at the full moon once again. Alone in my car on the side of the road, I stared at the beauty. I started to cry. The familiar tears reminded me of my desolation and loneliness.

Can Donna see the moon? I thought. *Is she looking at the same full moon on this same night with me? Are we looking at the moon together even if I don't know it? Is it possible in heaven? Where is she?*

I lowered my head no longer able to look at the beauty of the heavens. In my mind, the beauty of this full moon turned into the haunting glow of the azure moon of the gondola ride on the cavern river from years ago. All I could see of the moon was how its azure presence marked the end of Donna's life. Tears ran down my face and I silently sobbed. I fully understood what was happening. Not until I saw the full moon in the midst of the darkest night did I comprehend what the white rose petals had done to me.

I had lost my faith.

My faith vanished.

I had no idea if Donna lived with the Lord. I could not think if she was looking at the moon with me. Everything came to a complete stop, and I ceased to breathe as the tears continued.

How can I have faith if I don't even know where my beloved is?

All of a sudden, the tears stopped. Grief no longer had a place in my world of nothingness. Loneliness no longer mattered. Weariness no longer mattered. All had vanished. The moon continued to shine, but its light no longer appeared to make a difference in the dark vastness.

I drove home feeling as though my headlights only barely illuminated a few feet ahead of the car. But it didn't matter. I no longer worried about my safety or the sad days awaiting me. My Donna was forever gone. I would never see her again. Life and death. Simple beginning and end. Nothing more.

I drove into the garage and turned off the engine and watched the glow of the headlights on the wall in front of me. I waited until they automatically turned off. Darkness fell upon me, and I relaxed in its coldness.

I found myself no longer capable of experiencing the loss of love and a destroyed faith so I quickly sank into regret. Even though I knew the power of the conscience and the role of regret in changing lives, I always understood the danger of wallowing in regret.

In the darkness of the night, I allowed all regrets to flood into my thoughts. They had been waiting for just such an opportunity. As I sat in the midnight hour, the realization of how much I did not accomplish for my wife and family overwhelmed me. Regret led immediately to guilt, and remorse followed. Sadness and a sense of the futility of every wrong and every mistake filled me. My thoughts became clear in the midst of complete loathing of myself.

She will never see the white sand island surrounded by the crystal blue waters. We will never stand on the red cliffs and look out to all our tomorrows.

I knew tomorrow was gone forever.

"There's no reason to watch for the morning," I said out loud in the darkness. The words sounded as though spoken by someone else. I smiled and found the absence of faith and hope to be soothingly numbing.

"This is why people kill themselves."

The voice came from within me as I stared at the dark wall. The voice did not startle me. The notion did not frighten me. I accepted it as the logical conclusion of the void now defining me. I knew I would awaken each day to emptiness until I finally died.

I stepped out of my car and started slowly for the door. I almost hoped someone would try to rob me and end all of this confusion and my regrettable

Morning

life. As I opened the door, I walked through the pitch black of the hallway and up the stairs to the emptiness of the bedroom without turning on a light.

"Why bother with the light?" I told myself. "It only pretends to take away the darkness. It's actually powerless against the night. The night always overcomes the day. Nothing will ever change."

I crawled into bed and knew I could not end my life.

"It would be too devastating to Tyler and to the church," I told myself. "They would be harmed."

I wondered if I really cared about any of them. Then I comprehended the real reason I would not openly commit suicide: it would take too much effort to accomplish.

"Find a way that will seem completely accidental," the voice offered coldly and clearly. "You will know when the opportunity arises. It will happen soon. No one else will know and all of this will be over. Wait and see. Everything will then go away."

I pulled the duvet up to my chin even though I felt no chill.

I need to wash this thing tomorrow, I thought while looking at it. *How stupid of me to keep it as though it could ever remind me of her. She is gone. She is gone forever.*

Tearless and empty, I closed my eyes and went immediately to sleep.

Chapter 44

Morning

ANGER AWOKE ME. My eyes remained tightly and defiantly closed. In my weariness, I would not allow the bright light to pull me out of my long-awaited sleep. I struggled to breathe against the weariness weighing down my chest. I did not want to take up the strain of yet another day's burdens. Sleep would come back to me if I could only keep my eyes closed for a few seconds more.

Why is someone doing this? I thought as I awakened against my best efforts to regain unconsciousness.

I was certain Tyler stood near the side of the bed shining a very bright flashlight into my eyes, I could almost hear his laughter as he awaited my startled reaction.

My thoughts screamed in anger. Fighting away sleep, I decided to vent my anger and demand an explanation.

Doesn't he understand how tired I am?

Finally, my eyes opened to a sight I did not understand.

Morning had arrived.

The white duvet cover blinded me. Its searing light forced me to close my eyes tightly as though I had accidently looked directly into the sun. I did not jump nor angrily demand an explanation since I knew I was in the house alone.

Slowly I opened my eyes once again. The light from the cover forced me to squint. Now authentically startled, I knew the light must be coming from the head of the bed. Right behind me something was producing enough light that the white duvet cover blinded me with its reflected brilliance.

I started to turn my head and look at what could possibly be on the wall behind the bed. I hesitated out of fear since none of this made any sense. How could a wall be shining so brightly?

After a few seconds of waiting, I lifted my head from the pillow and quickly turned to look at the head of the bed. Even as I moved, I wondered if I should run from the bed without looking back to evade whatever was happening. Before I could run, I looked.

Unchanged in form, the headboard and wall simply glowed with the same intensity of the duvet cover. I realized I was seeing a reflection of light so intense it changed the wall into a gleaming mirror. Turning to look out the windows of the bedroom, I saw the source.

Morning

Through the dancing leaves of the trees, a single beam of light focused itself on the wall right above my head with great intensity.

Jumping from the bed, I pressed my hands on the window wishing it to break open and release me. The beam of light continued as though it would shine forever. As I watched in wonder, small sparkling flecks appeared to move through the light and come to me.

I stood with Donna and held her hand.

I felt her embrace. For an eternity I stood with her reliving our days together. She held me tightly as we laughed and walked up the aisle of the mountainside chapel with our backs to the raging storm.

We felt the night breeze of Jekyll as I hugged her tightly to protect against a summer's evening chill. We watched the glow of the island lighthouse reaching out forever to the farthest points of the sea.

She held my hand as I confessed my call to her, and she joyfully but reluctantly agreed to go on the journey with me. We walked along the roads of Sandy Springs looking at the distant vistas and once again I felt the thrill of youth and endless possibilities.

I squeezed her hand in excitement as we watched our newborn son crying through the window of the hospital nursery. I felt her gentle hands surrounding my arms as we cradled our sleeping son in our arms together.

On and on, without the necessity of beginning and end, we saw our life in the victory of completed love. I intended to stay here forever. Her love, her embrace, her hand holding mine. Our lives continuing to move in perfect rhythm. Just as it should be. Just as it should have been. Just as it was right at that moment.

She squeezed my hand as though to get my attention. We now stood on top of a red stone cliff. I looked over the beauty of the deserted island filled with fresh green trees waving in the morning breeze. The endless crystal-clear blue waters moved joyfully in the new light.

"I wanted to bring you here," I said as I looked at her. "I wanted us to see it together."

Her mahogany hair shone in the early light as she looked at me and smiled a peaceful and fully contented smile. She gently laughed and then turned to look beyond the red stone cliffs and the island surrounded by the fascinating waters.

"I know," she said. "Now we are here together. No regrets."

She moved from my side and spread her arms out in the sea breeze as though celebrating the joy of this new day. She did not let go of my hand as she gently pulled me closer to the edge of the cliff.

"There's something I want you to see," she said.

"Look! It's morning!"

I looked East across the waves and saw the day as it arose in glory. But I did not see the sun.

The eternal shone upon me. All mysteries came to an end. All pain ceased as I floated in grace. I felt Donna's hand in mine as she stepped forward with joy. I finally understand the reality of complete peace. Beyond anything I could imagine, I knew love. Love embraced me as I felt Donna's hand slide gently out of mine. I completely understood absolute acceptance of all things.

The light shone on those parts of me I could never love. All of the hidden became clearly visible as I was surrounded with understanding and the power of love present in the creation of light itself. No fear. No reprisal. The true light of morning banished all guilt.

The terror of the night and the constant presence of the voice of unending doubt vanished. Now I understood the totality of God's love, of divine acceptance of every mistake and every point of pain and confusion in my life.

I no longer experienced only faith in the risen Savior. I walked with Him in the morning.

Through blessed morning light, I was forever changed. With Donna at my side, I gained the strength to break through the surface of the dark waters and truly breathe again.

The light disappeared, and I stood completely alone looking out the bedroom window. Tears ran down my face as I closed my hand hoping beyond hope I could feel her hand in mine once again.

Even as the tears continued, I knew one bright morning I would.

Epilogue

LAVENDER SKY AT EVENTIDE. Lavender ocean with quiet white cresting waves. Lavender wet sand reflecting the colors of the sunset on the surface of the beach. My grandchild, Summer Lynn, not yet two years old, running ahead of me in a little turquoise swimming suit. I can barely hear her soft laughter. She giggles for no reason except that she is running on the wet lavender sand.

She spies some birds. Seagulls and sandpipers. They are the target of her fascination and she takes off for them laughing louder. The birds look confused as they see her approaching. They are not sure what to make of this pint-sized human who is determined to get as close as she can to where they are feeding.

At the last moment, they jump a few inches out and over the wet sand and glide a few yards away before landing and starting their feeding once again. Summer Lynn, still laughing, stops and reaches out her hand and tries to grasp them in her fingers. She seems confused that they don't understand she only wants to touch them.

Undaunted, she begins her journey up the beach toward the glowing high-rise buildings in the distance. She stops and looks at the gentle lavender waves and then decides the quest for the elusive birds must wait because now the water is calling her. She runs to the little waves and begins to startle me with her determination to continue out as far as she can.

When she senses I am behind her, she turns her head and looks at me and then reaches out her arm and points back to the beach. When I do not move, she shakes her finger and arm. The message is clear. She knows I am there to make sure she goes no further into the ocean, and she is telling me I am no longer needed.

A wicked little wave rushes up out of nowhere and knocks Summer Lynn off her feet. I quickly reach to pick her up thinking our reverie by the sea has come to a tearful end, but she begins to laugh. Before I can help, she is picking herself up from the warm water and begins to dance in the waves almost begging them to knock her down one more time.

Her world is lavender. Her sky, her waves, her sand, her time with the wind and the freedom of rejoicing in discovering her world are all lavender. I know this time is more precious than I can even imagine. I desire to keep it all just like this. A lavender world for a little girl. A lavender seaside with no cares, lavender laughter with no thought of tears. I ponder how I can contain these moments forever. The time passes too quickly and lavender begins to dissolve to darkness.

Summer Lynn would not want to live in the lavender world forever and could not even if I could preserve it for her. Her world, full of excitement and full of things that will cause pain, awaits her.

Now I no longer wait alone for the sunrise. Now I have seen it. Now I want her to see it as well and to know the promise of many days filled with joy. I pray that all might see the golden light and know that their dark night has passed.

Dear Lord, bless each of us with a life filled with lavender sunsets. In the evening as the darkness becomes night, please keep us safe and strong. When the golden rays of your presence come with the dawn, let us walk with you in the morning. Amen.

www.ingramcontent.com/pod-product-compliance
Lightning Source LLC
Chambersburg PA
CBHW072004110526
44592CB00012B/1194